Funded by a State Legislature Grant
Senator Suzi Oppenheimer

RYE FREE READING ROOM
Escape to the Library

Bloom's Classic Critical Views

WILLIAM BLAKE

Bloom's Classic Critical Views

Bloom's Classic Critical Views

WILLIAM BLAKE

Edited and with an Introduction by
Harold Bloom
Sterling Professor of the Humanities
Yale University

**BLOOM'S
LITERARY CRITICISM**
An imprint of Infobase Publishing

Bloom's Classic Critical Views: William Blake

Copyright © 2008 Infobase Publishing

Introduction © 2008 by Harold Bloom

Bloom's Literary Criticism
An imprint of Infobase Publishing
132 West 31st Street
New York NY 10001

Library of Congress Cataloging-in-Publication Data
William Blake / edited and with an introduction by Harold Bloom.
    p. cm. — (Bloom's classic critical views)
  Includes bibliographical references and index.
  ISBN 978-1-60413-138-3 (acid-free paper) 1. Blake, William, 1757–1827—Criticism and interpretation. I. Bloom, Harold. II. Title. III. Series.

  PR4147.W446 2008
  821.7—dc22

                        2008010498

Bloom's Literary Criticism books are available at special discounts when purchased in bulk quantities for businesses, associations, institutions, or sales promotions. Please call our Special Sales Department in New York at (212) 967-8800 or (800) 322-8755.

You can find Bloom's Literary Criticism on the World Wide Web at
http://www.chelseahouse.com

Contributing editor: Alexis Harley
Series design by Erika K. Arroyo
Cover design by Takeshi Takahashi
Printed in the United States of America
Bang EJB 10 9 8 7 6 5 4 3 2 1

This book is printed on acid-free paper.

All links and Web addresses were checked and verified to be correct at the time of publication. Because of the dynamic nature of the Web, some addresses and links may have changed since publication and may no longer be valid.

Contents

Series Introduction

Bloom's Classic Critical Views is a new series presenting a selection of the most important older literary criticism on the greatest authors commonly read in high school and college classes today. Unlike the Bloom's Modern Critical Views series, which for more than 20 years has provided the best contemporary criticism on great authors, Bloom's Classic Critical Views attempts to present the authors in the context of their time and to provide criticism that has proved over the years to be the most valuable to readers and writers. Selections range from contemporary reviews in popular magazines, which demonstrate how a work was received in its own era, to profound essays by some of the strongest critics in the British and American tradition, including Henry James, G.K. Chesterton, Matthew Arnold, and many more.

Some of the critical essays and extracts presented here have appeared previously in other titles edited by Harold Bloom, such as the New Moulton's Library of Literary Criticism. Other selections appear here for the first time in any book by this publisher. All were selected under Harold Bloom's guidance.

In addition, each volume in this series contains a series of essays by a contemporary expert, who comments on the most important critical selections, putting them in context and suggesting how they might be used by a student writer to influence his or her own writing. This series is intended above all for students, to help them think more deeply and write more powerfully about great writers and their works.

Introduction by Harold Bloom

I write these pages in April 2008, exactly fifty years since my first publication appeared, an essay on William Blake's *The Marriage of Heaven and Hell*. Since then I have published so much on Blake that I scarcely can compute the total. Nevertheless, I hope to keep these observations fresh, though haunted by a half-century's personal heritage.

Together with Shelley, Wallace Stevens, and Hart Crane, Blake was my first stimulus to think originally about the process of poetic influence, which still obsesses me after a lifetime's reflections. The strongest influence Blake ever knew was that of John Milton, as compounded with the Bible. Of all literary texts, Milton and the Bible most possessed Blake, though Shakespeare and Dante also had a strong impact on him.

Blake wrote three epic poems: *The Four Zoas*, *Milton*, and *Jerusalem*. As I age, I prefer *Milton* to the rest of Blake, partly because its vision is unclouded by the outer violence of *The Four Zoas* or the internalized violence of *Jerusalem*. In Book I, Milton descends from heaven in order to redeem his own creation, his poetry and the imaginative world he made, as well as his three wives and three daughters. The Miltonic descent—clearly distinct from Satan's precipitous fall—does not mean that the epic poet of *Paradise Lost* is to be confined to his voluntary coming down. In the poem *Milton,* an individual being has the power to exist simultaneously in various states of existence. Even as John Milton descends and "to himself he seem'd a wanderer lost in dreary night," his immortal self sleeps on in Eden. Later, he will wrestle steadily with Urizen (the "God" of *Paradise Lost*) in an agon ongoing through the poem while redeemed aspects of his being move to join Blake and Los, the artificer of the imagination.

Blake's shaking-up of spatial concepts is culminated when Milton descends as a comet:

The nature of infinity is this: That every
    thing has its
Own Vortex; and when once a traveler thro'
    Eternity
Has pass' that Vortex, he perceives it roll
    backward behind
His path, into a globe itself infolding, like
    a sun,
Or like a moon, or like a universe of starry
    majesty,
While he keeps onwards in his wondrous
    journey on the earth;
Or like a human form, a friend with
    whom he liv'd benevolent.
As the eye of man views both the east &
    west encompassing
Its vortex, and the north & south with all
    their starry host,
Also the rising sun & setting moon he views,
    surrounding
His corn-fields and his valleys of five
    hundred acres square,
Thus is the earth one infinite plane, and
    not as apparent
To the weak traveler confin'd beneath the
    moony shade.
Thus is the heaven a vortex pass'd already,
    and the earth
A vortex not yet pass'd by the traveler
    thro' Eternity

Blake's Vortex is not so much an esoteric conceptual image as it is a satire on Descartes's dualism in which subject rigorously is estranged from object. To pass *through* a vortex is to see an object from the object's own point of view, as it were. In Eden, subject and object are creator and creation; Milton journeys to heal the Cartesian-Newtonian split:

First Milton saw Albion upon the Rock of
    Ages,
Deadly pale outstretch'd and snowy cold,
    storm cover'd,
A Giant form of perfect beauty outstretch'd
    on the rock

In solemn death: the Sea of Time & Space
thunder'd aloud
Against the rock, which was inwrapped with
the weeds of death.
Hovering over the cold bosom in its vortex
Milton bent down
To the bosom of death: what was underneath
soon seem'd above:
A cloudy heaven mingled with stormy seas in
loudest ruin;
But as a wintry globe descends precipitant,
thro' Beulah bursting
With thunders loud and terrible, so Milton's
shadow fell
Precipitant, loud thund'ring, into the Sea
of Time & Space.

Milton's fusion with Blake has only begun, so that the "black cloud" represents a recalcitrant residiuum of Puritanism in the visionary of *Paradise Lost*. With sublime irony, Blake's Milton confuses all who behold his manifestation as a falling star, like Satan. Los the Artificer takes Milton as Satan, while the Shadowy Female or Female Will applauds his approach.

One being, the spectral or stony fallen Urizen, knows exactly what the return of Milton means, and he emerges to engage Milton in a wrestling match as dramatic and powerful as anything in Blake, a struggle that calls on Milton to be at once a Samson, a Jacob, and a new Moses for his people:

Urizen emerged from his Rocky Form & from
his Snows,
And he also darken'd his brows, freezing dark
rocks between
The footsteps and infixing deep the feet in
marble beds,
That Milton labour'd with his journey & his
feet bled sore
Upon the clay now chang'd to marble; also
Urizen rose
And met him on the shores of Arnon & by the
streams of the brooks.
Silent they met and silent strove among the
streams of Arnon
Even to Mahanaim; when with cold hand Urizen
stoop'd down

And took up water from the river Jordan,
     pouring on
To Milton's brain the icy fluid from his
     broad cold palm.
But Milton took of the red clay of Succoth,
     moulding it with care
Between his palms and filling up the furrows
     of many years,
Beginning at the feet of Urizen, and on the
     bones
Creating new flesh on the Demon cold and
     building him
As with new clay, a Human form in the Valley
     of Beth Peor.

This magnificent passage does assume the reader's knowledge of some crucial biblical references. The Arnon is a river flowing westward into the Dead Sea and dividing off the Trans-Jordan lands of the Israelites from Moab. Numbers 21:14 associates the Arnon and the Red Sea, by which the Israelites escaped the deathly bondage of Egypt. The Arnon in Blake has the same significance, as Milton Percival observes, for through it one passes from the body of death into the generative body, from Urizenic law to the sacrifice of Luvah for man. Mahanaim (Genesis 32:2) is where Jacob wrestled with God until he had secured a blessing and the name of Israel. Succoth is where Jacob went afterwards, to build a house and booths (Genesis 33:17), the booths giving the place its name, and associating the story with the harvest festival, where four plants represent four classes of men united as one man in worship. Beth Peor is the burial place of Moses in the land of Moab. Drawing all this together and applying it to Blake's passage, we suddenly behold the audacity and clarity with which Blake had molded his sources.

Urizen fears that Milton is coming to overturn his laws, for Milton began by taking off the robe and ungirding himself from the oath of Urizen-Jehovah's covenant with Moses. So Urizen goes forth to battle, turning the warm clay Milton walks on to freezing and purgatorial marble. They meet and wrestle, two silent and mighty champions, on the shores of Arnon, the body of law striving with the human form divine. Their struggle is like the wrestling of Jehovah and Jacob, except that Milton will not repeat Israel's mistake; he wants to reform God, and not merely to extract a blessing for himself.

As the battle continues, Urizen attempts an icy intellectual baptism of Milton with Jordan water, but Milton fights back by taking the Adamic red clay of Succoth, emblem of a human harvest, and sculpting the bare bones of the cold Urizen until he has made him into a human form in the same valley where the body of Moses or Urizenic law is forever buried. Milton's activity is artistic and gives the sculptor's gift of life, of red flesh to cold marble, making God into a Man, Urizen into Adam.

This extraordinary struggle attains an apotheosis in one of Blake's superb condensations of intellectual strife transmuted into saving metaphor:

But Milton entering my Foot, I saw in the
  nether
Regions of the Imagination—also all men on
  Earth
And all in Heaven saw in the nether regions
  of the Imagination
In Ulro beneath Beulah—the vast breach of
  Milton's descent.
But I knew not that it was Milton, for man
  cannot know
What passes in his members till periods of
  Space & Time
Reveal the secrets of Eternity: for more
  extensive
Than any other earthly things are Man's
  earthly lineaments.
And all this Vegetable World appear'd on my
  left Foot
As a bright sandal form'd immortal of precious
  stones & gold.
I stooped down & bound it on to walk forward
  thro' Eternity.

I offer this as an epitome of Blake's unique greatness. Few passages in Western poetry equal this in originality and soul-arousing eloquence.

BIOGRAPHY

WILLIAM BLAKE
(1757–1827)

William Blake was born in London on November 28, 1757. The son of a hosier, he did not go to school but instead was apprenticed to James Basire, an engraver, from 1772 until 1779. He then entered the Royal Academy; from 1779 he also worked as an engraver for the radical bookseller and publisher Joseph Johnson. In 1780, Blake met the Swiss artist Henry Fuseli, who became his closest friend, and two years later, he married Catherine Boucher, who remained a devoted wife throughout Blake's life. Through another artist friend, John Flaxman, Blake was introduced to the circle of Mrs. Henry Matthew, the Bluestocking wife of a minister, whose frequent guests included Anna Laetitia Barbauld, Hannah More, and Elizabeth Montagu. In 1783, Blake brought out *Poetical Sketches,* and in 1784, with the help of Mrs. Matthew, he opened his own printseller's shop in London; around the same period he also composed (though not for publication) the fragment *An Island in the* Moon (published 1907), in which he satirized scientific and cultural dilettantism. *Songs of Innocence* and *The Book of Thel* were both published with Blake's own engravings in 1789, the same year he wrote *Tiriel* (published 1874).

In 1790, Blake moved to Lambeth. Probably in that same year he engraved *The Marriage of Heaven and Hell,* his principal prose work, consisting of paradoxical aphorisms. Later works include *The French Revolution* (1791), *America: A Prophecy* (1793), and *Visions of the Daughters of Albion* (1793), in which Blake combined political radicalism with an ecstatic, visionary religiosity. In *Songs of Experience* (1794) he reconfirmed his talents as a lyric poet. The first edition combining *Songs of Innocence* and *Songs of Experience* appeared in 1795. Blake developed his own very personal mythology in *The Book of Urizen* (1794), *Europe: A Prophecy* (1794), *The Song of Los* (1795), *The Book of Ahania* (1795), *The Book of Los* (1795), and *The Four Zoas* (written 1795–1804), all engraved by himself.

In 1800, Blake moved to Felpham, Sussex, where he lived for three years, working for his friend, the poet William Hayley. In 1803, Blake was charged with treason for allegedly having made seditious remarks about the king but was soon acquitted. Later that year, Blake returned to London, where he worked on his poems *Milton* (written and etched 1804-08) and *Jerusalem: The Emanation of the Giant Albion* (written and etched 1804-20). Blake's later years were spent in obscurity and poverty, although he continued to be commissioned as an artist. His poem "The Everlasting Gospel" was written around 1818, and his famous illustrations for the Book of Job were published in 1826. Between 1825 and 1826, Blake executed the designs for an edition of Dante, but illness intervened before they could be engraved. Blake died on August 12, 1827.

PERSONAL

Blake died in 1827. In 1863, a version of William Blake was revived, with the publication of Alexander Gilchrist's *The Life of William Blake, "Pictor Ignotus." Pictor ignotus*, Latin for "unknown painter," was a telling subtitle. According to Gilchrist, the late Blake had lived, and then not lived, in a state of more or less unmitigated obscurity. Moreover, as the *pictor* suggests, those familiar with his work knew him primarily as an illustrator and engraver, not as a poet. Gilchrist's biography helped trigger a remarkable Blake renaissance. The work invigorated a narrative of Blake as a genius overlooked and ignored by the artistic establishment. This Blake was a radical not just because of what he said, but because no one listened, and in such a figure the artistic counterculture of the 1860s found a patron saint. While the portrait created of a neglected Blake was not without basis, the Blake revivalists—led by Alexander Gilchrist, Dante Gabriel and William Michael Rossetti, and Algernon Charles Swinburne—overplayed it. Certainly the conditions of Blake's artistic production (illuminated printing, print on demand), to say nothing of his theological and political unorthodoxies, meant that his work enjoyed only limited circulation and in the case of some manuscripts, no circulation. But as the following entries attest, there *was* a Blake who existed prior to Gilchrist's biography, just as there were biographical accounts and admirers of Blake before the publication of Gilchrist's pivotal work.

The accounts in this section are concerned primarily with Blake the private person and with his imaginative and artistic life. Most of the writers knew Blake personally, but two—Charles Lamb and Dante Gabriel Rossetti—extrapolate from their encounters with Blake's work.

The earliest surviving account of William Blake, and the first entry in this section, was published by Benjamin Heath Malkin in 1806 in the preface to his memoir of his late son. Blake had designed the frontispiece to Malkin's memoir, a depiction of

Malkin's son, and the printer-poet finds in Malkin an enthusiastic champion, eager to position Blake in the vanguard of an artistic revolution.

Blake is often anthologized today as an exemplary, albeit early, Romantic poet, but he did not engage in literary collaborations, as William Wordsworth and Samuel Taylor Coleridge did with the *Lyrical Ballads*, or in the sort of intellectual menagerie enjoyed by Percy Bysshe Shelley, Mary Shelley, and George Gordon, Lord Byron. Though Blake stood apart from the Romantic movement, such as it was, the accounts by Charles Lamb and Henry Crabb Robinson, both important figures in Romantic culture, show that the supposed disjunction between Blake and other Romantic writers and artists was not as profound as is supposed. Crabb Robinson, in particular, followed Blake's work with interest from as early as 1809 and befriended him in the 1820s, conducting lengthy interviews until Blake's death. He wrote to Dorothy Wordsworth, suggesting a meeting between Blake and William Wordsworth—of which, it seems, nothing came—and he mentions meetings between Blake and Coleridge.

The last two years of Blake's life saw the *pictor ignotus* surrounded by a circle of young artists. The Shoreham Disciples, or Shoreham Ancients, met at Blake's residence in Fountain Court, at the House of the Interpreter, as they called it. The group included Samuel Palmer, Frederick Tatham, Edward Calvert, John Linnell, and George Richmond. When Blake died in 1827, the disciples encouraged one another to record their memories of him. Tatham alone wrote a substantial memoir. He went on to form a close friendship with Blake's widow, Catherine, and after her death in 1831, claimed inheritance of William Blake's work. Upon his conversion to the millenarian Irvingite sect, Tatham destroyed many of Blake's works, believing them to have been inspired by Satan. Of the other disciples, Palmer and Linnell were still alive in the 1860s and supplied important firsthand biographical information to Gilchrist. Palmer's memorial letter, first published in Gilchrist's biography of Blake, is included in this section.

Benjamin Heath Malkin
"Letter to Thomas Johnes" (1806)

Benjamin Heath Malkin (1769–1842) wrote the earliest surviving account of Blake. This biographical and critical sketch, an important source for later biographers, appears in a "Letter to T. Johnes of Haford," which was published in Malkin's *A Father's Memoirs of His Child*, for which Blake designed the frontispiece (a depiction of Malkin's deceased son). Malkin is an enthusiastic Blake apologist; his defense of Blake, however, is an early indication that many of Blake's contemporaries thought him insane. Malkin was the headmaster at Bury St. Edmund's grammar school and the author of several monographs. His connections with the likes of Henry Fuseli and William Godwin suggest that, like Blake, he was a political radical. Malkin makes only cursory references to Blake's poetry—Blake was better known for most of the nineteenth century for his graphic art—but what Malkin does say is significant: Blake's "ancient simplicity," his "bold and careless freedom" are just the sort of qualities championed by Wordsworth less than six years earlier in the preface to the *Lyrical Ballads*. Malkin's observations suggest Blake as a forerunner in the Romantic reaction against eighteenth-century Augustan poetic formalism.

<hr />

Mr. William Blake, very early in life, had the ordinary opportunities of seeing pictures in the houses of noblemen and gentlemen, and in the king's palaces. He soon improved such casual occasions of study, by attending sales at Langford's, Christie's, and other auction-rooms. At ten years of age he was put to Mr. Pars's drawing-school in the Strand, where he soon attained the art of drawing from casts in plaster of the various antiques. His father bought for him the Gladiator, the Hercules, the Venus of Medicis, and various heads, hands, and feet. The same indulgent parent soon supplied him with money to buy prints; when he immediately began his collection, frequenting the shops of the printdealers, and the sales of the auctioneers. Langford called him his little connoisseur; and often knocked down to him a cheap lot, with friendly precipitation. He copied Raphael and Michael Angelo, Martin Hemskerck and Albert Durer, Julio Romano, and the rest of the historic class, neglecting to buy any other prints, however celebrated. His choice was for the most part contemned by his youthful companions, who were accustomed to laugh at what they called his mechanical taste. At the age of fourteen, he fixed on the engraver of Stuart's Athens and West's Pylades and Orestes for his master, to whom he served seven years apprenticeship. Basire, whose taste was like his own, approved of what he did. Two years passed over smoothly enough, till two other apprentices were added to the establishment, who completely destroyed its harmony. Blake, not chusing to take part with his master against his fellow apprentices, was sent out to make drawings. This circumstance he always mentions with gratitude to Basire, who said that he was too simple and they too cunning.

He was employed in making drawings from old buildings and monuments, and occasionally, especially in winter, in engraving from those drawings. This occupation led him to an acquaintance with those neglected works of art, called Gothic monuments. There he found a treasure, which he knew how to value. He saw the simple and plain road to the style of art at which he aimed, unentangled in the intricate windings of modern practice. The monuments of Kings and Queens in Westminster Abbey, which surround the chapel of Edward the Confessor, particularly that of King Henry the Third, the beautiful monument and figure of Queen Elinor, Queen Philippa, King Edward the Third, King Richard the Second and his Queen, were among his first studies. All these he drew in every point he could catch, frequently standing on the monument, and viewing the figures from the top. The heads he considered as portraits; and all the ornaments appeared as miracles of art, to his Gothicised imagination. He then drew Aymer de Valence's monument, with his fine figure on the top. Those exquisite little figures which surround it, though dreadfully mutilated, are still models for the study of drapery. But I do not mean to enumerate all his drawings, since they would lead me over all the old monuments in Westminster Abbey, as well as over other churches in and about London.

Such was his employment at Basire's. As soon as he was out of his time, he began to engrave two designs from the History of England, after drawings which he had made in the holiday hours of his apprenticeship. They were selected from a great number of historical compositions, the fruits of his fancy. He continued making designs for his own amusement, whenever he could steal a moment from the routine of business; and began a course of study at the Royal Academy, under the eye of Mr. Moser. Here he drew with great care, perhaps all, or certainly nearly all the noble antique figures in various views. But now his peculiar notions began to intercept him in his career. He professes drawing from life always to have been hateful to him; and speaks of it as looking more like death, or smelling of mortality. Yet still he drew a good deal from life, both at the academy and at home. In this manner has he managed his talents, till he is himself almost become a Gothic monument. On a view of his whole life, he still thinks himself authorized to pronounce, that practice and opportunity very soon teach the language of art: but its spirit and poetry, which are seated in the imagination alone, never can be taught; and these make an artist.

Mr. Blake has long been known to the order of men among whom he ranks; and is highly esteemed by those, who can distinguish excellence under the disguise of singularity. Enthusiastic and high flown notions on the subject of religion have hitherto, as they usually do, prevented his general reception, as a son of taste and of the muses. The sceptic and the rational believer, uniting their forces against the visionary, pursue and scare a warm and brilliant imagination, with the hue and cry of madness. Not contented with bringing down the reasonings of the mystical philosopher, as they well may, to this degraded level, they apply the test of cold calculation and mathematical proof to departments of the mind, which are privileged to appeal from so narrow and rigorous a tribunal. They criticise the representations of corporeal beauty, and the allegoric emblems of mental perfections; the image of the visible world, which appeals to the senses for a testimony to its truth, or the type of futurity and the immortal soul, which identifies itself with our hopes and with our hearts, as if they were syllogisms or theorems, demonstrable propositions or consecutive corollaries. By them have the higher powers of this artist been kept from public notice, and his genius tied down, as far as possible, to the mechanical department of his profession. By them, in short, has he been stigmatised as an engraver, who might do tolerably well, if he was not mad. But men, whose names will bear them out, in what they affirm, have now taken up his cause. On occasion of Mr. Blake engaging to illustrate the poem of The Grave, some of the first artists in this country have stept forward, and liberally given the sanction of ardent and encomiastic applause. Mr. Fuseli, with a mind far superior to that jealousy above described, has written some introductory remarks in the Prospectus of the work. To these he has lent all the penetration of his understanding, with all the energy and descriptive power characteristic of his style. Mr. Hope and Mr. Locke have pledged their character as connoisseurs, by approving and patronising these designs. Had I been furnished with an opportunity of shewing them to you, I should, on Mr. Blake's behalf, have requested your concurring testimony, which you would not have refused me, had you viewed them in the same light.

Neither is the capacity of this untutored proficient limited to his professional occupation. He has made several irregular and unfinished attempts at poetry. He has dared to venture on the ancient simplicity; and feeling it in his own character and manners, has succeeded better than those, who have only seen it through a glass. His genius in this line assimilates more with the bold and careless freedom, peculiar to our writers at the latter end of the sixteenth, and former part of the seventeenth century, than with the polished phraseology, and just, but subdued thought of the eighteenth.

—Benjamin Heath Malkin, from
"Letter to Thomas Johnes," *A Father's Memoirs of His Child,* 1806, pp. xviii–xxv

Charles Lamb (1824)

In 1824, Bernard Barton wrote to Charles Lamb to ask if he had written Blake's "The Chimney Sweeper," which Lamb had contributed to an anthology for chimney sweepers. The following letter is Lamb's reply. Lamb's acquaintance with Blake's work probably began when Henry Crabb Robinson invited him to Blake's 1809 exhibition. Lamb seems to have been attracted to Blake's work for its strangeness and mysticism. Obscurity, instability, and even madness were enjoying an increasingly privileged status as the Romantic movement gained popularity. Though Lamb tells Barton he knows nothing of Blake's fate and "must look on him as one of the most extraordinary persons of the age," in fact in 1824 Blake was living nearby in Fountain Court.

⸻

Blake is a real name, I assure you, and a most extraordinary man, if he be still living. He is the Robert Blake, whose wild designs accompany a splendid folio edition of the *Night Thoughts,* which you may have seen, in one of which he pictures the parting of soul and body by a solid mass of human form floating off, God knows how, from a lumpish mass (fac Simile to itself) left behind on the dying bed. He paints in water colours marvellous strange pictures, visions of his brain, which he asserts that he has seen. They have great merit. He has *seen* the old Welsh bards on Snowdon—he has seen the Beautifullest, the strongest, and the Ugliest Man, left alone from the Massacre of the Britons by the Romans, and has painted them from memory (I have seen his paintings), and asserts them to be as good as the figures of Raphael and Angelo, but not better, as they had precisely the same retro-visions and prophetic visions with themself. The painters in oil (which he will have it that neither of them practised) he affirms to have been the ruin of art, and affirms that all the while he was engaged in his Water paintings, Titian was disturbing him, Titian the 111 Genius of Oil Painting. His Pictures—one in particular, the Canterbury Pilgrims (far above Stothard's)— have great merit, but hard, dry, yet with grace. He has written a Catalogue of them with a most spirited criticism on Chaucer, but mystical and full of Vision. His poems have been sold hitherto only in Manuscript. I never read them; but a friend at my desire procured the 'Sweep Song.' There is one to a tiger, which I have heard recited, beginning:

Tiger, Tiger, burning bright,

Thro' the desarts of the night,

which is glorious, but alas! I have not the book; for the man is flown, whither I know not—to Hades or a Mad House. But I must look on him as one of the most extraordinary persons of the age.

—Charles Lamb, letter to
Bernard Barton, May 15, 1824

HENRY CRABB ROBINSON (1825–26)

Henry Crabb Robinson did not make Blake's acquaintance until 1825, but he had attended Blake's 1809 Exhibition, and in "William Blake: Künstler, Dichter und Religiöser Schwärmer" (published in *Vaterländisches Museum 2*, January 1, 1811, 107–31), he ranked Blake with the "whole race of ecstatics, mystics, seers of visions and dreams." Malkin's comparison, in *A Father's Memoirs*, of Blake to the Elizabethans struck a chord with Crabb Robinson, himself a student of German Romanticism and an enthusiastic admirer of the British Romantic revival of Elizabethan poetic practices. Crabb Robinson's essay of 1811 refers to Blake's "union of genius and madness." Thus, Blake's perceived madness was gradually reconfigured as a symptom of artistic genius. Between 1825 and 1827, Crabb Robinson met periodically with Blake and produced verbatim records of their conversations, on subjects ranging from Milton, Wordsworth, Dante, and Christ to free love and education. In 1852, Crabb Robinson compiled these records into the "Reminiscence of Blake" (reprinted in *Blake, Coleridge, Wordsworth, Lamb, Etc.*). They supplied Blake's first major biographer, Alexander Gilchrist, with important source material. Gilchrist did not question the accuracy of Crabb Robinson's record, but he did suggest that the diarist, a "friendly but very logical and cool-headed interlocutor," might "ruffle" Blake into "incoherences" or "extreme statements." Where Crabb Robinson had seen Blake's "interesting insanities" as signs of genius, Gilchrist defused Blakean volatility and brilliance—calling it ruffled incoherence—in order to defend Blake's sanity.

December 10th.—Dined with Aders. A very remarkable and interesting evening. The party at dinner Blake the painter, and Linnell, also a painter. In the evening, Miss Denman and Miss Flaxman came.

Shall I call Blake artist, genius, mystic, or madman? Probably he is all. I will put down without method what I can recollect of the conversation of this remarkable man. He has a most interesting appearance. He is now old (sixty-eight), pale, with a Socratic countenance and an expression of great sweetness, though with something of languor about it except when animated, and then he has about him an air of inspiration. The conversation turned on art, poetry, and religion. He brought with him an engraving of his "Canterbury Pilgrims." One of the figures in it is like a figure in a picture belonging to Mr. Aders. "They say I stole it from this picture," said Blake, "but I did it twenty years before I knew of this picture. However, in my youth, I was always studying paintings of this kind. No wonder there is a resemblance." In this he seemed to explain *humanly* what he had done. But at another time he spoke of his paintings as being what he had seen in his visions. And when he said "my visions," it was in the ordinary unemphatic tone in which we speak of every-day matters. In the same tone he said repeatedly, "The Spirit told me." I took occasion to say: "You express yourself as Socrates used to do. What resemblance do you suppose there is between your spirit and his?"—"The same as between our countenances.' He paused and added, "I was Socrates"; and then, as if correcting himself, said, "a sort of brother. I must have had conversations with him. So I had with Jesus Christ. I have an obscure recollection of having been with both of them." I suggested, on philosophical grounds, the impossibility of supposing an immortal being created, an eternity *a parte post* without an eternity *a parte ante*. His eye brightened at this, and he fully concurred with me. "To be sure, it is impossible. We are all coexistent with God, members of the Divine body. We are all partakers of the Divine nature." In this, by the by, Blake has but adopted an ancient Greek idea. As connected with this idea, I will mention here, though it formed part of our talk as we were walking homeward, that on my asking in what light he viewed the great question concerning the deity of Jesus Christ, he said: "He is the only God. But then," he added, "and so am I, and so are you." He had just before (and that occasioned my question) been speaking of the errors of Jesus Christ. Jesus Christ should not have allowed himself to be crucified, and should not have attacked the government. On my inquiring how this view could be reconciled with the sanctity and Divine qualities of Jesus, Blake said: "He was not then become the Father." Connecting, as well as one can, these fragmentary sentiments, it would be hard to fix Blake's station between Christianity, Platonism, and Spinozism. Yet he professes to be very hostile to Plato, and reproaches Wordsworth with being not a Christian, but a Platonist.

It is one of the subtle remarks of Hume, on certain religious speculations, that the tendency of them is to make men indifferent to whatever takes place, by destroying all ideas of good and evil. I took occasion to apply this remark to something Blake had said. "If so," I said, "there is no use in discipline or education,—no difference between good and evil." He hastily broke in upon me: "There is no use in education. I hold it to be wrong. It is the great sin. It is eating of the tree of the knowledge of good and evil. This was the fault of Plato. He knew of nothing but the virtues and vices, and good and evil. There is nothing in all that. Everything is good in God's eyes." On my putting the obvious question, "Is there nothing absolutely evil in what men do?"—"I am no judge of that. Perhaps not in God's eyes." He sometimes spoke as if he denied altogether the existence of evil, and as if we had nothing to do with right and wrong; it being sufficient to consider all things as alike the work of God. Yet at other times he spoke of there being error in heaven. I asked about the moral character of Dante, in writing his "Vision,"—was he pure?—"Pure," said Blake, "do you think there is any purity in God's eyes? The angels in heaven are no more so than we. 'He chargeth his angels with folly.'" He afterwards represented the Supreme Being as liable to error. "Did he not repent him that he had made Nineveh?" It is easier to repeat the personal remarks of Blake than these metaphysical speculations, so nearly allied to the most opposite systems of philosophy. Of himself, he said he acted by command. The Spirit said to him, "Blake, be an artist, and nothing else." In this there is felicity. His eye glistened while he spoke of the joy of devoting himself solely to divine art. Art is inspiration. When Michael Angelo, or Raphael, or Mr. Flaxman, does any of his fine things, he does them in the Spirit. Blake said: "I should be sorry if I had any earthly fame, for whatever natural glory a man has is so much taken from his spiritual glory. I wish to do nothing for profit. I wish to live for art. I want nothing whatever. I am quite happy."

Among the unintelligible things he expressed was his distinction between the natural world and the spiritual. The natural world must be consumed. Incidentally, Swedenborg was referred to. Blake said: "He was a divine teacher. He has done much good, and will do much. He has corrected many errors of Popery, and also of Luther and Calvin. Yet Swedenborg was wrong in endeavoring to explain to the rational faculty what the reason cannot comprehend. He should have left that." Blake, as I have said, thinks Wordsworth no Christian, but a Platonist. He asked me whether Wordsworth believed in the Scriptures. On my replying in the affirmative, he said he had been much pained by reading the Introduction to "The Excursion." It brought on a fit of illness. The passage was produced and read:—

Jehovah,—with this thunder and the choir

Of shouting angels, and the empyreal thrones,—

I pass them unalarmed.

This *"pass them unalarmed"* greatly offended Blake. Does Mr. Wordsworth think his mind can surpass Jehovah? I tried to explain this passage in a sense in harmony with Blake's own theories, but failed, and Wordsworth was finally set down as a Pagan; but still with high praise, as the greatest poet of the age.

Jacob Boehme was spoken of as a divinely inspired man. Blake praised, too, the figures in Law's translation as being very beautiful. Michael Angelo could not have done better.

Though he spoke of his happiness, he also alluded to past sufferings, and to suffering as necessary. "There is suffering in heaven, for where there is the capacity of enjoyment, there is also the capacity of pain."

I have been interrupted by a call from Talfourd, and cannot now recollect any further remarks. But as Blake has invited me to go and see him, I shall possibly have an opportunity of throwing connection, if not system, into what I have written, and making additions. I feel great admiration and respect for him. He is certainly a most amiable man,—a good creature. And of his poetical and pictorial genius there is no doubt, I believe, in the minds of judges. Wordsworth and Lamb like his poems, and the Aderses his paintings.

A few detached thoughts occur to me. "Bacon, Locke, and Newton are the three great teachers of Atheism, or of Satan's doctrine."

"Everything is Atheism which assumes the reality of the natural and unspiritual world."

"Irving is a highly gifted man. He is a *sent* man. But they who are sent go further sometimes than they ought."

"Dante saw devils where I see none. I see good only. I saw nothing but good in Calvin's house. Better than in Luther's,— in the latter were harlots."

"Parts of Swedenborg's scheme are dangerous. His sexual religion is so."

"I do not believe the world is round. I believe it is quite flat."

"I have conversed with the spiritual Sun. I saw him on Primrose Hill. He said, 'Do you take me for the Greek Apollo?'—'No,' I said; 'that' (pointing to the sky) 'is the Greek Apollo. He is Satan.'"

"I know what is true by internal conviction. A doctrine is told me. My heart says, 'It must be true.'" I corroborated this by remarking on the impossibility of the unlearned man judging of what are called the *external* evidences of religion, in which he heartily concurred.

I regret that I have been unable to do more than put down these few things. The tone and manner are incommunicable. There are a natural sweetness and gentility about Blake which are delightful. His friend Linnell seems a great admirer.

Perhaps the best thing he said was his comparison of moral with natural evil. "Who shall say that God thinks evil! That is a wise tale of the Mahometans, of the angel of the Lord that murdered the infant" (alluding to the "Hermit" of Parnell, I suppose). "Is not every infant that dies of disease murdered by an angel?"

December 17th.—A short call this morning on Blake. He dwells in Fountain Court, in the Strand. I found him in a small room, which seems to be both a working-room and a bedroom. Nothing could exceed the squalid air both of the apartment and his dress; yet there is diffused over him an air of natural gentility. His wife was a good expression of countenance.

I found him at work on Dante. The book (Cary) and his sketches before him. He showed me his designs, of which I have nothing to say but that they evince a power I should not have anticipated, of grouping and of throwing grace and interest over conceptions monstrous and horrible.

Our conversation began about Dante. He was an Atheist,—a mere politician, busied about this world, as Milton was, till in his old age he returned to God, whom he had had in his childhood."

I tried to ascertain from Blake whether this charge of Atheism was not to be understood in a different sense from that which would be given to it according to the popular use of the word. But he would not admit this. Yet when he in like manner charged Locke with Atheism, and I remarked that Locke wrote on the evidences of Christianity and lived a virtuous life, Blake had nothing to say in reply. Nor did he make the charge of wilful deception. I admitted that Locke's doctrine leads to Atheism, and with this view Blake seemed to be satisfied.

From this subject we passed over to that of good and evil, on which he repeated his former assertions more decidedly. He allowed, indeed, that there are errors, mistakes, &c; and if these be evil, then there is evil. But these are only negations. Nor would he admit that any education should be attempted, except that of the cultivation of the imagination and fine arts. "What are called the vices in the natural world are the highest sublimities in the spiritual world." When I asked whether, if he had been a father, he would not have grieved if his child had become vicious or a great criminal, he answered:

"When I am endeavoring to think rightly, I must not regard my own any more than other people's weaknesses." And when I again remarked that this doctrine puts an end to all exertion, or even wish to change anything, he made no reply.

We spoke of the Devil, and I observed that, when a child, I thought the Manichean doctrine, or that of two principles, a rational one. He assented to this, and in confirmation asserted that he did not believe in the omnipotence of God. The language of the Bible on that subject is only poetical or allegorical. Yet soon afterwards he denied that the natural world is anything. "It is all nothing; and Satan's empire is the empire of nothing."

He reverted soon to his favorite expression, "My visions." "I saw Milton, and he told me to beware of being misled by his *Paradise Lost*. In particular, he wished me to show the falsehood of the doctrine, that carnal pleasures arose from the Fall. The Fall could not produce any pleasure." As he spoke of Milton's appearing to him, I asked whether he resembled the prints of him. He answered, "All."—"What age did he appear to be?"—"Various ages,— sometimes a very old man." He spoke of Milton as being at one time a sort of classical Atheist, and of Dante as being now with God. His faculty of vision, he says, he has had from early infancy. He thinks all men partake of it, but it is lost for want of being cultivated. He eagerly assented to a remark I made, that all men have all faculties in a greater or less degree.

I am to continue my visits, and to read to him Wordsworth, of whom he seems to entertain a high idea. . . .

February 18th.—Called on Blake. An amusing chat with him. He gave me in his own handwriting a copy of Wordsworth's Preface to *The Excursion*. At the end there is this note:—

"Solomon, when he married Pharaoh's daughter, and became a convert to the heathen mythology, talked exactly in this way of Jehovah, as a very inferior object of man's contemplation. He also passed him by 'unalarmed,' and was permitted. Jehovah dropped a tear, and followed him by his Spirit into the abstract void. It is called the Divine mercy. Satan dwells in it, but mercy does not dwell in him."

Of Wordsworth Blake talked as before. Some of his writings proceed from the Holy Spirit, but others are the work of the Devil. However, on this subject, I found Blake's language more in accordance with orthodox Christianity than before. He talked of being under the direction of self. Reason, as the creature of man, is opposed to God's grace. He warmly declared that all he knew is in the Bible. But he understands the Bible in its spiritual sense. As to the natural sense, he says: "Voltaire was commissioned by God to expose that. I have had much intercourse with Voltaire, and he said to me, 'I blasphemed the Son of Man, and it shall be forgiven me'; but they (the enemies of Voltaire) blasphemed the Holy Ghost in me, and it shall not be forgiven them." I asked in what language Voltaire spoke. "To my sensations, it was English. It was like the touch of a musical key. He touched it, probably, French, but to my ear it became English." I spoke again of the *form* of the persons who appear to him, and asked why he did not draw them. "It is not worth while. There are so many, the labor would be too great. Besides, there would be no use. As to Shakespeare, he is exactly like the *old* engraving, which is called a bad one. I think it very good."

I inquired of Blake about his writings. "I have written more than Voltaire or Rousseau. Six or seven epic poems as long as Homer, and twenty tragedies as long as Macbeth." He showed me his vision (for so it may be called) of Genesis,—"as understood by a Christian visionary." He read a passage at random; it was striking. He will not print any more. "I write," he says, "when commanded by the spirits, and the moment I have written I see the words fly about the room in all directions. It is then published, and the spirits can read. My MS. is of no further use. I have been tempted to burn my MSS., but my wife won't let me."—"She is right," said I. "You have written these, not from yourself, but by order of higher beings. The MSS. are theirs, not yours. You cannot tell what purpose they may answer unforeseen by you." He liked this, and said he would not destroy them. He repeated his philosophy. Everything is the work of God or the Devil. There is a constant falling off from God, angels becoming devils. Every man has a devil in him, and the conflict is eternal between a man's self and God, &c, &c. He told me my copy of his songs would be five guineas, and was pleased by my manner of receiving this information. He spoke of his horror of money,—of his having turned pale when money was offered him.

—Henry Crabb Robinson, from *Diary*, 1825–26

Frederick Tatham
"The Life of William Blake" (1832)

Frederick Tatham (1805–1878) was one of the Shoreham Disciples (or Shoreham Ancients), a circle of young artists—including Samuel Palmer, Edward Calvert, John Linnell, and George Richmond—greatly influenced by Blake in the 1820s. When Blake died in 1827, the disciples encouraged each other to record their memories of their mentor. Tatham alone wrote a substantial memoir, one that importantly speaks of Blake not just as a visionary and an artist, but as a flesh-and-blood human. Tatham formed a close friendship with Blake's widow, Catherine, and after her death in 1831, claimed inheritance of her husband's work. Upon his conversion to the millenarian Irvingite sect, Tatham destroyed many of Blake's works, under the impression that they were inspired by the Devil.

———

William Blake in stature was short, but well made, and very well proportioned; so much so that West, the great history painter, admired much the form of his limbs; he had a large head and wide shoulders. Elasticity and promptitude of action were the characteristics of his contour. His motions were rapid and energetic, betokening a mind filled with elevated enthusiasm; his forehead was very high and prominent over the frontals; his eye most unusually large and glassy, with which he appeared to look into some other world. The best and only likeness of this glowing feature that can be produced is Shakespeare's description of the eye of the inspired poet in his *Midsummer Night's Dream:*

The poet's eye with a fine frenzy rolling—
Doth glance from heaven to earth, from earth to
heaven:
And as imagination bodies forth
The forms of things unknown, the poet's pen
Turns them to shapes, and gives to airy nothing
A local habitation and a name.

In youth he surprised everyone with his vigour and activity. In age he impressed all with his unfading ardour and unabated energy. His beautiful grey locks hung upon his shoulders; and dressing as he always did in latter years in black, he looked, even in person, although without any effort towards eccentricity, to be of no ordinary character. In youth, he was nimble; in old age, venerable. His disposition was cheerful and lively, and was never depressed by any cares but those springing out of his art. He was the attached friend of all who knew him, and a favourite with everyone but those who oppressed him, and against such his noble and impetuous spirit boiled, and fell upon the aggressor like a water-spout from the troubled deep. Yet, like Moses, he was one of the meekest of men. His patience was almost incredible: he could be the lamb; he could plod as a camel; he could roar as a lion. He was everything but subtle; the serpent had no share in his nature; secrecy was unknown to him. He would relate those things of himself that others make it their utmost endeavour to conceal. He was possessed of a peculiar obstinacy, that always bristled up when he was either unnecessarily opposed or invited out to show like a lion or a bear. Many anecdotes could be related in which there is sufficient evidence to prove that many of his eccentric speeches were thrown forth more as a piece of sarcasm upon the inquirer than from his real opinion. If he thought a question were put merely for a desire to learn, no man could give advice more reasonably and more kindly; but if that same question were put for idle curiosity, he retaliated by such an eccentric answer as left the inquirer more afield than ever. He then made an enigma of a plain question: hence arose many vague reports of his oddities. He was particularly so upon religion. His writings abounded with these sallies of independent opinion. He detested priestcraft and religious cant. He wrote much upon controversial subjects, and, like all controversies, these writings are inspired by doubt and made up of vain conceits and whimsical extravagances. A bad cause requires a long book. Generally advocating one in which there is a flaw, the greatest controversialists are the greatest doubters. They are trembling needles between extreme points. Irritated by hypocrisy and the unequivocal yielding of weak and interested men, he said and wrote unwarrantable arguments; but unalloyed and unencumbered by opposition, he was in all essential points orthodox in his belief. But he put forth ramifications of doubt, that by his vigorous and creative mind were watered into the empty enormities of extravagant and rebellious thoughts.

He was intimate with a great many of the most learned and eminent men of his time, whom he generally met at Johnson's, the bookseller of St. Paul's Churchyard. It was there he met Tom Paine, and was the cause of his escaping to America, when the Government were seeking for him for the punishment of his seditious and refractory writings. Blake advised him immediately to fly, for he said: "If you are not now sought, I am sure you soon will be." Paine took the hint directly, and found he had just escaped in time. In one of his conversations, Paine said that religion was a law and a tie to all able minds. Blake, on the other hand, said what he was always asserting, that the religion of Jesus was a perfect law of liberty. Fuseli was very intimate with Blake, and Blake was more fond of Fuseli than any other man on earth. Blake certainly loved him, and at least Fuseli admired Blake and learned from him, as he himself confessed, a great deal. Fuseli and Flaxman both said that Blake was the greatest man in the country, and that there would come a time when his works would be invaluable. Before Fuseli knew Blake, he used to fill his pictures with all sorts of fashionable ornaments and tawdry embellishments. Blake's simplicity imbued the minds of all who knew him; his life was a pattern, and has been spoken of as such from the pulpit. His abstraction from the world, his power of self-denial, his detestation of hypocrisy and gain, his hatred of gold and the things that perish, rendered him indeed well able to have exclaimed:

In innocency I have washed my hands. His poetry (and he has written a great deal) was mostly unintelligible, but not so much so as the works written in the manner of the present one. Generally speaking, he seems to have published those most mysterious. That which could be discerned was filled with imagery and fine epithet. What but admiration can be expressed of such poetry as ("London," "The Tiger," and "The Lamb.")

—Frederick Tatham, "The Life of William Blake,"
1832, *The Letters of William Blake,*
ed. A.G.B. Russell, 1906, pp. 37–41

Samuel Palmer (1855)

Samuel Palmer (1805–1881), an etcher, painter, and printmaker, was another member of the Shoreham Disciples (or Shoreham Ancients). Palmer first met Blake in 1824, when he was nineteen. Decades later, he and John Linnell were the most important personal sources for Blake's first major biographer, Alexander Gilchrist. In addition to supplying Gilchrist with personal anecdotes, Palmer contributed a description of the designs in *The Marriage of Heaven and Hell* and the following memorial letter, both of which Gilchrist published unaltered in his *Life of William Blake.* The letter displays Palmer's reverence and affection for Blake. That the missive stresses so heavily Blake's Christian faith probably says more of Palmer's own faith (and his desire to see Blake honored by Victorian society) than it reveals about Blake's inner life.

I regret that the lapse of time has made it difficult to recal many interesting particulars respecting Mr. Blake, of whom I can give you no connected account; nothing more, in fact, than the fragments of memory; but the general impression of what is great remains with us, although its details may be confused; and Blake, once known, could never be forgotten.

His knowledge was various and extensive, and his conversation so nervous and brilliant, that, if recorded at the time, it would now have thrown much light upon his character, and in no way lessened him in the estimation of those who know him only by his works.

In him you saw at once the Maker, the Inventor; one of the few in any age: a fitting companion for Dante. He was energy itself, and shed around him a kindling influence; an atmosphere of life, full of the ideal. To walk with him in the country was to perceive the soul of beauty through the forms of matter; and the high gloomy buildings between which, from his study window, a glimpse was caught of the Thames and the Surrey shore, assumed a kind of grandeur from the man dwelling near them. Those may laugh at this who never knew such an one as Blake; but of him it is the simple truth.

He was a man without a mask; his aim single, his path straightforwards, and his wants few; so he was free, noble, and happy.

His voice and manner were quiet, yet all awake with intellect. Above the tricks of littleness, or the least taint of affectation, with a natural dignity which few would have dared to affront, he was gentle and affectionate, loving to be with little children, and to talk about them. "That is heaven," he said to a friend, leading him to the window, and pointing to a group of them at play.

Declining, like Socrates, whom in many respects he resembled, the common objects of ambition, and pitying the scuffle to obtain them, he thought that no one could be truly great who had not humbled himself "even as a little child." This was a subject he loved to dwell upon, and to illustrate.

His eye was the finest I ever saw: brilliant, but not roving, clear and intent, yet susceptible; it flashed with genius, or melted in tenderness. It could also be terrible. Cunning and falsehood quailed under it, but it was never busy with them. It pierced them, and turned away. Nor was the mouth less expressive; the lips flexible and quivering with feeling. I can yet recal it when, on one occasion, dwelling upon the exquisite beauty of the parable of the Prodigal, he began to repeat a part of it; but at the words, "When he was yet a great way off, his father saw him," could go no further; his voice faltered, and he was in tears.

I can never forget the evening when Mr. Linnell took me to Blake's house, nor the quiet hours passed with him in the examination of antique gems, choice pictures, and Italian prints of the sixteenth century. Those who may have read some strange passages in his *Catalogue,* written in irritation, and probably in haste, will be surprised to hear, that in conversation he was anything but sectarian or exclusive, finding sources of delight throughout the whole range of art; while, as a critic, he was judicious and discriminating.

No man more admired Albert Dürer; yet, after looking over a number of his designs, he would become a little angry with some of the draperies, as not governed by the forms of the limbs, nor assisting to express their action; contrasting them in this respect with the draped antique, in which it was hard to tell whether he was more delighted with the general design, or with the exquisite finish and the depth of the chiselling; in works of the highest class, no mere adjuncts, but the last development of the design itself.

He united freedom of judgment with reverence of all that is great. He did not look out for the works of the purest ages, but for the purest works of every age and country—Athens or Rhodes, Tuscany or Britain; but no authority or popular consent could influence him against his deliberate judgment. Thus he thought with Fuseli and Flaxman that the Elgin Theseus, however full of antique savour, could not, as ideal form, rank with the very finest relics of antiquity. Nor, on the other hand, did the universal neglect of Fuseli in any degree lessen his admiration of his best works.

He fervently loved the early Christian art, and dwelt with peculiar affection on the memory of Fra Angelico, often speaking of him as an inspired inventor and as a saint; but when he approached Michael Angelo, the Last Supper of Da Vinci, the Torso Belvidere, and some of the inventions preserved in the Antique Gems, all his powers were concentrated in admiration.

When looking at the heads of the apostles in the copy of the *Last Supper* at the Royal Academy, he remarked of all but Judas, "Every one looks as if he had conquered the natural man." He was equally ready to admire a contemporary and a rival. Fuseli's picture of *Satan building the Bridge over Chaos* he ranked with the grandest efforts of imaginative art, and said that we were two centuries behind the civilization which would enable us to estimate his *Ægisthus*.

He was fond of the works of St. Theresa, and often quoted them with other writers on the interior life. Among his eccentricities will, no doubt, be numbered his preference for ecclesiastical governments. He used to ask how it was that we heard so much of priestcraft, and so little of soldiercraft and lawyercraft. The Bible, he said, was the book of liberty and Christianity the sole regenerator of nations. In politics a Platonist, he put no trust in demagogues. His ideal home was with Fra Angelico: a little later he might have been a reformer, but after the fashion of Savanarola.

He loved to speak of the years spent by Michael Angelo, without earthly reward, and solely for the love of God, in the building of St. Peter's, and of the wondrous architects of our cathedrals. In Westminster Abbey were his earliest and most sacred recollections. I asked him how he would like to paint on glass, for the great west window, his "Sons of God shouting for Joy," from his designs in the *Job*. He said, after a pause, "I could do it!" kindling at the thought.

Centuries could not separate him in spirit from the artists who went about our land, pitching their tents by the morass or the forest side, to build those sanctuaries that now lie ruined amidst the fertility which they called into being.

His mind was large enough to contain, along with these things, stores of classic imagery. He delighted in Ovid, and, as a labour of love, had executed a finished picture from the *Metamorphoses,* after Giulio Romano. This design hung in his room, and, close by his engraving table, Albert Dürer's *Melancholy the Mother of Invention,* memorable as probably having been seen by Milton, and used in his "Penseroso." There are living a few artists, then boys, who may remember the smile of welcome with which he used to rise from that table to receive them.

His poems were variously estimated. They tested rather severely the imaginative capacity of their readers. Flaxman said they were as grand as his designs, and Wordsworth delighted in his *Songs of Innocence.* To the multitude they were unintelligible. In many parts full of pastoral sweetness, and often flashing with noble thoughts or terrible imagery, we must regret that he should sometimes have suffered fancy to trespass within sacred precincts.

Thrown early among the authors who resorted to Johnson, the bookseller, he rebuked the profanity of Paine, and was no disciple of Priestley; but, too undisciplined and cast upon times and circumstances which yielded him neither guidance nor sympathy, he wanted that balance of the faculties which might have assisted him in matters extraneous to his profession. He saw everything through art, and, in matters beyond its range, exalted it from a witness into a judge.

He had great powers of argument, and on general subjects was a very patient and good-tempered disputant; but materialism was his abhorrence: and if some unhappy man called in question the world of spirits, he would answer him "according to his folly," by putting forth his own views in their most extravagant and startling aspect. This might amuse those who were in the secret, but it left his opponent angry and bewildered.

Such was Blake, as I remember him. He was one of the few to be met with in our passage through life, who are not, in some way or other, "double minded" and inconsistent with themselves; one of the very few who cannot be depressed by neglect, and to whose name rank and station could add no lustre. Moving apart, in a sphere above the attraction of wordly honours, he did not accept greatness, but confer it. He ennobled poverty, and, by his conversation and the influence of his genius, made two small rooms in Fountain Court more attractive than the threshold of princes.

—Samuel Palmer, letter to Alexander Gilchrist,
August 23, 1855, *Life of William Blake* by
Alexander Gilchrist, 1863, vol. 1, pp. 301–304

Seymour Kirkup (1870)

Seymour Kirkup (1788–1880), painter and antiquary, was a younger contemporary of Blake's. In 1864, Blake biographer Algernon Charles Swinburne visited Kirkup on the Continent, adding his recollections to Swinburne's *William Blake*. In 1866, Kirkup wrote to the art critic William Rossetti, explaining, much as he does in this letter to Lord Houghton, that he had once thought Blake mad but does not think so now. Kirkup's developing fascination with spiritualism may in part explain this conversion.

—◊◊◊— —◊◊◊— —◊◊◊—

Another person with whom I was intimate long ago is one in whom I know that your lordship has taken great interest, and has collected a great number of most valuable works of his genius—W. Blake. I was much with him from 1810 to 1816, when I came abroad, and have remained in Italy ever since. I might have learned much from him. I was then a student of the Royal Academy, in the antique school, where I gained a medal, and thought more of form than anything else. I was by nature a lover of colour, and my *beau ideal* was the union of Phidias and Titian. Blake was the determined enemy of colourists, and his drawing was not very academical. His high qualities I did not prize at that time; besides, I thought him mad. I do not think so now. I never suspected him of imposture. His manner was too honest for that. He was very kind to me, though very positive in his opinion, with which I never agreed. His excellent old wife was a sincere believer in all his visions. She told me seriously one day, "I have very little of Mr. Blake's company; he is always in Paradise." She prepared his colours, and was as good as a servant. He had no other. It was Mr. Butts who introduced me to him. I was a schoolfellow of his son's, whom he sent to Blake to learn engraving, which was his original art. Let me tell you now of a large picture he painted in my time. I thought it his best work—a battle from the Welsh Triads. The three last men who remained of Arthur's army, and who defeated the enemy—the strongest man, the handsomest man, and the ugliest man. As he was an enemy of oil painting, which he said was the ruin of painting, he invented a method of applying fresco to canvas, and this life-size picture was the result. It made so great an impression on me that I made a drawing of it fifty years afterwards, which I gave to Swinburne. You can see it. It (the picture) must have been about 14 feet by 10. In texture it was rather mealy, as we call it, and was too red; the sun seemed setting in blood. It was not Greek in character. Though the figures reminded one of Hercules, Apollo, and Pan, they were naked

Britons. If you should ever hear of it, it is worth seeking. There is more power and drawing in it than in any of his works that I have known, even in Blair's grave, respecting which he was enraged against Schiavonetti for correcting some defects. In general, engravers fail to do justice, and the most precious works have been etched by the painters themselves.

—Seymour Kirkup, letter to Lord Houghton,
March 25, 1870, cited in T. Wemyss Reid,
*The Life, Letters, and Friendships of
Richard Monckton Milnes, First Lord Houghton,*
1891, vol. 2, pp. 222–223

Dante Gabriel Rossetti "William Blake" (1880–81)

In 1860, halfway through writing his *Life of William Blake*, Alexander Gilchrist learned that Dante Gabriel Rossetti owned Blake's manuscript *Note-book*. Gilchrist applied to Rossetti for assistance, and soon Rossetti was so involved in Gilchrist's project he was suggesting the names of copyists and engravers. When Gilchrist died in November 1861, Rossetti volunteered his services, along with those of his brother, William Michael Rossetti, so beginning a fertile correspondence with Mrs. Gilchrist. Rossetti co-opted Blake as a proto-Pre-Raphaelite, seeing in Blake the sensuous and spiritual qualities he himself valued. This, coupled with the tremendous popularity of the Pre-Raphaelites in the 1870s and 1880s, helped Blake to belated fame.

———

This is the place. Even here the dauntless soul,
The unflinching hand, wrought on; till in that nook,
As on that very bed, his life partook
New birth, and passed. Yon river's dusky shoal,
Whereto the close-built coiling lanes unroll,
Faced his work-window, whence his eyes would stare,
Thought-wandering, unto nought that met them there,
But to the unfettered irreversible goal.
This cupboard, Holy of Holies, held the cloud
Of his soul writ and limned; this other one,
His true wife's charge, full oft to their abode
Yielded for daily bread the martyr's stone,

Ere yet their food might be that Bread alone,
The words now home-speech of the mouth of God.

—Dante Gabriel Rossetti, "William Blake,"
Five English Poets, 1880–81

GENERAL

The first volume of Alexander Gilchrist's *The Life of William Blake, "Pictor Ignotus," with Selections from His Poems and Other Writings* (1863) was a turning point in Blake biography, bringing a little known engraver, dead almost forty years, into the public eye. The second volume of Gilchrist's *Life*, the *Selections*, introduced Blake's writing—some of it, at least—to the general public for the first time. Virtually from Blake's death until 1863, his poetry was seen by few individuals beyond rare manuscript collectors and by such enthusiasts (Dante Gabriel Rossetti was one) who managed to gain access to private collections. Freely edited quotations had appeared in Allan Cunningham's *Lives of the Painters*. Transcriptions of isolated poems also sparingly surfaced (such as "The Chimney Sweeper," contributed by Charles Lamb to an anthology for chimney sweepers). An edition of *Songs of Innocence and Experience*, edited and with a preface by James John Garth Wilkinson, was published in 1839. But all of these publications, unlike the popular *Life of William Blake*, were not widely distributed.

The *Selections* made Blake available to a wide audience. Until its publication, Allan Cunningham's unsympathetic account in his *Lives of the Painters* (1830) had been the dominant, if not only, accessible resource. Cunningham ridiculed Blake's visions, mocked his preoccupation with angels, and propounded a version of Blake as gifted but insane. "Blake's misfortune," he wrote, "was that of possessing this precious gift [imagination] in excess." The madman tag stuck, and it was only with Gilchrist's discrediting of Cunningham's "pleasant mannered generalities, easy to read, hard to verify," that madness could be rewritten as genius. Now the growing number of Blake readers were free (or freer) to make up their own minds, based on their exposure to a carefully chosen selection of Blake's least unorthodox poetry.

The editors' desperation to produce a Blake acceptable to his newfound mid-Victorian audience meant that the *Selections* was woefully inadequate. The poems were bowdlerized, smoothed over, and Blake's prosody was "tidied up." Following Gilchrist's death two years before publication, there had been several editors and editorial advisers (including brothers Dante Gabriel and William Michael Rossetti, Algernon Charles Swinburne, and Anne Gilchrist), and thus an inconsistent editorial vision and principles. No work of Blake's written after 1794 was included, and, aside from the *Book of Thel,* none of the so-called Prophetic Books (*Tiriel*; *The Book of Thel*; *America a Prophecy*; *Europe a Prophecy*; *Visions of the Daughters of Albion*; *The Book of Urizen*; *The Book of Ahania*; *The Book of Los*; *Song of Los*; *Vala, or the Four Zoas*; *Milton, a Poem*; and *Jerusalem: The Emanation of the Giant Albion*). Rossetti initially intended to include an "extract" from *The French Revolution* (the word *extract* itself is a troubling index of the liberties these editors took), but he was discouraged by Swinburne and ended up omitting it.

Despite the careful vetting of Blake's writing, the debate over whether William Blake was a genius, a visionary, or an insane person raged on, and it reprises throughout the nineteenth-century commentary. Anna Jameson had anticipated the debate in 1848, when she invited a rereading of Blake's "madness" as a "telescope of truth," a "poetical clairvoyance." Conservative poet Coventry Patmore, reviewing the 1876 Burlington Fine Arts Club exhibition of Blake's work, denounced Blake's "craziness" and the way Patmore's own contemporary critics had configured madness as a symptom of genius rather than of moral and intellectual degeneration. (Patmore's critique is stunningly unforgiving, beginning: "Blake's poetry, with the exception of four or five lovely lyrics and here and there in the other pieces a startling gleam of unquestionable genius, is mere drivel.") The leaders of the visionary camp, Edwin J. Ellis and William Butler Yeats, argued in 1893 that Blake's texts, read together, comprised an elaborate Symbolic System, pointing to occult lore. The Symbolic System was theirs, not Blake's, but the implication of a latent order and meaning to what had long been read as burble prepared the way for some of the more enduring scholarly readings of the twentieth century.

The *Selections* were also important because they presented Blake as a poet. Beyond Allan Cunningham's skewed profile of Blake in *Lives of the Painters*, Anna Jameson in *Sacred and Legendary Art* and Walter Thornbury in *British Artists from Hogarth to Turner* also examined Blake's artistic endeavors.

When Dante Gabriel Rossetti wrote the "Supplementary" chapter to *The Life of William Blake*, he concentrated on Blake's linework and pigmentation, despite being a poet as well as an artist himself. Blake the engraver and Blake the illuminator had attracted far more attention than Blake the poet. As a writer, Blake seemed to operate outside established traditions. When Rossetti's "Supplementary" commentary does turn to the subject of Blake's poetry, it concentrates on its singularity, its disconnection from anything produced by the Romantics or the high Victorians. It was difficult to talk about Blake's verse because it was unlike anything else. Rossetti expects it to remain unappreciated and preemptively pens its eulogy.

In the flurry of critical and editorial activity that followed publication of *The Life of William Blake*, though, Blake's writing was anthologized in increasingly complete form. Where Blake had been once a "painter," now his poetry was in danger of being permanently severed from his engraving and illumination. Stripped of contextual clues, some of the earlier poems were read as childlike and conceptually simple: the anti-establishmentarian rancor of the *Songs of Innocence* and *Songs of Experience*, for instance, eluded many nineteenth-century commentators, who relied solely on print editions.

The second major book of the 1860s Blake revival came in 1866 with Algernon Swinburne's *William Blake: A Critical Essay*. With its publication, Swinburne redressed some of the deficiencies of Gilchrist's *Selections*, by writing extensively of the Prophetic Books, with substantial excerpted quotation. Swinburne was himself a controversial figure, decadent before decadence became fashionable, his poetry recurring to themes of sadomasochism, homosexuality, and irreligion. His reading of Blake, unsurprisingly, relishes the Prophetic Books' preemptive affront to Victorian pieties. Blake, he observes, deconstructs the categories of good and evil, Hell and Heaven, angel and devil. Swinburne is the first to catalogue these inversions, but he mistakenly reads Blake as being all and entirely on the side of the active, energetic, destructive, revolutionary—"of the devil's party" (as Blake himself writes of John Milton). He ignores Blake's insistence on a dialectic, explained in *The Marriage of Heaven and Hell*:

> Without Contraries is no progression. Attraction and Repulsion, Reason and Energy, Love and Hate, are necessary to Human existence.
>
> From these contraries spring what the religious call Good & Evil. Good is the passive that obeys Reason. Evil is the active springing from Energy.
>
> Good is Heaven. Evil is Hell. (Plate 3)

These sets of opposites all replicate one particular opposition: that of reason and religion against the creative energy of humanity. As Blake sees it, humanity needs both the disorderly will and the ordering principles of reason. Each represses and perverts the other, but so long as they remain adversaries, there will be progress. In his anxiety to incarnate Blake as forefather to his own apostasy, Swinburne misses Blake's point: that the force of rebellion is necessarily matched by a force of restraint. He does, however, give us a unified Blake, finding recurring concepts and narratives in the Prophetic Books.

Moncure Conway's review of Swinburne's *William Blake* offers a vigorous and distinctly American rereading of Blake. Revolutionary, abolitionist, republican Blake was deeply interested in the United States, and Conway's investigation of what Blake could mean for that country, just three years after the Civil War, is a serious study of the Prophetic Books in its own right. Conway's Blake envisages a "heavenly Jerusalem" for the United States, a "transcendentalized" (but still democratic) alternative to Thomas Paine's vision of concrete, material change.

Swinburne and Conway offered two of the few nineteenth-century studies of the Prophetic Books. For most of the century, Blake's critics confined their attentions to the *Songs of Innocence and of Experience*, the *Poetical Sketches*, and the *Marriage of Heaven and Hell*. The remainder of Blake's considerable oeuvre was regarded as impenetrable, confirmation of the enduring allegations of Blake's mental illness or instability. When William Butler Yeats and Edwin J. Ellis published *The Works of William Blake, Poetic, Symbolic, and Critical* in 1893, they revolutionized the status of the Prophetic Books. From the apparently daunting disorder of those books, they retrieved what they called "the Symbolic System," a map of Blake's myths and an illumination of the connections between them, a theory of Blake's overall purpose. The *Works* is regarded by contemporary scholars as brilliant but unsound, in many ways a resource better suited to showing us Yeats's and Ellis's minds than Blake's. Rather than focusing on specific poems, their intention is to read all of Blake's work—as much as survived to them—as so many stages in the development of his occult "System." This partly Platonic, partly Swedenborgian, entirely Yeatsian reading of Blake is outlined in the "Necessity of Symbolism," and clarified by Lionel Johnson in his reverent review of Ellis's and Yeats's *Works*.

Gilchrist's *Life*, Swinburne's *William Blake*, and Ellis's and Yeats's *Works* were undoubtedly the most pivotal Blake studies of the nineteenth century, each contributing radically new source material and analysis. They inspired a host of additional Blake commentary, much of which is included here, some of which reads against the grain of these major works. J. Comyns Carr and James Smetham both wrote in the wake of Swinburne but rejected the Prophetic Books on the grounds of obscurity and incoherence. Although sympathetic to Blake's early work, they were most interested in his graphic art. In 1892, the same year that Ellis and Yeats wrote their gravity-defying theory of Blake's "Symbolic System," Alfred Thomas Story produced a grave and stolid biographical study, *William Blake: His Life, Character and Genius.*

Finally, it is worth observing the progress of one of the most vexing questions for early Blake scholars: who were Blake's intellectual and artistic contemporaries? Blake did not correspond extensively with other writers, and he was older than the British poets seen as definitively Romantic. James John Garth Wilkinson, a young Swedenborgian, suggested a comparison between Blake and Percy Bysshe Shelley in his introduction to the first print edition of *Songs of Innocence and Experience* (1839). Walter Thornbury wrote in 1861 that Blake "anticipated Wordsworth, rivalled our old dramatists in sustained majesty and dignity, and at times vied with Shelley in nervous fire." And G.E. B. Saintsbury's 1896 study places Blake alongside Scottish poet Robert Burns (1759–96). Perhaps the best answer to this question is Bertrand Russell's: Blake "was a solitary Swedenborgian and hardly part of any 'movement.'"

ALLAN CUNNINGHAM
"WILLIAM BLAKE" (1830)

Allan Cunningham's account of Blake in *Lives of the Painters* is a generally unsympathetic one, ridiculing Blake's visions, and deploring his preoccupation with angels over flesh-and-blood nature. He depicts a Blake who is gifted but insane, and in any case too prone to squander his gifts on supernatural subjects. Cunningham comes in for criticism from later Blake commentators: the Shoreham Disciple Frederick Tate wrote his "Memoir of Blake" as a riposte to Cunningham, and Alexander Gilchrist refers to Cunningham's "pleasant mannered generalities, easy to read, hard to verify."

An overflow of imagination is a failing uncommon in this age, and has generally received of late little quarter from the critical portion of mankind. Yet imagination is the life and spirit of all great works of genius and taste; and, indeed, without it, the head thinks, and the hand labours in vain. Ten thousand authors and artists rise to the proper, the graceful, and the beautiful, for ten who ascend into "the heaven of invention." A work—whether from poet or painter—conceived in the fiery ecstasy of imagination, lives through every limb; while one elaborated out by skill and taste only will look, in comparison, like a withered and sapless tree beside one green and flourishing. Blake's misfortune was that of possessing this precious gift in excess. His fancy overmastered him—until he at length confounded "the mind's eye" with the corporeal organ, and dreamed himself out of the sympathies of actual life.

—Allan Cunningham, "William Blake,"
*The Lives of the Most Eminent British Painters
and Sculptors*, 1830, vol. 2

ANNA JAMESON (1848)

Anna Jameson (1794-1860) was the eldest daughter of Irish painter D. Brownell Murphy. Following a tour of France and Italy as governess in the family of the marquis of Winchester, she published *A Lady's Diary* in 1826, the beginning of a successful career as memoirist and art critic. Her critical work was belittled by her rival, John Ruskin (who compared her to his father's uneducated serving girl), but she exercised considerable influence over Dante Gabriel Rossetti. Rossetti, a Pre-Raphaelite devotee of

Blake, kept a heavily annotated copy of Jameson's *Sacred and Legendary Art* in his studio, famously concurring with her—and Blake's—disdain for Rubens. Jameson's reinvigoration of Blake's "madness" as "poetical clairvoyance" perhaps reflects the emerging enthusiasm for spiritualism, a preoccupation shared by the Pre-Raphaelites.

—————

The most original, and, in truth, the only new and original version of the Scripture idea of angels which I have met with, is that of William Blake, a poet painter, somewhat mad as we are told, if indeed his madness were not rather 'The telescope of truth,' a sort of poetical *clairvoyance,* bringing the unearthly nearer to him than to others. His adoring angels float rather than fly, and, with their half-liquid draperies, seem about to dissolve into light and love: and his rejoicing angels—behold them—sending up their voices with the morning stars, that 'singing, in their glory move!'

—Anna Jameson, *Sacred and Legendary Art,* 1848, vol. 1, p. 85

WALTER THORNBURY (1861)

Walter Thornbury (1828–1876) was a journalist, novelist, and art critic. His *British Artists* places Blake alongside a small collection of visionary artists: Cosway, Varley, Flaxman, and Loutherberg. In this passage, Thornbury makes the first extant comparison between Blake and Britain's Romantic poet *par excellence*, William Wordsworth. The comparison between Percy Bysshe Shelley and Blake, on the other hand, had been first suggested by a young Swedenborgian, James John Garth Wilkinson, in his introduction to the 1839 first print edition of *Songs of Innocence and Experience*. Wilkinson, who reveres Blake's genius, but shows a patchy comprehension of his poems and graphics, finds in both Blake and Shelley a movement toward "Pantheism, or natural-spiritualism."

—————

Good William Blake, the hosier's son, the prophet of Carnaby Market, Golden Square, a most poetic dreamer, an enthusiast of more than Swedenborgian calibre, and a poet of no mean order; for he anticipated Wordsworth, rivalled our old dramatists in sustained majesty and dignity, and at times vied with Shelley in nervous fire.

—Walter Thornbury, *British Artists from Hogarth to Turner,* 1861, vol. 2, p. 27

DANTE GABRIEL ROSSETTI
"SUPPLEMENTARY" (1863)

Alexander Gilchrist died before his *Life of William Blake* was completed. The biography was published in 1863 with a preface by Gilchrist's wife, Anne, who acknowledged the role of Dante Gabriel Rossetti and of his brother, William Michael Rossetti, in its completion. She noted particularly the addition to Gilchrist's manuscript of a supplementary chapter, Gilchrist having left a memorandum stating his intention to include such a section and outlining its contents. Dante Gabriel Rossetti was an artist and poet, a leading figure in the Pre-Raphaelite movement. That he writes here extensively of Blake's linework and pigmentation, and only cursorily of his poetry, is not for want of an intense appreciation for that poetry. Rather, Rossetti was confronted with the difficulty of writing about a poetry that operated outside the established traditions. Rossetti himself was engaged in producing a new poetry. That his limited commentary on Blake concentrates on its singularity, its disconnection from anything produced by the Romantics or the high Victorians, is perhaps the highest flattery the aesthetic radical could offer. The one literary confrere Rossetti summons for Blake is the desperately obscure Charles Jeremiah Wells (1798–1879). Wells was educated with the younger brother of Romantic poet John Keats and was later associated with essayist William Hazlitt. Hazlitt discouraged Wells from writing and, apart from receiving brief commendations from poet Thomas Wade in 1838 and from Richard Horne in 1844, Wells fell into complete obscurity. It took Rossetti's remarks in the *Life of William Blake* to thrust Wells back into the public eye. Rossetti's prediction that Wells would come into his own was fulfilled in the 1870s when Algernon Swinburne praised *Joseph and His Brethren* in the *Fortnightly Review* and the play was reprinted the following year, somewhat to its now elderly author's bemusement. Curiously, though envisioning a future for Wells, Rossetti fails to predict the far greater recognition that William Blake's poetry will eventually garner. In this, Rossetti is of, or at least aware of, his era; Blake's poetry remained subordinate to his paintings for decades, and even in the 1880s, the prophetic poems were dismissed as the effusions of an overwrought sensibility.

Having spoken so far of Blake's influence as a painter, I should be glad if I could point out that the simplicity and purity of his style as a lyrical poet had also exercised some sway. But, indeed, he is so far removed from ordinary apprehensions in most of his poems, or more or less in all, and they have been so little spread abroad, that it would be impossible to attribute to them any decided place among the impulses which have directed the extraordinary mass of poetry displaying power of one or another kind, which has been brought before us from his day to our own. Perhaps some infusion of his modest and genuine beauties might add a charm even to the most gifted works of our present rather redundant time. One grand poem, on the same footing as his own (or even a still more obscure one) as regards popular recognition, and which shares exactly, though on a more perfect scale than he ever realized in poetry, the exalted and primeval qualities of his poetic art, may be found in C. J. Wells's scriptural drama of *Joseph and His Brethren,* published in 1824 under the assumed name of Howard. This work is, perhaps, the solitary instance, within our period, of poetry of the very first class falling quite unrecognised and continuing so for a long space of years. Its time, however, will most assuredly still come. It is impossible here to make any but a passing allusion to it, as affording, in its command of various character, including even the strongest and most earthly passion, but all working within a circle of spiritual influence,—a perfect parallel with the productions of Blake's genius, though rather, perhaps, with its more complete development in painting, than its always somewhat fragmentary written expression. The same remarks would apply to Wells's prose *Stories after Nature* (1822).

—Dante Gabriel Rossetti, "Supplementary"
to *The Life of William Blake* by
Alexander Gilchrist, 1863, vol. 1, pp. 381–382

Mary Abigail Dodge "Pictor Ignotus" (1864)

Mary Abigail Dodge (1833–96), whose pen name was Gail Hamilton, was an American essayist, best remembered for her advocacy of education and employment opportunities for women. The title of this essay, Latin for "unknown painter," she borrows from Alexander Gilchrist's biography, *The Life of William Blake*, "*Pictor Ignotus*" (1863).

Yet, somewhere, through mediaeval gloom and modern din, another spirit breathed upon him,—a spirit of green woods and blue waters, the freshness of May mornings, the prattle of tender infancy, the gambols of young lambs on the hill-side. From his childhood, Poetry walked hand in hand with Painting, and beguiled his loneliness with wild, sweet harmonies. Bred up amid the stately, measured, melodious platitudes of the eighteenth century, that Golden Age of commonplace, he struck down through them all with simple, untaught, unconscious directness, and smote the spring of ever-living waters. Such woodnotes wild as trill in Shakspeare's verse sprang from the stricken chords beneath his hand. The little singing-birds that seem almost to have leaped unbidden into life among the gross creations of those old Afreets who

> Stood around the throne of Shakspeare,
> Sturdy, but unclean,

carolled their clear, pure lays to him, and left a quivering echo. Fine, fleeting fantasies we have, a tender, heart-felt, heart-reaching pathos, laughter that might at any moment tremble into tears, eternal truths, draped in the garb of quaint and simple story, solemn fervors, subtile sympathies, and the winsomeness of little children at their play,—sometimes glowing with the deepest color, often just tinged to the pale and changing hues of a dream, but touched with such coy grace, modulated to such free, wild rhythm, suffused with such a delicate, evanishing loveliness, that they seem scarcely to be the songs of our tangible earth, but snatches from fairy-land. Often rude in form, often defective in rhyme, and not un-frequently with even graver faults than these, their ruggedness cannot hide the gleam of the sacred fire.

> —Mary Abigail Dodge, "Pictor Ignotus,"
> *Atlantic*, April 1864, pp. 436–437

ALGERNON CHARLES SWINBURNE
"THE PROPHETIC BOOKS" (1866)

Algernon Charles Swinburne (1837–1909), poet and professional aesthete, wrote the second major book of the 1860s Blake revival, *William Blake: A Critical Essay*. Gilchrist's *Life of Blake* gives scant attention to Blake's Prophetic Books. The work instead is highly circumspect, low on quotation (a problem, particularly given that many of the poems had not yet been published), and prone to generalizations. The biography's coyness was owing to publisher Alexander Macmillan and to Mrs. Gilchrist, whose husband had died before its completion. Both shied away from the moral and religious heterodoxies of the prophetic books. These heterodoxies, however, were precisely what attracted Swinburne, who offered lengthy quotations from the books and a reading that emphasized and celebrated their preemptive affront to Victorian pieties. The apparent aim of the Prophetic Books (a category that includes *Tiriel; The Book of Thel; America*

*a Prophecy; Europe a Prophecy; Visions of the Daughters of Albion; The Book
of Urizen; The Book of Ahania; The Book of Los; Song of Los; Vala, or the Four
Zoas; Milton, a Poem*; and *Jerusalem: The Emanation of the Giant Albion,*
and read by Swinburne alongside *The Marriage of Heaven and Hell*) is
to give us a unified Blake, a coherent Blakean faith, to expose recurring
concepts and thoughts in the prophetic books. Importantly, Swinburne
envisions Blake as an apostate and rebel, exploring how he inverts the
categories of "Hell," "Heaven," "Angel," and "Devil." Swinburne's reading makes significant first initial strides toward an understanding of
the Prophetic Books, but he errs in telling us what he wants Blake to be
saying, rather than what Blake actually says. So caught up is Swinburne
in the appeal of a libertarian, active, energetic, Satanic Blake, that he
misses the dialectic quality in Blake's *Weltanschauung*: that for Blake the
force of rebellion is necessarily matched by a force of restraint. A final
word on Swinburne's comparison between Blake and Walt Whitman in
the passage below: Whitman was a child when Blake died in 1827, and
it is unlikely he had read any Blake until Mercure Conway alerted him to
Swinburne's coupling of their names here. That coupling, which goes on
for pages, and takes a fairly generalized form, is probably motivated prin-
cipally by Swinburne's reading of both poets as advocates of sexual and
political freedom—the former, at least, a subject dear to Swinburne's
own heart. Whitman was uneasy with the comparison.

———— ———— ————

Here then the scroll of prophecy is finally wound up; and those who have cared
to unroll and decipher it by such light as we can attain or afford may now look
back across the tempest and tumult, and pass sentence, according to their
pleasure or capacity, on the message delivered from this cloudy and noisy
tabernacle. The complete and exalted figure of Blake cannot be seen in full by
those who avert their eyes, smarting and blinking, from the frequent smoke
and sudden flame. Others will see more clearly, as they look more sharply, the
radical sanity and coherence of the mind which put forth its shoots of thought
and faith in ways so strange, at such strange times. Faith incredible and love
invisible to most men were alone the springs of this turbid and sonorous
stream. In Blake, above all other men, the moral and the imaginative senses
were so fused together as to compose the final artistic form. No man's fancy,
in that age, flew so far and so high on so sure a wing. No man's mind, in that
generation, dived so deep or gazed so long after the chance of human
redemption. To serve art and to love liberty seemed to him the two things (if
indeed they were not one thing) worth a man's life and work; and no servant

was ever trustier, no lover more constant than he. Knowing that without liberty there can be no loyalty, he did not fear, whether in his work or his life, to challenge and to deride the misconstruction of the foolish and the fraudulent. It does not appear that he was ever at the pains to refute any senseless and rootless lie that may have floated up during his life on the muddy waters of rumour, or drifted from hand to hand and mouth to mouth along the putrescent weed-beds of tradition. Many such lies, I am told, were then set afloat, and have not all as yet gone down. One at least of these may here be swept once for all out of our way. Mr. Linnell, the truest friend of Blake's age and genius, has assured me—and has expressed a wish that I should make public his assurance—that the legend of Blake and his wife, sitting as Adam and Eve in their garden, is simply a legend—to those who knew them, repulsive and absurd; based probably, if on any foundation at all, on some rough and rapid expression of Blake's in the heat and flush of friendly talk, to the effect (it may be) that such a thing, if one chose to do it, would be in itself innocent and righteous,—wrong or strange only in the eyes of a world whose views and whose deeds were strange and wrong. So far Blake would probably have gone; and so far his commentators need not fear to go. But one thing does certainly seem to me loathsome and condemnable; the imputation of such a charge as has been brought against Blake on this matter, without ground and without excuse. The oral flux of fools, being as it is a tertian or quotidian malady or ague of the tongue among their kind, may deserve pity or may not, but does assuredly demand rigid medical treatment. The words or thoughts of a free thinker and a free speaker, falling upon rather than into the ear of a servile and supine fool, will probably in all times bring forth such fruit as this. By way of solace or compensation for the folly which he half perceives and half admits, the fool must be allowed his little jest and his little lie. Only when it passes into tradition and threatens to endure, is it worth while to set foot on it. It seems that Blake never cared to do this good office for himself; and in effect it can only seem worth doing on rare occasions to any workman who respects his work. This contempt, in itself noble and rational, became injurious when applied to the direct service of things in hand. Confidence in future friends, and contempt of present foes, may have induced him to leave his highest achievements impalpable and obscure. Their scope is as wide and as high as heaven, but not as clear; clouds involve and rains inundate the fitful and stormy space of air through which he spreads and plies an indefatigable wing. There can be few books in the world like these; I can remember one poet only whose work seems to me the same or similar in kind; a poet as vast in aim, as daring in detail, as unlike others, as coherent to himself, as strange without and as sane within. The points of contact and sides of likeness between William Blake and Walt Whitman are so many and so grave, as to afford some ground of reason to those who preach the transition of souls or transfusion of spirits. The great American is not a more passionate preacher of sexual or political freedom than the English artist. To each the imperishable form of a possible and universal Republic is equally requisite and adorable as the temporal and spiritual queen of ages as of men. To each all sides and shapes of life are alike acceptable or endurable. From the fresh free ground of either workman nothing is excluded that is not exclusive. The words of either strike deep and run wide and soar high. They are both full of faith and passion, competent to love and to loathe, capable of contempt and of worship. Both are spiritual, and both democratic; both by their works recall, even to so untaught and tentative a student as I am, the fragments vouchsafed to us of the Pantheistic poetry of the East. Their casual audacities of expression or speculation are in effect wellnigh identical. Their outlooks and theories are evidently the same on all points of intellectual and social life. The divine devotion and selfless love which make men martyrs and prophets are alike visible and palpable in each. It is no secret now, but a matter of public knowledge, that both these men, being poor in the sight and the sense of the world, have given what they had of time or of money, of labour or of love, to comfort and support all the suffering and sick, all the afflicted and misused, whom they had the chance or the right to succour and to serve. The noble and gentle labours of the one are known to those who live in his time; the similar deeds of the other deserve and demand a late recognition. No man so poor and so obscure as Blake appeared in the eyes of his generation ever did more good works in a more noble and simple spirit. It seems that in each of these men at their birth pity and passion, and relief and redress of wrong, became incarnate and innate. That may well be said of the one which was said of the other: that "he looks like a man." And in externals and details the work of these two constantly and inevitably coheres and coincides. A sound as of a sweeping wind; a prospect as over dawning continents at the fiery instant of a sudden sunrise; a splendour now of stars and now of storms; an expanse and exultation of wing across strange spaces of air and above shoreless stretches of sea; a resolute and reflective love of liberty in all times and in all things where it should be; a depth of sympathy and a height of scorn which complete and explain each other, as tender and as bitter as Dante's; a power, intense and infallible, of pictorial concentration and absorption, most rare when combined with the sense and the enjoyment of the widest and the highest things; an exquisite and lyrical excellence of form when the subject is well in keeping with the poet's tone of spirit; a strength and security of touch in small sweet sketches of colour and outline, which bring before the eyes of their student a clear glimpse of the thing designed—some little inlet of sky lighted by moon or star, some dim reach of windy water or gentle growth of meadow-land or wood; these are qualities common to the work of either. Had we place or time or wish to touch on their shortcomings and errors, it might be shown that these too are nearly akin; that their poetry has at once the melody and the laxity of a fitful storm-wind; that, being oceanic, it is troubled with violent groundswells and sudden perils of ebb and reflux, of shoal and reef, perplexing to the swimmer or the sailor; in a word, that it partakes the powers and the faults of elemental and eternal things; that it is at times noisy and barren and loose, rootless and fruitless and informal; and is in the main fruitful and delightful and noble, a necessary part of the divine mechanism of things. Any work of art of which this cannot be said is superfluous and perishable, whatever of grace or charm it may possess or assume. Whitman has seldom struck a note of thought and speech so just and so profound as Blake has now and then touched upon; but his work is generally more frank and fresh, smelling of sweeter air, and readier to expound or expose its message, than this of the prophetic books. Nor is there among these any poem or passage of equal length so faultless and so noble as his "Voice out of the Sea," or as his dirge over President Lincoln—the most sweet and sonorous nocturn ever chanted in the church of the world. But in breadth of outline and charm of colour, these poems recall the work of Blake; and to neither poet can a higher tribute of honest praise be paid than this.

We have now done what in us lay to help the works of a great man on their way towards that due appreciation and that high honour of which in the end they will not fail. Much, it need not be repeated, has been done for them of late, and admirably done; much also we have found to do, and have been compelled to leave undone still more. If it should now appear to any reader that too much has been made of slight things, or too little said of grave errors, this must be taken well into account: that praise enough has not as yet been given, and blame enough can always be had for the asking; that when full honour has been done and full thanks rendered to those who have done great things, then and then only will it be no longer an untimely and unseemly labour to map out and mark down their shortcomings for the profit or the pleasure of their inferiors and our own; that however pleasant for common palates and feeble fingers it may be to nibble and pick holes, it is not only more profitable but should be more delightful for all who desire or who strive after any excellence of mind or of achievement to do homage wherever it may be due; to let nothing great pass unsaluted or unenjoyed; but as often as we look backwards among past days and dead generations, with glad and ready reverence to answer the noble summons—"Let us now praise famous men, and our fathers who were before us." Those who refuse them that are none of their sons; and among all these "famous men, and our fathers," no names seem to demand our praise so loudly as theirs who while alive had to dispense with the thanksgiving of men. To them doubtless, it may be said, this is now more than ever indifferent; but to us it had better not be so. And especially in the works and in the life of Blake there is so strong and special a charm for those to whom the higher ways of work are not sealed ways that none will fear to be too grudging of blame or too liberal of praise. A more noble memory is hardly left us; and it is not for his sake that we should contend to do him honour.

—Algernon Charles Swinburne, from
"The Prophetic Books," *William Blake:
A Critical Essay,* 1866, pp. 298–304

MONCURE D. CONWAY (1868)

Moncure Conway was born in Virginia in 1832. Though trained for Methodist ministry, ordained into the Unitarian Church, and engaged to South Place Chapel in London, by 1868, Conway had abandoned theism altogether, keeping one foot in the Emersonian transcendentalist camp, the other in a humanist one, devoting himself to abolitionism, the move for women's suffrage, and social justice. The following is his review of Algernon Charles Swinburne's *William Blake: A Critical Essay* (1866), which he reads through the lens of a (distinctly American) transcendentalism and political liberalism. Conway's Blake envisages a "heavenly Jerusalem" for America, a "transcendentalized" (but still democratic) alternative to revolutionary Thomas Paine's vision for concrete, material change. Blake, Conway writes, began an "era of rebound" against the "prevalent and inadequate materialism" of Paine (whose biography Conway would publish in 1892). He goes on to discuss at length the effects of Swinburne's understating Blake's philosophical attachment to Emanuel Swedenborg. The extent of that attachment is still debated today.

A century ago the human spirit was gaining its first successes in a rebellion against heaven, refusing to accept alleged Divine authority for earthly wrongs, or the joys of a future world as compensation for the inequalities of this.

Thomas Paine was the Coryphasus of this movement, whose great success was the independence of America—a land thenceforth to be pitted against the heavenly Jerusalem by the materialists who made it a republic, and their allies in England and France who attempted to create an America on this side of the Atlantic. But it is hard to reason down the facts of the human soul. Without subscribing exactly to Mr. Swinburne's phrase of "the tape-yard infidelities of Paine," their impotence toward any measurement of the mysterious nature of man will be conceded by his friends, and Blake was already inaugurating by his side the era of the rebound. It is an incident to which I have lately recurred with enhanced interest, that the first time I ever heard the name of William Blake mentioned, was on the occasion of an assemblage of the friends of Thomas Paine in a city of the Far West, to celebrate the anniversary of his birth. He was there named with honour as a faithful friend of Paine, whom he had rescued from his political pursuers; but no one in the meeting seemed to have any further association with Blake. Immediately after the disciple who made this allusion, there arose a "spiritualist," who proceeded to announce that the work of Paine was good, but negative; he was but the wild-honey-fed precursor of the higher religion; he prepared the way for the new revelation of the Spirits. So close did Paine and Blake come to each other again, without personal recognition, in the New World, where each had projected his visions. America was, indeed, the New Atlantis of many poets and prophets: Berkeley, Montesquieu, Shelley, Coleridge, Southey, and many others, saw the unfulfilled dreams of Humanity hovering over it; but thus far only the dreams of Paine and Blake have descended upon it—that of the former in its liberation from the governmental and religious establishments of the Old World—that of Blake, in the re-ascent of mystical beliefs which have taken the form of transcendentalism amongst the cultivated, and spiritism with the vulgar.

The tendency of mysticism throughout its history to simplify its symbols and illuminate its images, has kept pace with the extension of civil liberty. In its inception and expansion it has always been in the direction of emancipation from the letter. In the curious picture of the Stonehenge arch, with the almost fully eclipsed sun shining through, which Mr. Swinburne has happily chosen as the frontispiece of his work, Blake, however unconsciously, traced his pedigree; but in the long journey from the astronomical circles on Salisbury Plain to *The Marriage of Heaven and Hell*, the eclipse has perpetually waned, and the harmony of the altar with universal laws been steadily attained. Nature, ostracised by priests in every age, has been admitted in larger measure by each successive revival of mysticism; and its encroachments upon hell are notorious. Madame Guion saw an angel with a pitcher of water going to quench those flames, that man might not love God through fear. It could have been wished that Mr. Swinburne had felt equal to the rather heavy task of showing the relation of Blake to Swedenborg. Superficially there is reason enough for Blake's dislike of Swedenborg, whose temperament was without poetry or humour, and acted like a Medusa upon his hells, heavens, and angels; the English artist demonstrated the vast difference between himself and the Swedish seer in one exquisite stroke where he describes himself as using Swedenborg's volumes as weights to sink himself from a certain "glorious clime" to an iron void between the fixed stars and Saturn. Nevertheless, hard as were the fetters of Calvinism upon him, Swedenborg, in sundry passages, ingeniously overlooked by his followers, had the germs of the optimist faith in him. He sees spirits in hell quite happy in a belief that they are in heaven, and giving thanks. And where they were suffering he saw hope brooding over them. "Moreover, I desire to state this fact. . . . that many of them have been raised from hell and torments into heaven, where they now live; and that it appeared to a certain one who had been in the greatest torment as though God Messiah embraced and kissed him." With Blake the soul of the current theology which still haunted Swedenborg is utterly dead and trampled on; but he has not been able to rid himself of its body of language and images, however he may force these to strange and for them suicidal services. Nature, without and within, with all her powers and passions, is vindicated and worshipped; but these claim to be baptized and struggle for Christian shrines, and to supersede church saints in the same niches. Perhaps Mr. Swinburne is right in thinking that Blake's prophetic works would have been in his age unbearable if they had not been generally incomprehensible. This strange fire needed a deep cistern, no doubt. It has burst forth again, however, and now in the large and free genius of Walt Whitman, by whom the traditional and theological language and form are entirely ignored, and Nature and Life, without regard to lines of good and ill, are everywhere loved and celebrated as the physiognomical expressions of the all-fair unity. On this re-appearance of William Blake in America Mr. Swinburne has touched in the spirit of literary, rather than historical or philosophical criticism; but the passage is remarkable.

> The points of contact and sides of likeness between William Blake and Walt Whitman are so many and so grave as to afford some ground of reason to those who preach the transition of souls or transfusion of spirits. A sound as of a sweeping wind; a prospect as

over drawing continents at the stars and now of storms; an expanse and exultation of stretches of sea; a resolute and reflective love of liberty in all times and in all things where it should be; a depth of sympathy and a height of scorn which complete and explain each other, as tender and bitter as Dante's; a power, intense and infallible, of pictorial concentration and absorption, the most rare when combined with the sense and the enjoyment of the excellence of form when the subject is well in keeping with the poet's tone of feeling; a strength and security of touch in small sweet sketches of colour and outline, which bring before the eyes of their student a clear glimpse of the thing designed—some little inlet of sky lighted by moon or star, some dim reach of windy water, or gentle growth of meadowland or wood; these are qualities common to the work of either. Whitman has seldom struck a note of thought and speech so just and profound as Blake has now and then touched upon; but his work is generally more frank and fresh, smelling of sweet air, and readier to expound its message, than this of the prophetic books.

To one who has studied the works of the two writers in question, the furtherance of the thought and, measurably, of the accent of the one by the other—any knowledge of his predecessor's works by whom is felt to be out of the question— will seem even understated in the above extract. I think it may be justly added that there is a theological defiance bristling on much of Blake's poetry which is significantly absent from that of the American, to whom religions also are "leaves of grass." "All deities reside in the human breast." This should be taken as the keystone of Blake's splendid arch. It is necessary again and again to recur to this, for there are some writings of his, especially the later, where he seems to have fallen into the hands of the Nemesis that pursues mysticism, and surrendered himself to the dangerous idea that his thoughts were personal spirits. As Cicero feared that the populace might, in course of time, believe that the statues of the gods are the gods themselves, there is always a peril besetting the imagination when introduced into religious speculations that it will confuse the planes of substance and form; of which Swedenborg is the saddest example, and Blake came too near being another. By bearing in mind, however, his declaration that all deities reside in the human breast, we may find a coherence in his wildest prophecies, especially when aided by the clear and consistent analysis of Mr. Swinburne. Blake's inversion of the average Christian creed amounts almost to a method. With him things are not only not what they seem, but the exact reverse of what they seem. Popular virtues are for the most part vices, and so-called vices virtues. Humility is egotism, revenge is love.

> Both read the Bible day and night,
> But thou read'st black where I read white.

Jehovah is an envious Saturn, devouring his own children, and Jesus is the real Zeus—theologically, but little different from Satan—with whose effort to dethrone Jehovah he heartily joins. Of course, it is only with this use of words that any student of his works will quarrel. If Jehovah and Jesus be reduced to expressions for thoughts, Christian philosophy itself will agree that the latter dethroned the former, and superseded his laws. "The most wonderful part of his belief or theory," says Mr. Swinburne, "is this: 'That after Christ's death he became Jehovah.'" But this would seem to be the logical necessity of his position, supposing that the place and not the nature of Jehovah is meant. The relation of all this, though wrought in many and inconsistent forms, to the general truth seems to be about this: a religion victorious in any country over the previous religion of that country, outlaws the divinities of the conquered rival religion, and gradually converts those divinities into devils. The serpent was worshipped as a god before it was cursed as a devil. The god Odin is now the diabolical wild huntsman of the Alps; and every Bon *Diable,* clad in fruitful green, may trace his lineage to Pan. Jehovah, whom so-called Christianity worships still even under the name of Christ, really crucified Christ, and Christ is leader of the outlawed gods—theologically, devils—of Nature. Pharisaism, now surviving as Morality, represents the dominion of Jehovah; that Jesus, the Forgiver, overthrows, thus restoring the passions and impulses to freedom and power. Blake ardently vindicates Christ from having been virtuous in the theological sense; he is a rebel, an outlaw, a defender of the unchaste, an agitator for the freedom of the instincts and of the mind, and his sure triumph is to be the downfall of Jehovah, and his law the victory of divine man. Then "Heaven, Earth, and Hell henceforth shall live in harmony." Mr. Swinburne well describes his belief as "moral pantheism."

> The pride of the peacock is the glory of God;
> The lust of the goat is the bounty of God;
> The wrath of the lion is the wisdom of God;
> The nakedness of woman is the work of God.

It is impossible here to give any idea of the rare, flashing, fiery gems that Blake has strung on this thread; for this the reader must be referred to the works themselves—of which an edition may now be hoped for—and to the essay of Mr. Swinburne, who has polished those that were rough almost to transparency, and shown the grain and the lustre of all in their best lights. The patient labour which has been put into this essay could only have been wrought by love and reverence; and the personal portrait of Blake laid before us suggests that its author has in literature anticipated the period when the stereoscope shall add to its powers that of catching and retaining the colours and shades of nature. Indeed, if there were any censure of Mr. Swinburne's work to be suggested, it must be that its pictorial affluence is excessive. The metaphors at times almost crowd one another. We are reminded, for instance, of the antagonism of the priestly and prophetic offices when the critic speaks of pulpit logic as "chopped or minced on the altar of this prophet's vision." In his hands words blossom again into the flowers from which they were once scattered as seed, and even letters hint the forms of which they were originally copies. The work is a very important contribution to both the poetical and philosophical literature of our time; and it should be added that the publisher, and the artist who has reproduced in it some of the most characteristic works of Blake's pencil, have spared no pains to present worthily things of which poor Blake, sitting in his comfortless room, said, "I wrote and painted them in ages of eternity, before my mortal life."

—Moncure D. Conway, *Fortnightly Review,*
February 1868, pp. 216–220

JAMES SMETHAM "WILLIAM BLAKE" (1869)

James Smetham (1821–89) was a poet, a painter, a deeply religious Methodist, an acquaintance of William Blake disciple, John Linnell, and a close friend of Dante Gabriel Rossetti, the Pre-Raphaelite painter-poet who oversaw the completion of Alexander Gilchrist's *The Life of William Blake* (1863). Smetham's "William Blake" first appeared as a review of that biography, as "Gilchrist's *Life of William Blake*", in the *London Quarterly Review*, 31 (Jan. 1869), pp. 265–311. He is mostly concerned with Blake's paintings and illustrations, to which he sees the poetry as subordinate.

He stands, and must always stand, eminently alone. The fountain of thought and knowledge to others, he could never be the head of a school. What is best in him is wholly inimitable. "The fire of God was in him"; and as all through his works this subtle element plays and penetrates, so in all he did and said the ethereal force flamed outward, warming all who knew how to use it aright, scorching or scathing all who came impertinently near to it. He can never be popular in the ordinary sense of the word, write we never so many songs in his praise, simply because the region in which he lived was remote from the common concerns of life, and still more by reason of the truth of the "mystic sentence" uttered by his own lips, and once before cited in these pages—

Nor is it possible to thought
A greater than itself to know.

—James Smetham, "William Blake,"
1869, *Literary Works*, ed. William Davies,
1893, pp. 193–194

Charles Eliot Norton "Blake's Songs and Political Sketches" (1869)

Six years after the publication of Alexander Gilchrist's *Life of William Blake*, American belletrist Charles Eliot Norton summarizes the state of Blake scholarship. Norton's assessment of Blake as "caviare to the general" is some measure of the way the Pre-Raphaelite Blake revivalists had turned devotion to Blake into a test of sensibility.

During the last six years Blake has been a "fancy'" with many people who had before hardly known his name; but the peculiar characteristics of his genius are such as to make him "caviare to the general." With two classes, however, he is likely to hold a high place permanently: with the mystics, as the most spiritual, intense, and imaginative of English mystics; and with artists, and true lovers of art, as painter and poet, with a genius of a curiously individual stamp, and as pure and lofty as it was original. Among modern artists, Blake forms a class by himself. With great inequalities, alike in conception and execution, his work is instinct with a spirit which distinguishes it from that of any of his predecessors or contemporaries. "William Blake, his mark," ineffaceably stamps every production of his pencil or his pen. In his highest reach of imagination he has never been surpassed; in the perfection of his technical execution at its best he is one of the great masters.

But the qualities of Blake's genius have been so much discussed of late years, that, tempting as the subject is, and imperfect, in our judgment, as the treatment of it has been, we refrain from entering on it, and continue ourselves to the simpler task of giving an account of the books before us.

In spite of some obvious defects, Mr. Gilchrist's *Life*, with Mr. Rossetti's reprint of selections from Blake's poems and other writings, in the second volume of the *Life*, will not only be hereafter the main source of information in regard to Blake's career and works, but will, in fact, supply all that is needed for a tolerably just conception of the nature and limits of his genius. Mr. Swinburne's wordy and pretentious volume *(William Blake: A Critical Essay)* has no value except that which it derives from the extracts it contains from some of Blake's unpublished writings, and the facsimiles with which it is illustrated of a few of his designs in colors.

The larger part of Blake's poems, including most of his early *Poetical Sketches*, and of the *Songs of Innocence and of Experience*, as well as *Poems Hitherto Unpublished*, were given by Mr. Rossetti, and it might seem as if a reprint of them were superfluous. But the student of Blake, touched with enthusiasm for his genius, will be grateful to Mr. Pickering for the publication of the two little volumes in which he gives an exact reprint of the poems as they were originally printed or engraved, save that the spelling is modernized, and includes a few that Mr. Rossetti apparently did not think worthy of preservation.

The text of some of the poems in this edition varies more or less from that in Mr. Rossetti's volume, and in the preface to each of these reprints the editor speaks with more severity than was needed of the arbitrary changes made by Mr. Rossetti. For the most part, however, the differences in the text are very slight, chiefly metrical or grammatical,—Blake, like some of the great elder poets, holding himself *super grammaticam,*—and only in rare instances, which may be accounted for by Mr. Rossetti's access to Blake's manuscript, do they show any essential variation in the sense or form.

It would be difficult to overestimate the force and originality of Blake's poetical genius. It is marvellous that a youth born in 1757, in the very depth of the stagnation of English poetry, should, before his twentieth year, have written such a poem as that in the *Poetical Sketches* addressed to the Muses, or the song beginning,

My silks and fine array,
My smiles and languish'd air
By love are driven away.

Blake's sensitive and imaginative soul felt the earliest breath of the reviving spirit of Nature in poetry, and his torch was the first to be re-lighted at her altar. He was the first to restore truth and simplicity to poetry, and was in this respect the forerunner of Wordsworth and of Burns. His *Poetical Sketches* were all written in the years from 1768 to 1777, though not published till 1783. The *Songs of Innocence* appeared in 1789, and the *Songs of Experience* in 1794. Cowper's first volume of *Poems* came out in 1782; Burns's *Poems in the Scottish Dialect* were published in 1786. It was not till 1793 that Wordsworth's *Evening Walk* appeared.

Even in Blake's early poems an exquisite sensibility to Art is as apparent as his truth to Nature. In his best pieces, such as those to which we just now referred, it is very manifest in the beauty of their form and the sweetness of their music. But in these juvenile pieces his art is often imperfect, and his full mastery is shown only in his later work, especially in some of the *Songs of Innocence,* which were engraved, and had such publication as Blake could give to them, in 1789, when he was thirty-two years old. In the best and most characteristic of these poems there is the perfect simplicity of natural feeling expressed with an art exquisitely appropriate, and manifesting in its own simplicity the true temper of the artist.

—Charles Eliot Norton, "Blake's Songs
and Poetical Sketches," *North American
Review,* April 1869, pp. 641–643

J. COMYNS CARR "WILLIAM BLAKE" (1880)

Partly because of personal connections and partly because the late Victorian Blakeans were united by their membership of an aesthetic counter-culture, Blake scholars after the 1860s revival tended to be mutually supporting. The contribution of Joseph Williams Comyns Carr (1849–1916) is no exception to this principle. An art critic and playwright, Comyns Carr was editor of the *Pall Mall Gazette, Art and Letters*, the English edition of *L'Art*, and the *English Illustrated Magazine*. He wrote in defense of the Pre-Raphaelites and from 1873 co-directed the Grosvenor Gallery, where Dante Gabriel Rossetti, one of the chief figures in the 1860s Blake revival, frequently exhibited. In his "William Blake," we see Comyns Carr duly deferential to his Blakean connections, writing reverently of Algernon Charles Swinburne's and William Rossetti's additions to the study of Blake. Like James Smetham a decade earlier, Comyns Carr is most interested in Blake's graphic art; and like Smetham, he reads Blake's early work with sympathy, but dismisses the rest, the prophetic books particularly, on the grounds of obscurity and incoherence.

The poetry of Blake holds a unique position in the history of English literature. Its extraordinary independence of contemporary fashion in verse, and its intuitive sympathy with the taste of a later generation, would alone suffice to give a peculiar interest to the study of the poet's career. Nor is this interest in any way diminished by a knowledge of Blake's singular and strongly marked individuality. Indeed, it is scarcely possible to do justice to the great qualities of his imagination, or to make due allowance for its startling defects, unless the exercise of the poetic gift is considered in relation to the other faculties of his mind. He appealed to the world in the double capacity of poet and painter; and such was the peculiar nature of his endowment and the particular method of his work, that it is difficult to measure the value of his literary genius without some reference to his achievements in design. For it is not merely that he practised the two arts simultaneously, but that he chose to combine them after a fashion of his own. An engraver by profession and training, he began at a very early age to employ his technical knowledge in the invention of a wholly original system of literary publication. With the exception of the *Poetical Sketches,* issued in the ordinary form through the kindly help of friends, nearly all of Blake's poems were given to the world in a fantastic dress of his own devising. He became in a special sense his own printer and his own publisher. The typography of his poems and the pictorial illustration by which they were accompanied were blended in a single scheme of ornamental design, and from the engraved plate upon which this design was executed by the artist's own hand copies were struck off in numbers more than sufficient to satisfy the modest demands of his admirers.

This peculiar process of publication cannot of course be held to affect Blake's claims as a poet. It bears a more obvious relation to those powers of a purely artistic kind which are not here in question; but its employment by him is nevertheless well deserving of remark in this place, because it indicates a certain quality of mind that deeply affected his poetic individuality. That happy mingling and confusion of text and ornament which give such a charm to *Songs of Innocence* was the symbol of a strongly marked intellectual tendency that afterwards received a morbid development. Blake has been called mad, and within certain well-defined limits the charge must, we think, be admitted. He possessed only in the most imperfect and rudimentary form the faculty which distinguishes the functions of art and literature; and when his imagination was exercised upon any but the simplest material, his logical powers became altogether unequal to the labour of logical and consequent expression. That this failure arose rather from morbid excess and excitement of visionary power than from any abnormal defect of intellectual energy is sufficiently indicated by the facts of his career. For while his hold over the abstract symbols of language grew gradually feebler, his powers of pictorial imagery became correspondingly vigorous and intense. The artistic faculty in Blake strengthened and developed with advancing life, and he produced no surer or more satisfying example of his powers than the series of illustrations to the Book of Job, executed when he was already an old man.

Indeed if Blake had never committed himself to literature we should scarcely be aware of the morbid tendency of his mind. It is only in turning from his design to his verse that we are forced to recognise the imperfect balance of his faculties: nor could we rightly understand the strange limitation of his poetical powers without constant reference to this diseased activity of the artistic sense. For there is a large portion of Blake's verse which is not infected at all with the suspicion of insanity, and it seems at first sight almost inexplicable that a writer who has produced some of the simplest and sweetest lyrics in the language should also have left behind him a confused mass of writings such as no man can hope to decipher. All that can be done for these so-called *Prophetic Books* has been accomplished by Mr. Swinburne, in his sympathetic study of the poet's work; but although Mr. Swinburne rightly asserts the power that is displayed in them, his eloquent commentary does not substantially change the ordinary judgment of their confused and inconsequent character. The defects of such work are too grave for any kind of serious vindication to be really possible, and if Blake had produced nothing more or nothing better, his claims to rank among English poets could not be successfully maintained. But these defects, although they are in their nature incurable, are not altogether incapable of explanation. For it cannot be questioned by any one who has seriously attempted to decipher these 'prophetic' writings, that to Blake himself the ordinary modes of intellectual expression had become charged with something of mysterious and special meaning. Words were no longer mere abstract symbols: they had assumed to his imagination the force of individual images. As they passed into his work they lost the stamp of ordinary currency and became impressed with a device of his own coinage, vivid and eloquent to him, but strange to all the world beside. To Blake's mind, in short, these prophetic writings doubtless formed a series of distinct and coherent pictures; but without the key that he alone possessed, they must ever remain a chaos through which not even the most wary guide can hope to find a path.

Putting aside the prophetic books, the quantity of verse which Blake has left behind him is by no means large. His lyrical poems have been collected in a small volume edited by Mr. W. M. Rossetti, and the contents of this volume are found to be mainly derived from the *Poetical Sketches* and the *Songs of Innocence and Experience*. It is to these essays of his youth and early manhood that we must look for the true sources of his fame. The *Poetical Sketches*, begun when the author was only twelve years of age, and finished when he was no more than twenty, must assuredly be reckoned among the most extraordinary examples of youthful production; and it is profoundly characteristic of the man and his particular cast of mind that many of these boyish poems are among the best that Blake at any time produced. For his was a nature that owed little to development or experience. The perfect innocence of his spirit, as it kept him safe from the taint of the world, also rendered him incapable of receiving that enlargement of sympathy and deepening of emotion which others differently constituted may gain from contact with actual life. His imagination was not of the kind that could deal with the complex problems of human passion; he retained to the end of his days the happy ignorance as well as the freshness of childhood: and it is therefore perhaps less wonderful in his case than it would be in the case of a poet of richer and more varied humanity that he should be able to display at once and in early youth the full measure of his powers.

But this acknowledgment of the inherent limitation of Blake's poetic gift leads us by a natural process to a clearer recognition of its great qualities. His detachment from the ordinary currents of practical thought left to his mind an unspoiled and delightful simplicity which has perhaps never been matched in English poetry. The childlike beauty of his poems is entirely free from the awkward lisp of wisdom that condescends. It is always unconscious and always unstrained, and even the simplicity of a poet like Wordsworth must often seem by comparison to be tinged with a didactic spirit. Blake's verse has indeed, both as regards intellectual invention and executive skill, a kind of unpremeditated charm that forces comparison with the things of inanimate life. Where he is successful his work has the fresh perfume and perfect grace of a flower, and at all times there is the air of careless growth that belongs to the shapes of outward nature. And yet this quality of simplicity is constantly associated with an unusual power of rendering the most subtle effects of beauty. In the actual processes of his art Blake could command the utmost refinement and delicacy of style. He possessed in a rare degree the secret by which the loveliness of a scene can be arrested and registered in a line of verse, and he often displays a faultless choice of language and the finest sense of poetic melody.

We have said already that he worked in absolute independence of the accepted models of his time. This is strictly true: but it would be absurd therefore to assume that he laboured without any models at all. Blake's isolation, if we look to the character of the man, is indeed less extraordinary than it would otherwise appear. He did not mingle in the concerns of life in such a way as to expose him to the dangers of being unduly swayed by the caprices of fashion. His was a world of his own creating, and to his vivid imagination the poets of an earlier generation would seem as near as the versifiers of his own day. That he should have chosen from the past those models whose example was most needed in order to infuse a new life into English poetry proves of course the justice of his poetic instinct. In fixing upon the great writers of the Elizabethan age he anticipated, as we have already observed, the taste of a succeeding generation, and it is only to be regretted that he did not absolutely confine himself to these nobler models of style. Unfortunately however his own intellectual tendency towards mysticism, found only too ready encouragement in the prophetic vagueness of the Ossianic verse, and we may fairly trace a part at least of Blake's obscurer manner to this source.

—J. Comyns Carr, "William Blake,"
The English Poets, ed. Thomas Humphry
Ward, 1880, vol. 3, pp. 596–600

MARGARET OLIPHANT (1882)

An established popular author, Margaret Oliphant (1828–97) was com-missioned by Macmillan (publisher of Alexander Gilchrist's *Life of Blake*) to write a literary history of England in the end of the eighteenth and beginning of the nineteenth century. While the resulting history proph-esies a future of obscurity for Blake, he was clearly, by this stage, suffi-ciently known for Oliphant to include him. Oliphant finds a Blake in *Songs of Innocence and of Experience* who is meek and mild, and in this—like most of Blake's Victorian readers—she misses the rebellious and ironic qualities in these poems (particularly in the *Songs of Experience*). Oliphant says nothing overtly critical about the prophetic books, but this should be considered in light of her *History*, which is unstintingly generous in its treatment of other authors; she is clearly uncomfortable with Blake in full visionary flight.

<hr/>

His poems are scarcely more easy to characterise than his pictures. *The Songs of Innocence* and *Songs of Experience* were both the productions of his youth, most artless, sometimes most sweet—striking accidental melodies out of the simplest words, out of an idea half suggested, a sentiment of the ineffable sort, such as an infant, new out of the unseen, might give utterance to, could it give utterance at all. The reader is struck silent by the surprise of the little verse, a sort of babble, yet divine, which is beyond all dogmas of criticism or art, and yet touches the soul with a momentary soft contact as of angels' wings: nay, it is a silly angel, one might suppose a spoiled child of heaven, petted for its tender foolishness, as sometimes a child is on earth, but yet in its way celestial. The little snatches of verses should be sung by children in fair spring landscapes, among the new-born lambs, or under the blossoming trees, but to criticise them as literary productions is impossible; it would be a kind of offence to simplicity and innocence. Sometimes, indeed, there strikes in suddenly a stronger note, as, when after all that ethereal babble of lambs, and flowers, and little children, the dreamer, in his bewildered Arcadia, suddenly dreams of a Tiger—and running off in his wonder into a few wild glowing stanzas, asks suddenly, *Did He who made the lamb make thee?* ...

He left Felpham in three years, renouncing the attempt to make money, and recurred to his original compositions and to a very precarious and limited livelihood. "I am again emerged into the light of day," he cries after his emancipation. "I have conquered, and shall go on conquering. Nothing can withstand the fury of my course among the stars of God and in the abysses of the accuser." This is wild enough in all conscience. A little later he speaks of the composition of "a sublime allegory which is now perfectly completed into a great poem. I may praise it since I dare not attempt to be other than the secretary; the authors are in eternity. I consider it the grandest poem this world contains." Whether this was the *Jerusalem: the Emanation of the Giant Albion,* we are not exactly informed; but as it is the first "prophetic" work which follows this announcement, it is to be supposed this is what he means. Such language has been heard since from believers in the fantastic system which draws its tenets from the teachings of a piece of furniture. There is no tangible medium of communication mentioned in Blake's descriptions, but the disciples of this faith write as he did, utterances of which they do not claim to be more than the secretary, and of which they sometimes assert that they are great poems. His is a curious antedating of a mystery which is often very vulgar, and often very foolish, but which cannot be quite accounted for either by mere imposture or credulity. There was no imposture in Blake, and it is strange to find in him the phraseology which was utterly strange to his time, but has come to be a comparatively well-known jargon now. The great poem is the wildest rhapsody that can be conceived. But his early songs last, and will continue to do so: even they cannot be said to be appreciated by the uninitiated. They are little known and little likely to be known: but in their ineffable artlessness they are unlike anything else of the time, or perhaps it might be safe to say, of the language, in which he remains a unique figure, unapproachable and alone.

—Margaret Oliphant, *The Literary History of England, 1790-1825,* 1882, vol. 2, pp. 287–94

COVENTRY PATMORE "BLAKE" (1889)

In 1876, an exhibition of Blake's work was presented by the Burlington Fine Arts Club. Many who had encountered Blake via the extravagantly partial media of Alexander Gilchrist, Dante Gabriel and William Michael Rossetti, and Algernon Charles Swinburne were now able to see Blake for themselves, unmediated. Many, in turn, were disappointed; the fault obviously lying with those who had raised public expectation. The essay below first appeared as Coventry Patmore's review of the Burlington exhibition, and was initially published in 1876 in the *St James' Gazette.* Patmore (1823–96), best known these days for *The Angel in the House,* a celebration of marriage and wifeliness, was a Roman Catholic (since conversion in the late 1850s) and, politically, an archconservative. This conservatism discloses itself immediately, with Patmore's sally against William Rossetti as an "enthusiast" for the Paris Commune. Where the Rossettis and Swinburne had admired Blake as a revolutionary, and, themselves members of an aesthetic counterculture, had identified with and celebrated his rebelliousness, Patmore deplored revolution and disorder. He was, consequently, intolerant of the apparent formal disorderliness of Blake's writing and especially averse to Blake's "craziness" and the way his own contemporary critics had configured madness as a symptom of genius rather than moral and intellectual degeneration. Patmore led the anti-Blake reaction, a reaction that could not have happened, of course, had Blake remained neglected. His views helped secure Blake's reputation for radicalism.

Blake's poetry, with the exception of four or five lovely lyrics and here and there in the other pieces a startling gleam of unquestionable genius, is mere drivel. A sensible person can easily distinguish between that which he cannot understand and that in which there is nothing to be understood. Mr. W. Rossetti, who is an enthusiast for "the much-maligned Paris Commune" and for Blake's poetry, says of some of the latter, where it is nearly at its worst,

"We feel its potent and arcane influence, but cannot dismember this into articulated meanings." This sentence, if put into less exalted English, expresses tolerably well the aspect of mind with which we regard much of the writing of the Prophets and of the great ancient and modern mystics. Some light of their meaning forces itself through the, in most cases, purposely obscure cloud of their words and imagery; but when, by chance, a glimpse of the disk itself is caught, it is surprisingly strong, bright, and intelligible. Such writers are only spoken of with irreverence by those that would have given their verdict in favour of the famous Irishman who, being confronted with one witness swearing to having seen him take a handkerchief from another gentleman's pocket, brought four who testified with equal solemnity to not having seen him do any such thing. The obvious rule in regard to such writers is, "When you cannot understand a man's ignorance, think yourself ignorant of his understanding." Again, if a man's sayings are wholly unintelligible to us, he may claim the benefit of a small possibility of a doubt that his meanings may be too great and necessarily "arcane" for our powers of reception. But when a writer's works consist of a few passages of great beauty and such simplicity that a child may understand them—like Blake's "Chimney-Sweep," "Tiger," "Piping down the valleys wild," "Why was Cupid a boy?" and "Auguries of Innocence"—and a great deal more that is mere ill-expressed but perfectly intelligible platitude and commonplace mixed with petty spite, and a far larger quantity still which to the ear of the natural understanding is mere gibberish, he has no right to claim, as Blake does, that the latter shall be regarded as plenarily inspired, or, indeed, as being anything better than the delirious rubbish it obviously is.

Mr. W. Rossetti, though he goes a great way further in his admiration of Blake than reason can be shown for, does the cause of reason a good service in declaring his opinion that the poet was probably mad. "When," says he, "I find a man pouring forth conceptions and images for which he professes himself not responsible, and which are in themselves in the highest degree remote, nebulous, and intangible, and putting some of these, moreover, into words wherein congruent sequence and significance of expression or analogy are not to be traced, then I cannot resist a strong presumption that that man was in some true sense of the word mad." As Pope "could not take his tea without a stratagem," so Blake could not "mix his colours with diluted glue" without declaring that "the process was revealed to him by St. Joseph"; and it was the ghost of his brother who taught him the new, though, had we not been told otherwise, the not supernaturally wonderful device of saving the expense of ordinary typography by etching the words of his verses on the copper plate which bore their illustrations. Blake was morally as well as intellectually mad; proposing on one occasion, for example, that his wife should allow him to introduce a second partner to his bed, and doing so with a *bona fide* unconsciousness of anything amiss in such a suggestion as perfect as that with which Shelley urged his wife to come and share the delights of a tour in Switzerland with him and his mistress Mary Godwin.

That "great wits to madness nearly are allied" is not true; but it is not only true but psychologically explicable that small "geniuses" often are so. Most children are geniuses before the dawn of moral and intellectual responsibilities; and there are some who remain, not children, but moral and intellectual manikins, all their lives. It must be confessed that conscience makes, not only cowards, but more or less dullards, of us all. The child, that

> Mighty prophet, seer blest,
> On whom those truths do rest
> Which we are toiling all our lives to find,

owes his power of vision to his not being able to see the flaming sword of conscience which turns every way, and hinders all men but a very few from getting a glimpse through the closed gates of Paradise. Yet it is better to be a purblind man with a conscience than a seeing manikin with none. It is better still, and best of all, when the man of developed intellect and fully accepted responsibilities retains a cherished memory of and an innocent sympathy with the knowledge that came to him in childhood and early youth, and uses his trained powers of expression in order to make the world partakers of those thoughts and feelings which had no tongue when they first arose in him, and leave no memory in the mass of men until the man of true and sane genius touches chords of recollection that would otherwise have slept in them for ever. One of the few really good things ever said by Hazlitt is that "men of genius spend their lives in teaching the world what they themselves learned before they were twenty."

For the time, however, the manikin type of genius is all the fashion, especially with a class of critics who have it in their power to give notoriety, if they cannot give fame. Craziness alone passes at present for a strong presumption of genius, and where genius is really found in company therewith it is at once pronounced "supreme." This is partly because most people can see that craziness has something abnormal about it, and are ready, therefore, to identify it with genius, of which most persons only know that it also is "abnormal"; and partly because the manikin mind is always red republican, and ardent in its hatred of kings, priests, "conventions," the "monopoly" of property and of women, and all other hindrances put in the way of virtue, liberty, and happiness by the wicked "civilizee."

Blake, as an artist, is a more important figure than Blake the poet; and naturally so, for the smallest good poem involves a consecutiveness and complexity of thought which are only required in paintings of a character which Blake rarely attempted. Yet, even as a painter his reputation has until lately been much exaggerated. The recent exhibition of his collected drawings and paintings was a great blow to the fame which had grown up from a haphazard acquaintance by his admirers with a few sketches or an illustrated poem. Here and there there was a gleam of such pure and simple genius as is often revealed in the speech of a finely natured child amid its ordinary chatter; here and there the expression of a tender or distempered dream, which was not like anything else in the spectator's experience; now and then an outline that had a look of Michael Angelo, with sometimes hints which might have formed the themes of great works, and which justified the saying of Fuseli that "Blake is damned good to steal from"; but the effect of the whole collection was dejecting and unimpressive, and did little towards confirming its creator's opinion that Titian, Reynolds, and Gainsborough were bad artists, and Blake, Barry, and Fuseli good ones.

—Coventry Patmore, "Blake,"
Principle in Art, 1889, pp. 97–102

RICHARD HENRY STODDARD (1892)

Stoddard (1825–1903) was an American critic and poet. His *Under the Evening Lamp* (1892) is a collection of essays, mostly regarding modern English poets.

If we wish to understand Blake as a poet, we must discard his Ossianic and prophetic aberrations, and read him as we would any other poet, not when he is at his worst, but when he is at his best, in his Songs of Innocence, and Songs of Experience, which was published five years later. Here we find a poet who differed from all his contemporaries, who had no predecessor, and has had no successor, but who was altogether unique, original and individual, primitive and elemental. The qualities which distinguish his verse at this time were simplicity and sincerity, sweetness and grace, an untutored, natural note which reminds one of the singing of a child who croons to himself in his happy moments, not knowing how happy he is, wise beyond his years, superior to time or fate. They seem never to have been written, but to have written themselves, they are so frank and joyous, so inevitable and final.

—Richard Henry Stoddard, *Under the Evening Lamp*, 1892, pp. 174–75

W.B. YEATS AND EDWIN J. ELLIS (1893)

For most of the nineteenth century, Blake's critics confined their attentions to the *Songs of Innocence and of Experience*, the *Poetical Sketches*, and the *Marriage of Heaven and Hell*. In 1866, Algernon Charles Swinburne wrote a sustained study of the so-called prophetic books, but it did little to dispel the impression that the greater body of Blake's work was, at best, impenetrable. When William Butler Yeats and Edwin J. Ellis published *The Works of William Blake, Poetic, Symbolic, and Critical* in 1893, they revolutionized the status of the prophetic books. From the apparently daunting disorder of those books, they retrieved what they called "the Symbolic System", a map of Blake's myths and an illumination of the connections between them, a theory of Blake's overall purpose. As literary criticism, *The Works* is generally regarded as brilliant but unsound. The authors display an impressive erudition, deploying knowledge about the *Kabbala*, the Illuminati, and Greek and Celtic languages in their consideration of Blake, but they write with an obscurity to rival Blake's, and are certainly as (or more) invested in mystical doctrine of a questionable stripe. Nonetheless, they adduce—as Swinburne did not—an overall coherence in Blake, elucidating his prophetic books as no previous commentator had done. Their treatment of the prophetic books as a poetic-graphic corpus founded on sustained deliberation, as the work of a serious thinker, not a madman, has made a lasting impact on twentieth-century scholarship. Rather than focusing on specific poems, their intention is to read all of Blake's work—as much as survived to them—as so many stages in the development of his occult System.

There is strong ground for arguing that Yeats and Ellis make Blake over in their own image: in Ellis's edition of Blake's *Vala, or The Four Zoas*, for instance, he alters words, passages and metrical arrangements; Yeats claimed that Blake was (like himself) of Irish descent, via a paternal grandfather originally named Cornelius O'Neal. Yeats' Blake becomes, like Yeats, an Irish symbolist poet. That Blake used ordinary words symbolically, and that the mythic figures in the prophetic books have a symbolic function, seems, these days, self-evident. But by "symbol," Yeats means more than "metaphor." In the "Necessity of Symbolism" (below), he explains that the "symbolism of mysticism" differs from the "metaphors of poetry," in that it forms a complete system, an occult system. Yeats goes on to claim that in Blake there are three separate planes of being, natural, emotional, and intellectual. Natural and intellectual things, he explains, have a material reality, are consciousness shrunk to the size of physical facts, whereas the emotional transcends space. There are vague traces of Plato's philosophy of forms in this theory, and more discernible traces of Emanuel Swedenborg, but it is emphatically Yeats' theory, not Blake's.

"The Preface" (below), appears in the first of the three volumes that comprise *The Works of William Blake*, along with a "Memoir" of Blake, a preliminary exposition of the editor's approach entitled "The Literary Period," and a description of "The Symbolic System" (which "The Necessity of Symbolism" [also below] begins).

The reader must not expect to find in this account of Blake's myth, or this explanation of his symbolic writings, a substitute for Blake's own works. A paraphrase is given of most of the more difficult poems, but no single thread of interpretation can fully guide the explorer through the intricate paths of a symbolism where most of the figures of speech have a two-fold meaning, and some are employed systematically in a three-fold, or even a four-fold sense. "Allegory addressed to the intellectual powers while it is altogether hidden from the corporeal understanding is my definition," writes Blake, "of the most sublime poetry," *Letter to Butts from Felpham, July 6th,* 1803.

Such allegory fills the *Prophetic Books*, yet it is not so hidden from the corporeal understanding as its author supposed. An explanation, continuous throughout, if not complete for side issues, may be obtained from the enigma itself by the aid of ordinary industry. Such an explanation forms, not perhaps the whole, but certainly the greater part, of the present volumes. Every line, whether written for the "understanding" or the "intellect," is based on a line of Blake's own.

Two principal causes have hitherto kept the critics,— among whom must be included Mr. Swinburne himself, though he reigns as the one-eyed man of the proverb among the blind,—from attaining a knowledge of what Blake meant.

The first is the solidity of the myth, and its wonderful coherence. The second is the variety of terms in which the sections of it are named.

The foundation of Blake's symbolic system of speech is his conception of the Four-fold in Man, and the covering that concealed this system was a peculiar use of synonyms. The four portions of Humanity are divided under the names of the Four Zoas in the myth, and the reader who does not understand the relation of the Four Zoas to each other, and to each living man, has not made even the first step towards understanding the Symbolic System which is the signature of Blake's genius, and the guarantee of his sanity. Mr. Swinburne, Mr. Gilchrist, and the brothers, Dante and William Rossetti, deserve well of literature for having brought Blake into the light of day and made his name known throughout the length and breadth of England. But though whatever is accessible to us now was accessible to them when they wrote, including the then published *Vala*, not one chapter, not one clear paragraph about the myth of Four Zoas, is to be found in all that they have published.

With regard to the use of synonyms, which must be understood before the Four Zoas can be traced through their different disguises, the earliest idea of this, as a mere guess, occurred to the editor whose name stands first on the present title-page, in the year 1870. The suggestion arose through a remark in the first edition of Gilchrist's *Life of Blake*, where the poem "To the Jews," from *Jerusalem*, was printed with a challenge at the beginning, calling on those who could do so, to offer an interpretation.

In the later edition this challenge was withdrawn, probably under the impression that it had not been accepted. The glove, however, had been quietly taken up. "What if Blake should turn out to use the quarters of London to indicate the points of the compass, as he uses these to group certain qualities of mind associated with certain of the senses and the elements?" This was the idea that presented itself, and eventually led us to shape the master-key that unlocked all the closed doors of the poet's house.

It happened, however, that the idea was fated to be laid aside almost unused for many years. The maker of the lucky guess had only given a week or two of study, and barely succeeded in assuring himself that he was on the right track, when the course of destiny took him to Italy and kept him there, with only brief and busy visits to England and other countries, until a few years ago. In the meantime the other editor had grown up, and become a student of mysticism. He came one day and asked to have Blake explained. Very little could be given him to satisfy so large a demand, but with his eye for symbolic systems, he needed no more to enable him to perceive that here was a myth as well worth study as any that has been offered to the world, since first men learned that myths were briefer and more beautiful than exposition as well as deeper and more companionable. He saw, too, that it was no mere freak of an eccentric mind, but an eddy of that flood-tide of symbolism which attained its tide-mark in the magic of the Middle Ages.

From that moment the collaboration which has produced the present work was begun, and it has gone on, notwithstanding some unforeseen and serious interruptions, for four years. The fellow labourers have not worked hand in hand, but rather have been like sportsmen who pursue the game on different tracks and in the evening divide their spoils. Each has learned in this way that the other was indispensable. The result is not two different views of Blake, so much as one view, reached by two opposite methods of study, worked out in order to satisfy two different forms of mental enjoyment.

Except in connection with the Memoir, very little assistance was to be had from outside. The biographical matter has been added to considerably, the greater part of the space being given to hitherto unpublished facts, while some twenty or thirty pages are condensations of the story as told in the accounts of Blake's life which have already been given to the world. A satisfactory and complete narrative has yet to be written, if all that is now known be set forth at its natural length. But this may well wait. Fresh material comes in from time to time, and now that readers are relieved of their discouraging inability to prove that they are not studying the life or works of a madman, it is probable that much will be done in the near future. A "Blake Society" would find plenty of occupation. It would probably be able, not only to gather together new facts for the biography, but it might even find some of the lost books by Blake, printed and in manuscript. The Society could also take up the task of interpretation, and work out details, for which space has not been found in this book, large as it is.

Blake's was a complex message—more adapted than any former mystical utterance to a highly complex age. Yet it claims to be but a personal statement of universal truths, "a system to deliver men from systems."

The only other European mystics worthy to stand by his side, Swedenborg and Boehmen, were to a large extent sectaries, talking the language of the Churches, and delivering a message intended, before all else, for an age of dogma. They brought the Kingdom of the soul nearer to innumerable men; but now their work is nearly done, and they must soon be put away, reverently, and become, as Blake says, "the linen clothes folded up." As the language of spiritual utterance ceases to be theological and becomes literary and poetical, the great truths have to be spoken afresh; and Blake came into the world to speak them, and to announce the new epoch in which poets and poetic thinkers should be once more, as they were in the days of the Hebrew Prophets, the Spiritual leaders of the race. Such leadership was to be of a kind entirely distinct from the "temporal power" claimed to this day elsewhere. The false idea that a talent or even a genius for verse tends to give a man a right to make laws for the social conduct of other men is nowhere supported in Blake's works. The world in which he would have the poet, *acting as a poet,* seek leadership is the poetic world. That of ordinary conduct should be put on a lower level. It belongs to Time, not to Eternity. It is only so far as conduct affects imagination that it has any importance, or, to use Blake's term, "existence."

The whole of Blake's teaching,—and he was a teacher before all things,—may be summed up in a few words.

Nature, he tells (or rather he reminds) us, is merely a name for one form of mental existence. Art is another and a higher form. But that art may rise to its true place, it must be set free from memory that binds it to Nature.

Nature,—or creation,—is a result of the shrinkage of consciousness,—originally clairvoyant,—under the rule of the five senses, and of argument and law. Such consciousness is the result of the divided portions of Universal Mind obtaining perception of one another.

The divisions of mind began to produce matter (as one of its divided moods is called), as soon as it produced contraction (Adam), and opacity (Satan), but its fatal tendency to division had further effects. Contraction, or divided into male and female,—mental and emotional egotism. This was the "fall." Perpetual war is the result. Morality wars on Passion, Reason on Hope, Memory on Inspiration, Matter on Love.

In Imagination only we find a Human Faculty that touches nature at one side, and spirit on the other. Imagination may be described as that which is sent bringing spirit to nature, entering into nature, and seemingly losing its spirit, that nature being revealed as symbol may lose the power to delude.

Imagination is thus the philosophic name of the Saviour, whose symbolic name is Christ, just as Nature is the philosophic name of Satan and Adam. In saying that Christ redeems Adam (and Eve) from becoming Satan, we say that Imagination redeems Reason (and Passion) from becoming Delusion,—or Nature.

The prophets and apostles, priests and missionaries, prophets and apostles of this Redemption are,—or should be,—artists and poets. Art and poetry, by constantly using symbolism, continually remind us that nature itself is a symbol. To remember this, is to be redeemed from nature's death and destruction.

This is Blake's message. He uttered it with the zeal of a man, who saw with spiritual eyes the eternal importance of that which he proclaimed. For this he looked forward to the return of the Golden Age, when "all that was not inspiration should be cast off from poetry." Then, whenever the metaphors and the rhythms of the poet were heard, while the voices of the sects had fallen dumb, should be the new Sinai, from which God should speak in "Thunder of Thought and flames of fierce desire."

The Necessity of Symbolism

The Hindu, in the sculptured caverns of Elephanta; the gipsy, in the markings of the sea shell he carries to bring him good fortune; the Rosicrucian student, in the geometric symbols of medieval magic, the true reader of Blake in the entangled histories of Urizen and his children, alike discover a profound answer to the riddle of the world. Do they find anything in their obscure oracles that cannot be known from the much more intelligible dialectics and experiments of modern science and modern philosophy? To answer this question it is necessary to analyze the method whereby the mystic seeks for truth, and to inquire what the truth is he seeks for. Blake has discussed the first portion of this problem in many places, but particularly in two tractates called "There is no Natural Religion." By Natural Religion he understood attempts to build up a religious or spiritual life from any adjustment of "ratio" of the impressions derived from the five senses. These impressions may, indeed, be used in poetry and prophesy as a key to unlock religious truths, but "correspondence," as Swedenborg called the symbolic relation of outer to inner, is itself no product of nature or natural reason, beginning as it does with a perception of a something different from natural things with which they are to be compared. "Natural Religion" was two-fold to Blake. It was a solution of problems and a restraint of conduct: when only a restraint it was deadening, when only a solution it was dead. All such solutions, according to him, arise from the belief that natural and spiritual things do not differ in kind; for if they do so differ, no mere analysis of nature as its exists outside our minds can solve the problems of mental life. This absolute difference may be described as the first postulate of all mystics. Swedenborg, whose writings were familiar to Blake, has carefully explained it in his doctrine of "discrete" degrees. "Degrees are of two kinds," he writes, "there being continuous degrees and degrees not continuous. Continuous degrees are like the degrees of light, decreasing as it recedes from flame, which is its source, till it is lost in obscurity; or like the degrees of visual clearness, decreasing as the light passes from the objects in the light to those in the shade; or like the degrees of the purity of the atmosphere from its base to its summit; these degrees being determined by the respective distances. But degrees that are not continuous but discrete, differ from each other like that which is prior and what is posterior, like cause and effect, and like that which produces and that which is produced. Whoever investigates this subject will find, that in all the objects of creation, both general and particular, there are such degrees of production and composition, and that from one thing proceeds another and from that a third, and so on. He that has not acquired a clear apprehension of these degrees cannot be acquainted with the difference between the exterior and interior faculties of man; nor can he be acquainted with the difference between the spiritual world and the natural, nor between the spirit of man and his body" *(Heaven and Hell,* page 38).

The materialistic thinker sees "continuous" where he should see "discrete degrees," and thinks of the mind not merely as companioning but as actually one with the physical organism. The mistake has brought into the world many curious dogmas, such as that of the scientific German who has pronounced the soul "a volatile liquid capable of solution in glycerine," and thereby shown a confusion of mind as great as if he had asked, with the religious man in Professor Clifford's story, "How many foot-pounds are there to the top of St. Paul's?" The scientific German has, however, a great advantage over the mystic, in the perfect intelligibility of his statement. He has not been forced by the essential obscurity of truth to wrap his utterance about with symbol and mystery, and to expound the nature of mind and body by "correspondence," or "signature," as Boehmen called it. For discrete degrees are related to each other by "correspondence" and by that alone, for all other methods imply identity. This relation is set forth by Blake in an MS. note on the margin of a copy of Swedenborg's *Divine Love and Wisdom,* now in the British Museum. The words "science" and "demonstration" he here applies to investigations of external nature, and "intellect" to the world of man's thoughts existing in and for themselves. "Is it not evident," he writes, "that one degree will not open the other." He is combatting a statement of Swedenborg's that a child is born in the merely "natural degree," and that he passes from that to the others. As readers of the *Songs of Innocence* know, childhood was to him a divine and no mere animal or natural state. "And that science," he goes on, "will not open intellect, but that they are discrete and not continuous, so as to explain each other only by correspondence, which has nothing to do with demonstration, for you cannot demonstrate one degree by the other, for how can science be brought to demonstrate intellect without making them continuous and not discrete." The materialist, and not the child, exists in the natural degree he is contending; for no increase of natural observations, and sensations could of itself awake into being or "open" the intellectual faculties. They must accompany the action of the observations and sensations from the first, and are indeed the primary condition of their existence. The sensations and observations are merely the symbols or correspondence whereby the intellectual nature realizes or grows conscious of itself in detail. Thus Blake met a number of materialistic thinkers at the bookseller Johnston's, and recognised in them an expression, external to himself, of certain elements he knew in his own mind, and created from this double perception the gigantic "spectre" of denial and soulless reason called Hand, in *Jerusalem*. Had he never gone to the house in St. Paul's Churchyard he might never have become conscious of this "spectrous" reason, but it would have existed in his mind all the same. In this way study of external events, not merely the elaborate and laborious study we call mysticism, but the emotional and flying observation that embodies itself in the metaphors of poetry, explains to us the nature of the mind. Whoever has understood the correspondence asserted by Blake between (say) sight, hearing, taste and smell, and certain mental qualities, feels at once that much in his own intellect is plainer to him, and when Shakespeare compares the mind of the mad Lear to the "vexed sea," we are told at once something more laden with meaning than many pages of psychology. A "correspondence," for the very reason that it is implicit rather than explicit, says far more than a syllogism or a scientific observation. The chief difference between the metaphors of poetry and the symbols of mysticism is that the latter are woven together into a complete system. The "vexed sea" would not be merely a detached comparison, but, with the fish it contains, would be related to the land and air, the winds and shadowing clouds, and all in their totality compared to the mind in its totality. This relation of sea to land and of thought to thought, is by continuous and not discrete degrees. Water changes into land, and air into vapour, and thought melts into thought, not as "prior" into "posterior," "cause" into "effect," "spirit" into "nature," but by a transformation that lifts them into no new world. These changes are, however, symbols of the "discrete degrees," and we will hear much in *The Mystical Writings* of flood, air, and fire, as representing the difference between natural, intellectual, and emotional things. In Swedenborg and Blake the difference between the two kinds of degrees is symbolized by perpendicular and longitudinal motion. We pass upward into higher discrete degrees and merely outward into the continuous ones.

As natural things correspond to intellectual, so intellectual things correspond to emotional. In the second of the two tractates on "Natural Religion" Blake goes further and asserts that "the poetic genius," as he calls the emotional life, "is the true man, and that the body or outward form of man is derived from the poetic genius. Likewise, that the forms of all things are derived from their genius, which by the ancients was called an Angel and Spirit and Demon." The growing genius of the child forms about it by affinity a complex series of thoughts, and these in their turn have much to do in moulding unconsciously the no less complex symbol, or series of symbols, known as the physical body. In the same way the oak-tree shows that it differs in essence or genius from the beech by the different nature of its symbol, and the man of mere commonplace activities gathers about him a body nowise resembling the refined body of the man of culture. To hear a man talking, or to watch his gestures, is to study symbolism, and when we restate our impressions in what are thought to be straightforward and scientific sentences, we are in reality giving a more limited, and therefore more graspable, symbolic statement of this impalpable reality. Mysticism, poetry and all creative arts, for the very reason that they explain but seldom, are more profound than the explanatory sciences. Sometimes the mystical student, bewildered by the different systems, forgets for a moment that the history of moods is the history of the universe, and asks where is the final statement—the complete doctrine. The universe is itself that doctrine and statement. All others are partial, for it alone is the symbol of the infinite thought which is in turn symbolic of the universal mood we name God.

As natural things and intellectual differ by discrete degrees, so do intellectual things differ by discrete degrees from emotional. We have thus three great degrees the first of which is external: the first two possessing form, physical and mental respectively, and the third having neither form nor substance—dwelling not in space but in time only. We shall presently hear of the great emotional or inspired principle, named Los, as God of Time. The absolute separation of these degrees was a thought that pleased Blake, "Study science till you are blind, study intellectuals till you are cold," he writes in the before quoted notes to *Divine Love and Wisdom*, "yet science cannot teach intellect much less can intellect teach affection." Emotion or affection is defined in *The Marriage of Heaven and Hell* as what the religious call evil, its tendency being to burst bounds, as it were, and shatter forms. The idea is that of a saying, used recently in conversation by a Brahmin, who was denying the possibility of a science of conduct. "The ethical impulse," he said, "always breaks the ethical law." Blake's peculiar use of the word "evil" often causes obscurity, for he does not always take the trouble to say when he restricts his meaning to what "the religious" so call. The emotional Degree is associated with will by Swedenborg, hence Blake wrote on the fly-leaf of *Divine Love and Wisdom*, "There is no good will. Will is always evil." The rest is illegible, having been rubbed out, probably, by heresy-hating Tatham, in whose possession the book was originally. The second Degree, with its definite forms, is, on the other hand, associated with what the religious call good. "The passive that obeys reason." Reason in its turn being "the outward bound or circumference of energy." Good is, in fact, the passive symbol, and good and evil are "the contraries, without which there is no progression."

These two degrees are the most important, and much of Blake's system is but the history of their opposing lives differing from and yet completing one another, as love does wisdom—will, understanding—substance, form. The systems of philosophy and the dogmas of religion are to the mystic of the Blakean school merely symbolic expressions of racial moods or emotions—the essences of truth—seeking to express themselves in terms of racial memory and experience—the highest degree cloaking itself, as it were, in the second. The German produces transcendental metaphysics, the Englishman positive science, not because either one has discovered the true method of research, but because they express their racial moods or affections. The most perfect truth is simply the dramatic expression of the most complete man. "No man can think, write, or speak," says Blake in the second "Natural Religion" booklet, "from his heart but he must intend truth. Thus all sects of philosophy are from the poetic genius adapted to the weaknesses of every individual." And again, "The religions of all nations are derived from each nation's different reception of the poetic genius which is everywhere called the Spirit of Prophesy." This poetic genius or central mood in all things is that which creates all by affinity—worlds no less than religions and philosophies. First, a bodiless mood, and then a surging thought, and last a thing. This triad is universal in mysticism, and corresponds to Father, Son, and Holy Spirit. In Swedenborg it is divided under the names celestial, spiritual and natural degrees; in the Kabala as Neschamah, Ruach and Nesphesch, or universal, particular and concrete life. In Theosophical mysticism we hear of the triple logos—the unmanifest eternal, the manifest eternal, and the manifest temporal; and in Blake we will discover it under many names, and trace the histories of the many symbolic rulers who govern its various subdivisions. As mood differs from mood, and emotion from emotion, not by discrete but continuous degrees, it will be seen that there is something common to them all—a mood that goes through all the moods. This is what Blake means when he speaks of "the poetic genius," as he sometimes does, as if there were but one genius for all men. "As all men are alike in outward form," he writes, "so (and with the same infinite variety) all are alike in the poetic genius"; and again, "as all men are alike (though infinitely various), so all religions, as all similars, have one source. The true man is the source, he being the poetic genius." This true or universal man he sometimes calls Christ, the centre of the universe, the truth self-existing in its own essence. He is infinite, all-pervading, but yet we are compelled to describe him to ourselves as a man, not merely because that is the least limited symbol to remember the unlimited by, but because our "genius," or central mood, is a direct, and our intellectual and physical natures an indirect, derivation from him. "Man can have no idea of anything greater than a man," writes Blake in the MS. notes to *Divine Love and Wisdom*, "as a cup cannot contain more than its capaciousness. But God is a man not because He is so perceived but because He is the creator of man." It is important to us to love this universal life that we may test ourselves and all else by it, and therefore we must be careful of the symbol we use, and not employ some merely intellectual abstraction or material correspondence. Swedenborg complains that many Christians have no other idea of a spirit "than as a particle of cloud," and Blake comments— "Think of a white cloud as holy! you cannot love it; but think of a holy man within the cloud, love springs up in your thought, for to think of holiness distinct from man is impossible to the affections. Thought makes monsters, but the affections cannot." The man he speaks of is the inner and not the outer being—the spiritual not the physical—the highest ideal, "the human form divine," as he calls it, and not the extrinsic body.

The mind or imagination or consciousness of man may be said to have two poles, the personal and impersonal, or, as Blake preferred to call them, the limit of contraction and the unlimited expansion. When we act from the personal we tend to bind our consciousness down as to a fiery centre. When, on the other hand, we allow our imagination to expand away from this egoistic mood, we become vehicles for the universal thought and merge in the universal mood. Thus a reaction of God against man and man against God— which is described by Swedenborg as good and evil, and by Blake as really two forms of good (MS. notes to Swedenborg)—goes on continually. The "genius" within us is impatient and law-breaking, and only becomes peaceful and free when it grows one with "the poetic genius"—the universal mood. It does so not by surrender of its own nature, but by expanding until it contains that which is the essence of all. Blake refuses to consider the personal as in itself evil for by it we obtain experience. It is continually feeding the universal life, as it were, with fuel of individual emotion. It becomes evil in the true sense of the word only when man invents a philosophy from reasoning upon it, asserts that its limited life is alone real, and that there is nothing but what is perceived by the five senses of individual man. "The outward bound or circumference of energy" then becomes an iron band closing in the man. Having denied the existence of that for which his bodily life exists, man begins an unceasing preoccupation with his own bodily life, neglecting to regard it as a symbol.

Hence Blake's denunciation of "demonstration" which is "only by the bodily senses," and of "the most holy reasoning power in which is the abomination of desolation." It is this and not the personal energies, "the little devils which fight for themselves," that he denounces. When this reason has obtained power "the limit of contraction" becomes "the limit of the opaque." The creative mystic and the man of genius, on the other hand, live unenslaved by any "reason" and pass at will into the universal life. All our highest feelings come in this way. "He who loves," say the notes on Swedenborg, "feels love descend into him, and if he has wisdom, may perceive it is from the Poetic Genius which is the Lord." No man can see or think of anything that has not affinity with his mood or "state," as Blake preferred to call it. The materialist sees only what belongs to his contracted consciousness. The creative visionary or man of genius has all the thoughts, symbols, and experiences that enter within his larger circle. If he has developed his perception of mental sound it will give him music; if his perception of thought, philosophic generalizations; and if his sense of mental sight, visions, strong or faint, according to his power of concentration upon them. The mood of the seer, no longer bound in by the particular experiences of his body, spreads out and enters into the particular experiences of an ever-widening circle of other lives and beings, for it will more and more grow one with that portion of the mood essence which is common to all that lives. The circle of individuality will widen out until other individualities are contained within it, and their thoughts, and the persistent thought-symbols which are their spiritual or mental bodies, will grow visible to it. He who has thus passed into the impersonal portion of his own mind perceives that it is not a mind but all minds. Hence Blake's statement that "Albion," or man, once contained all "the starry heavens," and his description of their flight from him as he materialized. When once a man has re-entered into this, his ancient state, he perceives all things as with the eyes of God. The thoughts of nature grow visible independent of their physical symbols. He sees when the body dies the soul still persisting and ascending, perhaps as Blake saw his brother Robert's, clapping its hands with joy. He discovers by "his enlarged and numerous senses" the "spiritual causes" that are behind "natural events." It was in this way that Blake perceived those spiritual forms with which, as Tatham tells us, he talked and argued as with old friends. But most men can only see the thoughts of nature through their physical effects. Inattention has robbed them of the universe and they have shrunk up into the "worm of sixty winters." When we do not listen to the voice of one who is talking, it first becomes an unintelligent hum, and then ceases for us altogether and leaves us alone in the circle of our minds. It is going on, however, and others may hear and even begin to move about in obedience to its commands, and jostle us while doing so. It is thus with ordinary men, they dwell wrapped up in their own narrow circles, like the creatures with whom Urizen talks in the book of *Vala*, and finds "cursed beyond his curse." For them the natural degree, the world of effects, is alone visible when they turn their eyes outward. For them, and they include well nigh all of us, no spirit passes by with placid tread. How then should it be strange that the grave seems the end of all, and life a mere lichen growing upon the cliff side?

—Ewin J. Ellis and William Butler Yeats,
preface to *The Works of William Blake:*
Poetic, Symbolic, and Critical, ed. Edwin J. Ellis
and W.B. Yeats, 3 vols., 1893

LIONEL JOHNSON (1893)

A member of W. B. Yeats' circle, Lionel Pigot Johnson (1867–1902) was a poet and classicist, whom Yeats consulted about the possible Greek and Celtic derivations of some of Blake's names. Here Johnson reviews Ellis's and Yeats's *The Works of William Blake: Poetic, Symbolic, and Critical*. He offers a clear paraphrase of one of the work's key arguments—that ordinary words in Blake's writing have a symbolic meaning, and that the symbols collaborate to form a system—but he also takes the work very much at its word, claiming uncritically, after Yeats, that "Blake refused phenomenal facts."

⚬⚬⚬

Take all the seemingly grotesque nomenclature of his enormous myths, Enitharmon, Los, Golgonooza, Bath, Felpham, Oro, Canterbury, Battersea; see how each name is employed throughout the books; compare its meaning here with its meaning there; examine the bearing of one myth upon another, of this narrative with that; you will be forced to acknowledge that these vast stories, vast powers and personifications, "moving about in worlds not realised," are thoroughly consistent and harmonious. You will also see that Blake, exercising his liberty of vision, discerns his actors in various relations and positions: one power will appear under many aspects; but you will never find him inextricably confusing his myths. I only claim that a careful study of Blake's text, and of these commentaries, will show that Blake's prophetic books, if mad, are admirably methodical in their madness; that he was not under the spell of chance dreams and monstrous imageries, turbidly and rhapsodically thrown together as by some unbalanced faculty. Test the books as you would test the *Iliad,* or *Hamlet,* or *Faust.* Some allowances you must perforce make; but the general result will be a conviction that one great imaginative mind, precise, determinate, consistent, presided over their construction. I do not claim to have mastered them; that demands some years of patient study. I do claim to have applied to them the most prosaic tests, and never to have found them wanting. Ask a novice in Platonic philosophy to collate the various passages of Plato, in which the word "idea" occurs. He will say, with all due diffidence, that he discovers one prominent usage and meaning of the word, together with certain passages in which it appears to vary somewhat, yet not to the overthrow of Plato's general consistency. Just that is my position: no scholar in Blake, I have still tested these commentaries by ordinary methods, and found that, upon the whole, they disclose to me one persistent purpose in Blake's prophetic books. True, I cannot presume to say, in a few words, what that is. Blake is not Plato or Aristotle, a man whose philosophy is a common possession of many ages, easily sketched, because all can fill up the gaps and interspaces. I can but say that (in their edition of Blake's works) Mr. Ellis and Mr. Yeats seem to me, one out of many readers, to have proved their point, the rational consistency of Blake's conceptions: in fact, that he had a system. When I read in the *Jerusalem,* that "the Faeries lead the Moon along the Valley of Cherubim," I am personally content, in my sloth, to admire the vague beauty of the picture; but I know that Faeries, Moon, Valley, Cherubim, have definite meanings, above or underneath their pictorial charm. Blake's life, Blake's writings, Blake's art of design, are shown incontestably by Mr. Ellis and Mr. Yeats to have a single, simple coherence, a perfect unity: he lived, wrote, designed under one inspiration, obedient to one service of the imagination, without extravagance, without absurdity.

But why this symbolism, this apparatus of mystical mythology? Why not say what you have to say in plain language? Mill and Mr. Spencer use plain language, and yet their conceptions are difficult. What is the profit of this somewhat suspect and perplexing phraseology, this pseudo-systematic machinery? Surely, after all, Blake was a splendid fanatic, an innocent charlatan, half deluding and half deluded? Why not say Space and Time, if you mean them, instead of using crackjaw names of fantastic personages? Mr. Ellis and Mr. Yeats contrive to use fairly lucid English to explain it all: why did not Blake in the first instance?

In reply, we may refer to the chapter upon the "Necessity of Symbolism," perhaps the finest piece of writing in the whole work. It probably escapes many readers and critics, that any wholesale condemnation of Blake applies also to the literatures and writers whom they revere. Most of us, nominally, are some sort of Christians. What of Job, Isaiah, Ezekiel, the Song of Songs, the Apocalypse? Waiving all vexed questions of inspiration, it remains true that the Biblical writers, Israelite and Christian, did not always use plain language; they wrote visions, allegories, parables. The early Christian exegesis was frankly mystical. Moab, and Edom, and Egypt, and Babylon did not mean Moab, and Edom, and Egypt, and Babylon, but the spiritual significance of those names, exemplified in history. In the name of honesty, let us make a clean sweep of all this, if at heart we revolt against it; orthodox, or heretic, or neither, we need not be superstitious. Let us be honest positivists or materialists, and reject all mystical fables, however ancient and venerable. After all, if much of Blake seem ludicrous, undignified, unpoetical, Blake does not stand alone in that, but he is openly modern, a man of his day, not afraid of its terms. Ancient mystics are saved by their antiquity. Sincerely, if Gilead be admissible, why not Gloucester? if Gog and Magog, why not Urizen and Orc? Bibliolatry, and a false reverence for antiquity, have deadened alike our spiritual appreciation and our spiritual humour.

But the whole question, ultimately, is this: are we bound within the limits, and by the bonds, of the five senses? If not, and metaphysics for the most part say no, what is the ruling principle? Blake, like so many others, found it in imagination, the power of the spirit, soul, mind, at their highest. Like any Kantian, he drew distinctions between reason and understanding; like any Coleridgian, between fancy and imagination; and, like any Spinozist, he saw all things *sub specie aeternitatis*. The "thing in itself" haunted him, he refused phenomenal facts; he pondered upon the nature of things, as Lucretius calls the universe, and upon bygone, though not obsolete, systems. "He loved St. Theresa." His students know how much else he loved, how wide and deep was his mystical erudition, his "science of being," his ontology. He found his end in a reaction, almost Manichaean, against nature, the material world: against nature, he set up art, the power that divines and sees. Like any theologian, he discerned a "fall of man," a severance and division of his powers, a perpetual war: and, in imagination, he saw that royal faculty which interprets to fallen and distracted man the material witness of his natural senses. That is to say, imagination supplies to nature its interpretative symbols. And here we join hands with all poets. For, though we should begin with drawing elementary distinctions between metaphor and simile, and end by reading the history of aesthetics from Plato and Aristotle to Lessing and Hegel, we shall not comprehend the incomprehensible mystery of poetry. Why did Wordsworth fall from the highest altitudes to the deepest depths, utterly unconscious? Why does the quest after rhyme sometimes lead to the highest beauty of thought, the rhyming words mutually charged with spiritual significance, though the poet was ignorant of it? One may read scores of treatises upon poetry, learned, imaginative, from Aristotle to Sidney, from Sidney to Shelley, and remain wholly unenlightened. Blake delighted in the doctrine of correspondences, foolishly attributed to Swedenborg as a discovery, but the most ancient wisdom of the world. It may flippantly be termed, saying one thing when you mean another; more truly it means, seeing that one thing is the sign and symbol of another. Imagination at work among the common things of human experience, descries and discovers their divine counterparts: the world is the shadow of eternal truth, and imagination their go-between. Though in Blake, as our authors explain to us, this doctrine or theory took a special form and feature, systematised itself peculiarly, it is the property of all imaginative writers, each in his degree. Thus, to take a living author, the magnificent Odes and Essays of Mr. Patmore are largely unintelligible, apart from the doctrine of symbolic correspondences, as utilised by a Catholic. Assuredly here is the essence of poetry: the perception of spiritual resemblances. Blake chose to take these resemblances, and to personify them, and to embody or envisage them, and to make them in his prophetic books as real and live as Hector and Helen: he saw significance in the points of the compass, he found nothing common or unclean, he was utterly fearless in applying his doctrine to visible and actual things. To a prosaic man he would talk of the weather or the Ministry with all imaginable courtesy and practical address; but in himself, at least with his friends, to his wife, he talked of the eternal world of imagination in which he lived, discerning everywhere its types and images in this. Now and again, he burst out telling of that world before company unfit; and strange stories went about, how Mr. Blake said the sun was the Greek Apollo and the Devil, but the real sun cried "Holy, Holy, Holy." Most of us are content to find adumbrations of eternal truth and absolute being in material things. Blake, greatly daring, dared to proclaim that not the material image, but the eternal thing signified, was the reality. Many men think that Voltaire's and Johnson's jesting refutations of Berkeley are not only amusing, but adequate: such men will see nothing in Blake. A most imperfect poet, best remembered by the praises of Browning and Rossetti, has these lines:

> The essence of mind's being is the stream of thought;
> Difference of mind's being is difference of the
>   stream;
> Within this single difference may be brought
> All countless differences that are or seem.
> Now thoughts associate in the common mind

By outside semblance, or from general wont;
But in the mind of genius, swift as wind,
All similarly influencing thoughts confront.
Though the things thought, in time and space, may
    lie
Wider than India from the Arctic zone;
If they impress one feeling, swift they fly,
And in the mind of genius take one throne.

Garth Wilkinson, in the epilogue to those strange poems, *Improvisations from the Spirit*, writes: "Writing from an influx which is really out of yourself, or so far within yourself as to amount to the same thing, is either a madness or a religion. I know of no third possibility." Here is a man, drunk with mysticism, though no mean master in science, confessing the two alternatives; it is impossible to study Blake, without seeing that his inspiration was religious, spiritual, not fanatical and insane. Further, this perception of spiritual correspondences and analogies has often led to the wildest moral licence. Blake, understood *literatim et verbatim,* is unconventional enough, but never irresponsibly, enthusiastically so. As Mr. Dowden puts it: "An antinomian tendency is a characteristic common to many mystics; it is rarely that the antinomianism is so pure and childlike, yet so impassioned, as it was in the case of Blake." Behmen is poetical enough, but exceedingly vague; Swedenborg is lucid enough, but exceedingly prosaic; Blake is both poetical and—laboriously studied—lucid. Take away his nomenclature, his mythical imagery, and substitute its actual meaning; he reads like *The Dark Night of the Soul,* by St. John of the Cross, and many another masterpiece of Christian mysticism. We are always hearing that the epic is out of date and impossible. Blake wrote epics, an epic including epics, upon very high matters, and he has paid the penalty. Had he cast his work into another form, into his excellent and vigorous prose, he would have won applause: as it is he recorded the truth, as his literary imagination gave it to him, and the world, the little English world that knows of him, stands aghast. Yet Blake is far more intelligible than Emerson, because far more precise. Precision, said Palmer, was his word. As Arnold maintained against Carlyle, speaking of the second part of *Faust,* a fitful, vague adumbration of many things is detestable. Blake knew that "grandeur of ideas is founded upon precision of ideas," and was definite to the verge of absurdity.

—Lionel Johnson, *Academy,*
August 26, 1893, pp. 163–165

ALFRED T. STORY (1893)

In the same year that Edwin J. Ellis and William Butler Yeats produced their remarkable study of Blake's "Symbolic System," Alfred Thomas Story (1842–1934) published a reflection on Blake's merits as artist and poet. The task followed naturally from his previous project, *The Life of John Linnell* (1892), Linnell having been one of the young artisan-disciples who gathered around Blake in the 1820s. Story uses the evaluative, judgmental, vague tone of Victorian belletrism, contrasting markedly with Yeats' analytic (if muddled) passages. Of the differences between these two major contemporary works, he writes, simply, "Indeed, the great fault of Messrs. Ellis and Yeates's work is that they push this symbolism too far, and make too complex a system of it. Blake, we feel convinced, never evolved all that confused and laborious system; his genius was too intuitive, too instantaneous for that."

————

I have not in these pages attempted to deal with Blake's art, except in so far as it constitutes a part of his literature; but before coming to a close, it may be well to say that, in judging of the products of his brush, as of his pen, it behoves us to consider the limitations put upon him by his opportunities. The charge is frequently brought against him that he was not able to draw; but as a matter of fact he could draw as well as any man of his time. We have abundant material in proof of this. But he was unfortunate, in the first place, in being apprenticed to a man like Basire, whose style of engraving was hard and dry and conventional, the result being to cramp and fetter the genius of the pupil. In the second place, a great deal of the technique of painting he had to find out for himself. Where other men had instruction and guidance, he had none; while they were gaining knowledge of methods and facility of treatment, he was spending years of solitary toil in ecclesiastical edifices.

The significance of the time thus spent can hardly be over-estimated as regards the working out of his genius. It kindled in him a fervent love of the Gothic spirit, which remained with him to the end, and, doubtless, as his principal biographer has noted, fostered "the romantic turn of his imagination" and his "natural affinities for the spiritual in art." But while it did this, it rooted in him some of his worst mannerisms. In short, though it strengthened, if it did not actually create, in him that leaning towards the gloomy and supernatural, the moral and religious, in art which characterised his genius, it caused him to become indifferent to execution and finish. In his art, as in his writings, form was nothing; the thought was everything. If the conception were fully set forth, the rest was of little moment. In other words, he held that the power to conceive or invent a work carried with it that of adequately executing it.

His central idea, both as regards poetry and art, is essentially the same. "Shall painting," he asks, "be confined to the sordid drudgery of *facsimile* representation of merely mortal and perishing substance, and not be, as poetry and music are, elevated into its own proper sphere of invention and visionary conception? No, it shall not be so. Painting, as well as poetry and music, exists and exults in immortal thoughts."

In these words are contained the vitalising principle that underlay all Blake's work. In art his aim was not merely to excite and satisfy the aesthetic sense; it was to move and instruct—to elevate the soul above its mundane surroundings—to create a desire for that life of the imagination in which alone "all things exist." If that end were accomplished, all was accomplished.

In short, as I have already pointed out, his aim was largely and chiefly literary: it was to point a moral—to illustrate a theme, and that theme the grandest and noblest. This is the primary object of all great art; subsidiary thereto is the object of creating a sensation of pleasure, similar to what we experience in seeing a beautiful thing in nature, an exquisite harmony of colour, a bit of perfect form, a sentiment in light and shade.

Sometimes Blake neglected this secondary aim in his zeal for the first. But how well he could compass it if he liked we may see by turning to any of his earlier, and some of his later, illustrated and illuminated books. There we not only have his story told, but the emotion of beauty stirred, now by his fine perception of form, now by his tender feeling for colour.

In all this, however, he did no better than other men have done; often, indeed, he fell short of his own previous achievement. But in one respect he has had no equal. It would be hard to find a better word to specify the quality in question than that which he applied to his designs for the Book of Job, namely, "Inventions." His faculty of invention was supreme. Such was his originality and fecundity in this respect that he was not only held to be good to steal from by the men of his own day, but ever since artists have found him suggestive and worthy of careful study.

It has frequently been pointed out that in some of his works there are indications of his having taken ideas from others. That is undoubtedly true; but the plagiarism, if plagiarism it can be called, was unconscious, and he adds thereto so many ideas of his own as practically to make the whole new. This is especially the case with his "Last Judgment," which is undoubtedly based on Michael Angelo's.

But when all has been said, it remains for ever true that as regards what is commonly known as creative work, in that, namely, wherein the imagination reigns supreme, there have been few to equal and none to excel Blake among our English artists. Though his drawing be faulty, and faulty much of his method and handling, these may be forgotten and forgiven in the grandeur and sublime pathos of most, if not all, of his purely imaginative work.

In this, as in his writing, it is important to note the effect of his imperfect education. But it is important also to note that this lack of education may have had its beneficial side both for himself and for us. For sometimes it is well to leave the beaten track of custom and authority, or to have one strong in power and individuality do so, in order that we may from time to time be presented with glimpses of the reverse of the shield. We can never keep too much in mind, or have too strongly impressed upon us, the fact that there is another way of looking at a thing. Education, as we understand it, is too much a matter of filling the brain with the currently accepted or authoritative view of things; in other words, it is a stereotyping and too often a stultifying process, and makes a man as incapable of preserving a delicate perception of the truth as an already overcrowded photographic plate of receiving and giving back a fresh image.

Here was an unsophisticated mind revelling in the universe of things as it appeared to him. The phenomenon is so rare that the result cannot but be precious, especially when the medium of transmission is of the translucent purity of Blake. It is next to impossible to rise from a study of his works without a feeling amounting almost to a conviction that to him was given a vision of a world closed to the eyes of ordinary mortals. We may occasionally feel that the transmitted image is blurred, that the thought has often become confused, but we cannot doubt his sincerity. Every line he wrote was as it were infused with his own life's blood. He was literally consumed with earnestness, while the fire of his spirit burned itself into every jot and particle of the work he did.

Conscious that "the sea of time roars and follows swiftly," engulfing men too often before their work is done, and that he has "spiritual enemies of formidable magnitude," who may tempt or turn him from his course; he, in his own phrase, roars and rages in the effort to get done what has been given him to do. "Nothing," he cries in his exultation, when he feels the stress and fervour of inspiration upon him—"Nothing can withstand the fury of my career among the stars of God and in the abysses of the accuser." And then, as it were in explanation and justification of his fiery zeal, he tells us the nature of his mission. "My mission is visionary—an endeavour to bring back the Golden Age." No wonder if, with such a mission and under such conditions, his thoughts are sometimes "scattered upon the winds in incoherent despair."

But notwithstanding the mass of what we must at present consider undigested verbiage in his prophetic poems, there still remains such an immensity of matter in them that one cannot pretend to examine, or even to state the whole of it in a treatise of this description. The fact that such is the case, and that it is so full of novel and startling thought, is almost enough in itself to indicate that he had struck some new vein or source of truth. That he believed himself to have been commissioned to deliver a message to mankind, as serious as that of Jonah, or of any other of the prophets, and that a terrible penalty attached to its non-fulfilment, is apparent not only from the passage previously noted, but from numberless others scattered through his writings.

In short, the more one studies these poems the more surely is one convinced that the writer had a purpose in view, and that that purpose was a very distinct and a very high and clear one. What strikes one with equal if not still greater force is that he for some reason failed to carry out his purpose with entire clearness and sanity. Before we have reached the end of his works the impression grows and strengthens upon us that his message is too great for him, that, as Hazlitt—profoundest of critics—said, "He is ruined by vain struggles to get rid of what presses on his brain; he attempts impossibilities."

No man in his day and generation—no man, perhaps, that ever stood on our English earth—struggled so hard to deliver the truth that was in him. How nigh his deliverance was to becoming a mere nullity and abortion we know; and yet it was providentially saved from that ignominy. Through the smoke and vapour of his fiery effort, through the roaring and confused thunder of his wrathful spirit, we see the tongue of clear flame ascending—we hear the voice proclaiming. Thus was he enabled in some sort to deliver his message—possibly to deliver it fully—albeit the utterance was accompanied by so much tempestuous uproar, and such a wild rush of words, that one is at times almost deafened.

And the pity of it is that the more we study him the more we feel convinced that, had he been able to put into his work that crystalline freshness and lucidity which, after all, must still remain a chief characteristic of all supremely great writing, he would to-day have stood side by side with the foremost in our literature, probably in all literatures. For in the splendour and magnitude of his imagination—it cannot too often be insisted—he has no superior; and though it is possible to point to his vast overplus of words utterly without meaning, except on some inane theory of magico-cabalistic mysticism, in proof of his insanity; yet, in spite of all, there burned through this incoherent windy drift, and for ever stands revealed as in golden letters of light, a treasury of thought so rich that it constitutes a veritable and almost unparalleled intellectual heritage for all the ages to come.

—Alfred T. Story, from *William Blake:*
His Life, Character and Genius, 1893, pp. 153–160

J.J. JUSSERAND (1894)

Jean Jules Jusserand (1855-1932), a French author and diplomat, produced monographs in French and English on several areas of English literature.

~~~

The poems of Blake appear the simplest in the world; they treat of the most ordinary subjects; but suddenly a deeper note, an allusion to hidden sufferings and wounds, reveals to us that we are not in the presence of a shepherd who pipes, but of a prophet who knows. The effect is grand and strange. Placed on the limit of two centuries, and on the boundary line of two periods, Blake is the first in date (but the least in genius) of that group of mysterious and symbol-loving poets, amongst whom are to be ranked Shelley, Rossetti and Browning, poets who shiver at the mere idea of the surrounding triviality, universal ease and fluency, staleness of the higher sentiments taught by rule in schools, and take refuge, out of scorn and vexation, in a thick-veiled darkness, where they know that ease-loving multitudes will not follow them. They mingle with the crowd, like "Longe Will," saluting no one; and the crowd long remains in ignorance of who they are, or, at most, wonders with an incredulous shake of the head, whether, by any possibility or chance, such men as they belong to the chosen people.

—J.J. Jusserand, *Piers Plowman:*
A Contribution to the History of English
Mysticism, trans. Marion Richards and
Elise Richards, 1894, pp. 218–219

JOHN VANCE CHENEY
"WILLIAM BLAKE" (1895)

John Vance Cheney (1848-1922) was an American librarian, poet, and writer. His inclusion of an essay on Blake in *That Dome in Air: Thoughts on Poetry and the Poets* is a measure of Blake's gaining canonical status. Cheney also considers the work of Ralph Waldo Emerson, James Lowell,

John Greenleaf Whittier, Henry Wadsworth Longfellow, William Bryant, Walt Whitman, William Cowper, and William Wordsworth, a select and transatlantic cohort.

—ᴠᴠᴠ— —ᴠᴠᴠ— —ᴠᴠᴠ—

Blake, in his lifetime, was known to many as a madman, but let us not be too hasty in consigning great gifts to the asylum; for Coleridge, De Quincey, Byron, and even Wordsworth, have been tracked beyond the bounds of sanity. The spice of madness demanded for the poet, Blake assuredly had; and this is all that concerns us at present.

The many make too little of such a mind, while a few make too much of it. Mr. Gilchrist and Swinburne are guilty on the side of over-appreciation. If, here and there, are applied to Blake adulatory adjectives larger than his erratic genius can well carry, he is very different from what he has been found to be by his detractors. The sympathetic reader finds a deal of queerness, a medley of Ezekiel, Ossian, and an innominable *tertium quid;* finds independence, intolerance, wildness; finds incoherence, vast scattering, rhapsody thinning away into nebula, mysticism slipping into nonsense,—in short, defiance of much that is right in thought and in method; finds this, but, mingled with it, strains and whole poems possible only to the poet pure and simple, to the singer by the grace of God. Indeed, Blake, at his best, is, what we should always joy to discover, an excellent illustration of the old notion, the true notion, of the poet; with imagination, vision, faith, enthusiasm, he has the poet's kind of thought, his straight sight, and his swift method, his fire and his music shining and singing along the native, inevitable lines. As we read the place of his birth, there is something prophetic in the names, "Broad Street, Golden Square"; of a truth, he was the babe for a spacious, radiant cradle.

It is a waste of time to look for system in the work of such a mind; as in the case of Emerson, the light is too white for more than gleams, flashes. Blake is a reporter, a flesh-and-blood conduit for the high might that descends, through certain rare organisms, to become the precious possession of men. We get from him occasional meteor streaks of prophecy; we get scattered blossoms of philosophy; we hear the voice of the teacher, indirect, trembling with passion; we listen to the joyous songs of nature and of "humble livers" from the lips of one the color of whose singing-robe matches the sunset purple of Wordsworth's; we hear the last echo of the days when youth and music ruled the English world; and, having this, we have something harder to find than theories and systems.

The vision is mightier in this poet than the faculty divine. He sees so much that he forgets the blindness of the world; with so much of the poet in himself, he forgets how little of the poet there is in us; he draws the rapid outlines, dashes off the sketch, and our own imagination is left to complete the picture. It should not be forgotten, however, that in many cases the poems are but half the artistic whole; that it was Blake's habit to engrave his poems, illustrating them with colored drawings round the page or on a separate page. To read the poems apart from the designs is like listening to Wagner's operas, blindfold. To be sure, the poems must stand or fall by themselves; still it is only right to bear in mind that without the illustrations we do not realize the full action of the author's imagination.

Emerson describes himself as a "transparent eyeball," yet his vision is normal; Blake's vision is abnormal. If Emerson sees more than he can tell, Blake is determined that language shall fellow his limitless vision:—

I assert for myself that I do not behold the outward creation, and that to me it is hindrance and not action. 'What!' it will be questioned, 'when the sun rises, do you not see a disc of fire, somewhat like a guinea?' 'Oh no, no! I see an innumerable company of the heavenly host, crying, 'Holy, holy, holy is the Lord God Almighty!' I question not my corporeal eye, any more than I would question a window, concerning a sight. I look through it, and not with it.

The more we inquire into the matter of art, the more evident it becomes that patience is of the very essence of success in it; but, unluckily, all the patience of the little Blake family was in the heart of faithful, black-eyed Catherine. Had it been among the temperamental treasures of the master of the house, what might he not have done, he that in green boyhood can remind us of the old masters of the drama? . . .

If on the one side is madness, on the other is good old-fashioned sanity; in fact, it is not difficult for Blake to be as worldly-wise as one could wish. Despite his abnormal vision and incoherent utterance, despite his inequality and his thousand vagaries, Blake was a close critic of life. While his vision was abnormally active, the range is round a few elementary principles. It is the safe circuit of Epictetus himself; the favorite themes, love, youth, and childhood, indicating not only sanity, but special qualification for the office of poet. Sweet-tempered and joyous, barring the few lapses unavoidable by one with so ardent a temperament, he saw the world as the old prophets saw it, beautiful, good; he trusted it, looked up from it to the Maker of all, and sang as he journeyed, angels overhead and lambs at his feet. No man has lived a more thoroughly poetic life; few men have come closer to a realization of his own happy phrase, a "shining lot."

—John Vance Cheney, "William Blake,"
*That Dome in Air: Thoughts on Poetry
and the Poets*, 1895, pp. 170–176

STOPFORD A. BROOKE (1896)

Stopford Augustus Brooke (1832–1916), born in Donegal, Ireland, was ordained into the Church of England and served as chaplain to Empress Frederick in Berlin, and later to Queen Victoria, before seceding from the Church of England in 1880 upon his conversion to Unitarianism. He wrote extensively on English literature and Irish literature in English, and in this latter connection had contact with William Butler Yeats. That Brooke calls Blake "a full Mystic" suggests familiarity with Edwin J. Ellis and Yeats's *The Works of William Blake, Poetic, Symbolic, and Critical* (1893). But unlike Ellis and Yeats, Brooke stresses the political radicalism of Blake's poetry. The implication of a poetic affinity with Wordsworth suggests Blake as a Romantic, if not as a member of anything so coherent as a Romantic Movement.

He anticipated in 1789 and 1794, when his *Songs of Innocence* and *Experience* were written, the simple natural poetry of ordinary life which Wordsworth perfected in the Lyrical Ballads, 1798. Moreover, the democratic element, the hatred of priestcraft, and the cry against social wrongs which came much later into English poetry spring up in his poetry. Then, he was a full Mystic, and through his mysticism appears that search after the true aims of life and after a freer theology which characterise our poetry after 1832.

He cast back as well as forward, and reproduced in his songs the spirit, movement, and music of the Elizabethan songs. The little poems in the *Songs of Innocence,* on infancy and first motherhood, and on subjects like the "Lamb," are without rival in our language for simplicity, tenderness, and joy. The *Songs of Experience* give the reverse side of the *Songs of Innocence,* and they see the evil of the world as a child with a man's heart would see it—with exaggerated horror. This small but predictive work of Blake, coming where it did, between 1777 and 1794, going back to Elizabethan lyrics and forward to those of Wordsworth, is very remarkable.

—Stopford A. Brooke,
English Literature, 1896, p. 223

GEORGE SAINTSBURY (1896)

George Edward Bateman Saintsbury (1845–1933) was a prominent historian of English and French literature, professor of rhetoric and English
literature at Edinburgh University from 1895 until 1915. He compares
Blake and Scottish poet, Robert Burns (1759–96), with good reason: anti-
clericalism and republicanism, a radical revisioning of gender roles and
class can be found in both. There is no evidence, however, to suggest
that they were aware of each other, and certainly Burns's poetry lacks
Blake's mysticism.

Yet, however one may sympathise with Cowper, however much one may
admire Crabbe, it is difficult for any true lover of poetry not to feel the sense
of a "Pisgah sight," and something more, of the promised land of poetry, in
passing from these writers to William Blake and Robert Burns. Here there
is no more allowance necessary, except in the first case for imperfection
of accomplishment, in the second for shortness of life and comparative
narrowness of range. The quality and opportuneness of poetry are in each
case undeniable. Since the deaths of Herrick and Vaughan, England had not
seen any one who had the finer lyrical gifts of the poet as Blake had them. Since
the death of Dunbar, Scotland had not seen such strength and intensity of
poetic genius (joined in this case to a gift of melody which Dunbar never had)
as were shown by Burns. There was scarcely more than a twelvemonth between
their births; for Blake was born in 1757 (the day appears not to be known),
and Burns in January 1759. But Blake long outlived Burns, and did not die
till 1828, while Burns was no more in July 1796. Neither the long life nor the
short one provided any events which demand chronicling here. Both poets
were rather fortunate in their wives, though Blake clave to Catherine Boucher
more constantly than Burns to his Jean. Neither was well provided with this
world's goods; Burns wearing out his short life in difficulties as farmer and
as exciseman, while all the piety of biographers has left it something of a
mystery how Blake got through his long life with no better resources than a
few very poorly paid private commissions for his works of design, the sale of his
hand-made books of poetry and prophecy, and such occasional employment
in engraving as his unconventional style and his still more unconventional
habits and temper allowed him to accept or to keep. In some respects the two
were different enough according to commonplace standards, less so perhaps
according to others. The forty years of Burns, and the more than seventy
of Blake, were equally passed in a rapture; but morality has less quarrel with

Blake, who was essentially a "God-intoxicated man" and spent his life in one long dream of art and prophecy, than with Burns, who was generally in love, and not unfrequently in liquor. But we need no more either of antithesis or of comparison: the purely literary matter calls us.

It was in 1783—a date which, in its close approximation to the first appearances of Crabbe and Cowper, makes the literary student think of another group of first appearances in the early "eighties" of the sixteenth century foreshadowing the outburst of Elizabethan literature—that Blake's first book appeared. His *Poetical Sketches,* now one of the rarest volumes of English poetry, was printed by subscription among a literary coterie who met at the house of Mr. and Mrs. Mathew; but the whole edition was given to the author. He had avowedly taken little or no trouble to correct it, and the text is nearly as corrupt as that of the *Supplices*; nor does it seem that he took any trouble to make it "go off," nor that it did go off in any appreciable manner. Yet if many ears had then been open to true poetical music, some of them could not have mistaken sounds of the like of which had not, as has been said, been heard since the deaths of Herrick and Vaughn. The merit of the contents is unequal to a degree not to be accounted for by the mere neglect to prepare carefully for press, and the influence of *Ossian* is, as throughout Blake's work, much more prominent for evil than for good. But the chaotic play of *Edward the Third* is not mere Elizabethan imitation; and at least half a dozen of the songs and lyrical pieces are of the most exquisite quality—snatches of Shakespeare or Fletcher as Shakespeare or Fletcher might have written them in Blake's time. The finest of all no doubt is the magnificent "Mad Song." But others—"How sweet I roamed from Field to Field" (the most eighteenth century in manner, but showing how even that manner could be strengthened and sweetened); "My Silks and Fine Array," beautiful, but more like an Elizabethan imitation than most; "Memory Hither Come," a piece of ineffable melody—these are things which at once showed Blake to be free of the very first company of poets, to be a poet who for real essence of poetry excelled everything the century had yet seen, and everything, with the solitary exception of the *Lyrical Ballads* at its extreme end, that it was to see.

Unfortunately it was not by any means as a poet that Blake regarded himself. He knew that he was an artist, and he thought that he was a prophet; and for the rest of his life, deviating only now and then into engraving as a mere breadwinner, he devoted himself to the joint cultivation of these two gifts, inventing for the purpose a method or vehicle of publication excellently suited to his genius, but in other respects hardly convenient. This method was to execute text and illustrations at once on copper-plates, which were then treated in slightly different fashions. Impressions worked off from these by hand-press were coloured by hand, Blake and his wife executing the entire process. In this fashion were produced the lovely little gems of literature and design called *Songs of Innocence* (1789) and *Songs of Experience* (1794); in this way for the most part, but with some modifications, the vast and formidable mass of the so-called "Prophetic" Books. With the artistic qualities of Blake we are not here concerned, but it is permissible to remark that they resemble his literary qualities with a closeness which at once explains and is explained by their strangely combined method of production. That Blake was not entirely sane has never been doubted except by a few fanatics of mysticism, who seem to think that the denial of complete sanity implies a complete denial of genius. And though he was never, in the common phrase, "incapable of managing" such very modest affairs as were his, the defect appears most in the obstinate fashion in which he refused to perfect and co-ordinate his work. He could, when he chose and would give himself the trouble, draw quite exquisitely; and he always drew with marvellous vigour and imagination. But he would often permit himself faults of drawing quite inexplicable and not very tolerable. So, too, though he had the finest gift of literary expression, he chose often to babble and still oftener to rant at large. Even the *Songs of Innocence and Experience*—despite their double charm to the eye and the ear, and the presence of such things as the famous "Tiger," as the two "Introductions" (two of Blake's best things), and as "The Little Girl Lost"—show a certain poetical declension from the highest heights of the *Poetical Sketches*. The poet is no longer a poet pure and simple; he has got purposes and messages, and these partly strangle and partly render turbid the clear and spontaneous jets of poetry which refresh us in the "Mad Song" and the "Memory." And after the *Songs* Blake did not care to put forth anything bearing the ordinary form of poetry. We possess indeed other poetical work of his, recovered in scraps and fragments from MSS., and some of it is beautiful. But it is as a rule more chaotic than the *Sketches* themselves; it is sometimes defaced (being indeed mere private jottings never intended for print) by personality and coarseness; and it is constantly puddled with the jargon of Blake's mystical philosophy, which, borrowing some of its method from Swedenborg and much of its imagery and nomenclature from *Ossian*, spreads itself unhampered by any form whatever over the Prophetic Books. The literary merit of these in parts is often very high, and their theosophy (for that is the best single word for it) is not seldom majestic. But despite the attempts of some disciples to evolve a regular system from them, students of philosophy as well as of literature are never likely to be at much odds as to their real character. "Ravings" they are not, and they are very often the reverse of "nonsense." But they are the work of a man who in the first place was very slightly acquainted with the literature and antecedents of his subject, who in the second was distinctly non *compos* on the critical, though admirably gifted on the creative side of his brain, and who in the third had the ill luck to fall under the fullest sway of the Ossianic influence. To any one who loves and admires Blake—and the present writer deliberately ranks him as the greatest and most delectable poet of the eighteenth century proper in England, reserving Burns as specially Scotch—it must always be tempting to say more of him than can be allowed on such a scale as the present; but the scale must be observed.

There is all the more reason for the observance that Blake exercised on the literary *history* of his time no influence, and occupied in it no position. He always had a few faithful friends and patrons who kept him from starvation by their commissions, admired him, believed in him, and did him such good turns as his intensely independent and rather irritable disposition would allow. But the public had little opportunity of seeing his pictures, and less of reading his books; and though the admiration of Lamb led to some appreciation from Southey and others, he was practically an unread man.

—George Saintsbury, from
*A History of Nineteenth Century
Literature*, 1896, pp. 9–13

W.B. Yeats "Academy Portraits: XXXII. William Blake" (1897)

Yeats understood Blake as operating within a mystical Symbolic System (see note to W. B. Yeats and Edwin J. Ellis, *The Works of William Blake, Poetic, Symbolic, and Critical* [1893]). But that complicated reading, with its weight of erudition and arguably crankish twists, is suppressed in the high oratory of this brief sketch for *Academy*. Yeats's characterization of Blake as the prophet in a religion of art resembles the utterances made by Blake's Pre-Raphaelite admirers. Throughout the nineteenth century, the moral and revelatory authority of the Bible was gradually transferred to the secular text. Yeats suggests that Blake anticipated this phenomenon, authoring what Northrop Frye will call the "secular scripture."

There have been men who loved the future like a mistress, and the future mixed her breath into their breath and shook her hair about them, and hid them from the understanding of their times. William Blake was one of these men, and if he spoke confusedly and obscurely it was because he spoke things for whose speaking he could find no models in the world about him. He announced the religion of art, of which no man dreamed in the world about him; and he understood it more perfectly than the thousands of subtle spirits who have received its baptism in the world about us, because, in the beginning of important things—in the beginning of love, in the beginning of the day, in the beginning of any work, there is a moment when we understand more perfectly than we understand again until all is finished. In his time educated people believed that they amused themselves with books of imagination, but that they "made their souls" by listening to sermons and by doing or by not doing certain things. When they had to explain why serious people like themselves honoured the great poets greatly they were hard put to it for lack of good reasons. In our time we are agreed that we "make our souls" out of some one of the great poets of ancient times, or out of Shelley or Wordsworth, or Goethe or Balzac, or Flaubert, or Count Tolstoy, in the books he wrote before he became a prophet and fell into a lesser order, or out of Mr. Whistler's pictures, while we amuse ourselves, or, at best, make a poorer sort of soul, by listening to sermons or by doing or by not doing certain things. We write of great writers, even of writers whose beauty would once have seemed an unholy beauty, with wrapped sentences like those our fathers kept for the beatitudes and mysteries of the Church; and no matter what we believe with our lips, we believe with our hearts that beautiful things, as Browning said in his one prose essay that was not in verse, have "lain burningly on the Divine hand," and that when time has begun to wither, the Divine hand will fall heavily on bad taste and vulgarity. When no man believed these things William Blake believed them, and began that preaching against the Philistine, which is as the preaching of the Middle Ages against the Saracen. He wrote:

> I know of no other Christianity, and of no other gospel, than the liberty both of body and mind to exercise the divine arts of imagination—imagination, the real and eternal world, of which this vegetable universe is but a faint shadow, and in which we shall live in our eternal or imaginative bodies when these vegetable mortal bodies are no more. The Apostles knew of no other gospel. What are all their spiritual gifts? What is the Divine Spirit? Is the Holy Ghost other than an intellectual fountain? What is the life of man but art and science? Answer this for yourselves, and expel from among you

those who pretend to despise the labours of art and science, which alone are the labours of the gospel.

And he wrote:

I care not whether a man is good or bad, all that I care is, whether a man is a wise man or a fool. Go, put off holiness and put on intellect.

He had learned from Jacob Boehme and from old alchemist writers that imagination was the first emanation of divinity, "the body of God," "the Divine members," and he drew the deduction, which they did not draw, that the imaginative arts were therefore the greatest of Divine revelations, and that the sympathy with all living things, sinful and righteous alike, which the imaginative arts awaken, is that forgiveness of sins commanded by Christ. The reason, and by the reason he meant deductions from the observations of the senses, binds us to mortality because it binds us to the senses, and divides us from each other by showing us our clashing interests; but imagination divides us from mortality by the immortality of beauty, and binds us to each other by opening the secret doors of all hearts. He cried again and again that every thing that lives is holy, and that nothing is unholy except things that do not live—lethargies, and cruelties, and timidities, and that denial of imagination which is the root they grew from in old times. Passions, because most living, are most holy—and this was a scandalous paradox in his time—and man shall enter eternity borne upon their wings.

> Men are admitted into heaven not because they have curbed or governed their passions, or have no passions, but because they have cultivated their understandings. The treasures of heaven are not negations of passion but realities of intellect from which the passions emanate uncurbed in their eternal glory.

And he understood this so literally that certain drawings to *Vala*, had he carried them beyond the first faint pencillings, the first faint washes of colour, would have been a pretty scandal to his time and to our time. The sensations of this "foolish body," this "phantom of the earth and water," were in themselves but half living things, "vegetative" things, but that "eternal glory" made them a part of the body of God.

This philosophy kept him more simply a poet than any poet of his time, for it made him content to express every beautiful feeling that came into his head without troubling about its utility or chaining it to any utility. Sometimes one feels, even when one is reading poets of a better time—Tennyson or Wordsworth, let us say—that they have troubled the energy and simplicity

of their imaginative passions by asking whether they were for the helping or
for the hindrance of the world, instead of believing that all beautiful things
have "lain burningly on the Divine hand." But when one reads Blake, it is as
though the spray of an inexhaustible fountain of beauty was blown into our
faces, and not merely when one reads *The Songs of Innocence,* or the lyrics he
wished to call *The Ideas of Good and Evil;* but when one reads those *Prophetic
Works* in which he spoke confusedly and obscurely because he spoke of things
for whose speaking he could find no models in the world about him. He was
a symbolist who had to invent his symbols; and his counties of England,
with their correspondence to tribes of Israel, and his mountains and rivers,
with their correspondence to parts of a man's body, are arbitrary as some of
the symbolism in the *Axel* of the symbolist Villiers d'Lisle Adam is arbitrary,
while they have an incongruity that *Axel* has not. He was a man crying out
for a mythology, and trying to make one because he could not find one to his
hand. Had he been a Catholic of Dante's time he would have been well content
with Mary and the angels; or had he been a scholar of our time he would have
taken his symbols where Wagner took his, from Norse mythology; or have
followed, with the help of Prof. Rhys, that pathway into Welsh mythology
which he found in *Jerusalem;* or have gone to Ireland—and he was probably
an Irishman—and chosen for his symbols the sacred mountains, along
whose sides the peasant still sees enchanted fires, and the divinities which
have not faded from the belief, if they have faded from the prayers of simple
hearts; and have spoken without incongruity because he spoke of things that
had been steeped in emotion from the old times; and have been less obscure
because a traditional mythology stood on the threshold of his meaning and
on the margin of his sacred darkness. If *Enitharmon* had been named Fylgga,
or Gwydeon, or Danu, and made live in Ancient Norway, or Ancient Wales,
or Ancient Ireland, we would have forgotten that her maker was a mystic; and
the hymn of her harping, that is in *Vala,* would but have reminded us of many
ancient hymns.

> The joy of woman is the death of her beloved,
> Who dies for love of her,
> In torments of fierce jealousy and pangs of adoration.
> The lover's night bears on my song,
> And the nine spheres rejoice beneath my powerful control.
> They sing unwearied to the notes of my immortal hand.
> The solemn, silent moon
> Reverberates the long harmony sounding upon my limbs.

The birds and beasts rejoice and play.
And every one seeks for his mate to prove his inmost joy
Furious and terrible they rend the nether deep,
The deep lifts up his rugged head,
And lost in infinite hovering wings vanishes with a cry.
The fading cry is ever dying,
The living voice is ever living in its inmost joy.

—W.B. Yeats, "Academy Portraits: XXXII.
William Blake," *Academy*, June 19, 1897,
pp. 634–635

G.K. CHESTERTON (1910)

Gilbert Keith Chesterton (1874–1936) was a prolific writer, known for his Christian apologetics. The following reflection on Blakean mysticism was written as an antidote to Yeats' and Ellis' account of Blake's occult system. In his youth, Chesterton had been interested in the occult, but by 1910 his creed was moving increasingly towards Catholicism. The ideas he espouses here about Blake's questing for the essence of things closely resembles Plato's theory of forms.

A verbal accident has confused the mystical with the mysterious. Mysticism is generally felt vaguely to be itself vague—a thing of clouds and curtains, of darkness or concealing vapours, of bewildering conspiracies or impenetrable symbols. Some quacks have indeed dealt in such things: but no true mystic ever loved darkness rather than light. No pure mystic ever loved mere mystery. The mystic does not bring doubts or riddles: the doubts and riddles exist already. We all feel the riddle of the earth without anyone to point it out. The mystery of life is the plainest part of it. The clouds and curtains of darkness, the confounding vapours, these are the daily weather of this world. Whatever else we have grown accustomed to, we have grown accustomed to the unaccountable. Every stone or flower is a hieroglyphic of which we have lost the key; with every step of our lives we enter into the middle of some story which we are certain to misunderstand. The mystic is not the man who makes mysteries but the man who destroys them. The mystic is one who offers an explanation which may be true or false, but which is *always* comprehensible—by which I mean, not that it is always comprehended, but that it always can be comprehended, because there is always something to comprehend. The man whose meaning remains mysterious fails, I think, as a mystic: and Blake, as we shall see, did, for certain peculiar reasons of his own, often fail in this way. But even when he was himself hard to be understood, it was never through himself not understanding: it was never because he was vague or mystified or groping, that he was unintelligible. While his utterance was not only dim but dense, his opinion was not only clear, but even cocksure. You and I may be a little vague about the relations of Albion to Jerusalem, but Blake is as certain about them as Mr Chamberlain about the relations of Birmingham to the British Empire. And this can be said for his singular literary style even at his worst, that we always feel that he is saying something very plain and emphatic, even when we have not the wildest notion of what it is.

There is one element always to be remarked in the true mystic, however disputed his symbolism, and that is its brightness of colour and clearness of shape. I mean that we may be doubtful about the significance of a triangle or the precise lesson conveyed by a crimson cow. But in the work of a real mystic the triangle is a hard mathematical triangle not to be mistaken for a cone or a polygon. The cow is in colour a rich incurable crimson, and in shape unquestionably a cow, not to be mistaken for any of its evolutionary relatives, such as the buffalo or the bison. This can be seen very clearly, for instance, in the Christian art of illumination as practised at its best in the thirteenth and fourteenth centuries. The Christian decorators, being true mystics, were chiefly concerned to maintain the reality of objects. For the highest dogma of the spiritual is to affirm the material. By plain outline and positive colour those pious artists strove chiefly to assert that a cat was truly in the eyes of God a cat and that a dog was preeminently doggish. This decision of tint and outline belongs not only to Blake's pictures, but even to his poetry. Even in his descriptions there is no darkness, and practically, in the modern sense, no distance. All his animals are as absolute as the animals on a shield of heraldry. His lambs are of unsullied silver, his lions are of flaming gold. His lion may lie down with his lamb, but he will never really mix with him.

Really to make this point clear one would have to go back to the twelfth century, or perhaps to Plato. Metaphysics must be avoided; they are too exciting. But the root of the matter can be pretty well made plain by one word. The whole difference is between the old meaning and the new meaning of the word "Realist." In modern fiction and science a Realist means a man who begins at the outside of a thing: sometimes merely at the end of a thing, knowing the monkey only by its tail or the motor by its smell. In the twelfth century a Realist meant exactly the opposite; it meant a man who began at the inside of a thing. The mediaeval philosopher would only have been interested in a motor because it moved. He would have been interested (that is) only in the central and original idea of a motor—in its ultimate motorishness. He would have been concerned with a monkey only because of its monkeyhood; not because it was like man but because it was unlike. If he saw an elephant he would not say in the modern style, "I see before me a combination of the tusks of a wild boar in unnatural development, of the long nose of the tapir needlessly elongated, of the tail of the cow unusually insufficient," and so on. He would merely see an essence of elephant. He would believe that this light and fugitive elephant of an instant, as dancing and fleeting as the May-fly in May, was nevertheless the shadow of an eternal elephant, conceived and created by God. When you have quite realised this ancient sense in the reality of an elephant, go back and read William Blake's poems about animals, as, for instance, about the lamb and about the tiger. You will see quite clearly that he is talking of an eternal tiger, who rages and rejoices for ever in the sight of God. You will see that he is talking of an eternal and supernatural lamb, who can only feed happily in the fields of Heaven.

It is exactly here that we find the full opposition to that modern tendency that can fairly be called "Impressionism." Impressionism is scepticism. It means believing one's immediate impressions at the expense of one's more permanent and positive generalisations. It puts what one notices above what one knows. It means the monstrous heresy that seeing is believing. A white cow at one particular instant of the evening light may be gold on one side and violet on the other. The whole point of Impressionism is to say that she really is a gold and violet cow. The whole point of Impressionism is to say that there is no white cow at all. What can we tell, it cries, beyond what we can see? But the essence of Mysticism is to insist that there is a white cow, however veiled with shadow or painted with sunset gold. Blessed are they who have seen the violet cow and who yet believe in the white one. To the mystic a white cow has a sort of solid whiteness, as if the cow were made out of frozen milk. To him a white horse has a solid whiteness as if he were cut out of the firm English chalk, like the White Horse in the valley of King Alfred. The cow's whiteness is more important than anything except her cowishness. If Blake had ever introduced a white cow into one of his pictures, there would at least have been no doubt about either of those two elements. Similarly there would have been no doubt about them in any old Christian illumination. On this point he is at one with all the mystics and with all the saints.

This explanation is really essential to the understanding of Blake, because to the modern mind it is so easy to understand him in the opposite sense. In the ordinary modern meaning Blake's symbols are not symbols at all. They are not allegories. An allegory nowadays means taking something that does not exist as a symbol of something that does exist. We believe, at least most of us do, that sin does exist. We believe (on highly insufficient grounds) that a dragon does not exist. So we make the unreal dragon an allegory of the real sin. But that is not what Blake meant when he made the lamb the symbol of innocence. He meant that there really is behind the universe an eternal image called the Lamb, of which all living lambs are merely the copies or the approximation. He held that eternal innocence to be an actual and even an awful thing. He would not have seen anything comic, any more than the Christian Evangelist saw anything comic, in talking about the Wrath of the Lamb. If there were a lamb in one of Aesop's fables, Aesop would never be so silly as to represent him as angry. But Christianity is more daring than Aesop, and the wrath of the Lamb is its great paradox. If there is an immortal lamb, a being whose simplicity and freshness are forever renewed, then it is truly and really more creepy idea to horrify that being into hostility than to defy the flaming dragon or challenge darkness or the sea. No old wolf or world-worn lion is so awful as a creature that is always young—a creature that is always newly born. But the main point here is simpler. It is merely that Blake did not mean that meekness was true and the lamb only a pretty fable. If anything he meant that meekness was a mere shadow of the everlasting lamb. The distinction is essential to anyone, at all concerned for this rooted spirituality which is the only enduring sanity of mankind. The personal is not a mere figure for the impersonal; rather the impersonal is clumsy term for something more personal that common personality. God is not a symbol of goodness. Goodness is a symbol of God.

Some very odd passages in Blake become clear if we keep this in mind. I do not wish this book to dwell unduly on the other side of Blake, the literary side. But there are queer facts worth remarking, and this is one of them. Blake was sincere; if he was insane he was insane with the very solidity and completeness of his sincerity. And the quaintest mark of his sincerity is this, that in his poetry he constantly writes things that look like mere mistakes. He writes one of his most colossal convictions and the average reader thinks it is a misprint. To give only one example not connected with the matter in hand, the fine though somewhat frantic poem called "The Everlasting Gospel" begins exactly as the modern humanitarian and essential Christian would like it to begin—

"The vision of Christ that thou dost see
Is my vision's greatest enemy."

It goes on (to the modern Christian's complete satisfaction) with denunciations of priests and praise of the pure Gospel Jesus; and then comes a couplet like this—

"Thine is the friend of all mankind,
Mine speaks in parables to the blind."

And the modern humanitarian Christian finds the orthodox Christ calmly rebuked because he is the friend of all mankind. The modern Christian simply blames the printer. He can only suppose that the words "Thine" and "Mine" have been put in each other's places by accident. Blake, however, as it happens, meant exactly what he said. His private vision of Christ was the vision of a violent and mysterious being, often indignant and occasionally disdainful.

"He acts with honest disdainful pride,
And that is the cause that Jesus died;
Had he been Antichrist, creeping Jesus,
He would have done anything to please us,
Gone sneaking into their synagogues,
And not use the elders and priests like dogs."

When the reader has fully realised this idea of a fierce and mysterious Jesus, he may then see the sense in the statement that this Jesus speaks in parables to the blind while the lower and meaner Jesus pretends to be the friend of all men. But you have to know Blake's doctrine before you can understand two lines of his poetry.

—G.K. Chesterton, *William Blake*,
London: Duckworth & Co.; New York:
E. P. Dutton & Co., 1910

WORKS

In 1830, poet Robert Southey wrote to Caroline Bowles, describing both Blake's 1809 Exhibition and Blake, whom he thought brilliant and insane. Southey recalled that when he had tried to buy a copy of *Songs of Innocence and of Experience*, Blake had none available. The majority of Blake's writings—aside from the quantity that remained in manuscript—Blake engraved and printed on demand himself. The demand was limited, because Blake was on principle resistant to the business of bookselling and advertising. The exceptions to print-on-demand were the *Poetical Sketches*, printed and then left to Blake to distribute, and *The French Revolution: Book One*, of which only a single copy survived. The book was suppressed by its publisher, who was fearful of the British government's treatment of radicals in the years after the French Revolution.

Blake's poetry was haltingly published over the course of the nineteenth century, though the first remotely adequate critical edition of Blake's *Poetical Works* (edited by John Samson) was not released until 1905, and some manuscript texts remained unpublished well into the twentieth century. James John Garth Wilkinson published an edition of *Songs of Innocence and of Experience* in 1839. The first major work of Blake scholarship, Alexander Gilchrist's *The Life of William Blake, "Pictor Ignotus," with Selections from His Poems and Other Writings* (1863) offered only the *Book of Thel*, the lyrical poems (mostly from the *Poetical Sketches*, the *Songs of Innocence*, and the *Songs of Experience*), and a very limited selection of prose works. Gilchrist's anthology was riddled with unauthorized emendations. Later projects, Algernon Charles Swinburne's *William Blake: A Critical Essay* (1868), *The Poetical Works of William Blake, Lyrical and Miscellaneous* (the Aldine Blake), edited by William Michael Rossetti and published in 1874, and the Ellis-Yeats edition of 1893, presented slightly expanded repertoires of Blake's work. It is fair to say that for most of the century Blake's work was close to unavailable, and for the latter part, only the *Songs of Innocence*, the *Songs of Experience*, the *Poetical Sketches* and a miscellany of lyrics were widely read.

Useful nineteenth-century critical commentary on Blake's works is, therefore, scarce (the scarcity, perhaps, more telling than what is actually written in such commentary). James Thomson's frustration is palpable, when he writes in 1864, reviewing Gilchrist's *Life*: "As to the longer poems produced after the *Songs of Experience—Visions of the Daughters of Albion, Europe, Jerusalem, Ahania, Urizen,* &c,—the Selections given by Mr. Gilchrist are not sufficient to enable one to form a settled opinion." What nineteenth-century textual criticism there is, as the following essays show, is generally confined to discussing the lyric poetry; critics were understandably loathe to write of what they had not themselves read. Exceptions to the trend of writing only on the lyrics (Swinburne, Moncure Conway, W. B. Yeats) are presented in the previous section of this book. The essays in the following section, however, are more indicative of what any late century critic but the most devout Blake scholar was able to read and think of Blake.

There are three themes that surface repeatedly in the following essays: the place of Blake in literary history; the childlike quality of, variously, the poet and his poems; and whether the poems have aesthetic merit.

James Thomson addresses the first of these in this reflection on the *Poetical Sketches*:

> Never, perhaps, was a book of verse printed more strange to the literature of its period; and one scarcely knows whether to account the novelty more or less wonderful because relative and not absolute, because the novelty of the long dead past come back to life rather than of a new future just born. The spirit of the great Elizabethan Age was incarnate once more, speaking through the lips of a pure and modest youth.

Thomson goes on to make a convincing case for Blake's role in the revival of an Elizabethan poetry, where "Elizabethan" signals not only the culture of the English Renaissance, but approximates what we mean today by "Romantic." Henry Hewlett's essay accepts Blake's debt to the Elizabethans, but uses evidence of that debt to portray the lyrics as derivative and unoriginal. Lucy Allen Paton, in "A Phase of William Blake's Romanticism" (1893) exercises a related question, whether Blake had artistic contemporaries, and Henry Justin Smith labors Blake's "perfect unlikeness to his age."

The insistence on Blake's childishness is remarkably consistent. It relies on an elision between the narrator of the *Songs of Innocence* and their author. Victorian readers, with the exception of Swinburne, were apparently unable to see the ironic distance between the two. Thomson writes that the *Songs of Innocence* showed us "the strange fact that he who was mature in his childhood and youth became in his manhood a little child." Henry Justin Smith writes, "The Blake I know is a child, grasping manhood at intervals. Childhood is mercury, manhood is strength." And A.C. Benson, that "Blake's poetry is, from beginning to end, childish; it has the fresh simplicity, but also the vapid deficiencies of its quality." Benson goes on to enumerate these "deficiencies," pouncing on what he sees as poetic infelicities. By century's end, Blake's commentators were strictly divided between those who thought his poetry the stuff of genius, and those who—perhaps in reaction—declared it ill-formed, derivative and, not "brilliantly immature" (as Henry Justin Smith puts it), but dangerously unripened.

James Thomson "The Poems of William Blake" (1864)

James Thomson (1834–1882) was a poet and literary critic, described by Yeats and Ellis as one of the century's most important Blake commentators (alongside Algernon Charles Swinburne, the Rossettis, and James Smetham). "The Poems of William Blake" first appeared as a review of Alexander Gilchrist's 1863 Blake biography. Thomson wrote it without having read Blake's prophetic books, which at that stage were only publicly accessible via the brief extracts supplied by Gilchrist. "As to the longer poems produced after the *Songs of Experience—Visions of the Daughters of Albion, Europe, Jerusalem, Ahania, Urizen,* &c,—the Selections given by Mr. Gilchrist are not sufficient to enable one to form a settled opinion," writes Thomson, who goes on to offer an eloquent defense of those longer poems, with conjectures of a systematized symbolism that prefigure the system adduced by Yeats and Ellis. Besides this defense, Thomson's essay performs two significant tasks. It gives a biographical reading of the *Songs of Innocence* and *Songs of Experience*, with their narrative persona, or singer, identified absolutely with Blake (Swinburne will be the first, probably, not to elide the poems' narrator with the poet). Secondly, it makes a compelling case for Blake's role in the revival of an Elizabethan poetry. Thomson uses "Elizabethan" to signify a set of poetic practices similar to those that contemporary critics designate with the term "Romantic" (this latter term, incidentally, was only available in the 1860s as a pejorative). Elizabethan poetry, more concerned with naturalness than orderliness, contrasts with the highly ordered and organized poetic diction of the Augustans, the poets of the early and mid-eighteenth century. The poets Thomson enlists as representative neo-Elizabethans are all today considered Romantics. Thomas Malkin had also identified an Elizabethan quality in Blake's work, in 1806.

Before the publication of these volumes[1] I knew but one of Blake's poems, that on the Human Form, or Divine Image, quoted by James John Garth Wilkinson in his great work. The wisdom and the celestial simplicity of this little piece prepared one to love the author and all that he had done; yet the selections from his poems and other writings were a revelation far richer than my hopes. Not only are these selections most beautiful in themselves, they are also of great national interest as filling up a void in the cycle of our poetic literature. I had long felt, and probably many others had felt, that much of the poetry of the present and the last age *must* have had an antecedent less remote in time than the Elizabethan works, and less remote in resemblance than the works of Cowper and Burns; yet, since Macaulay's essay on Byron appeared, Cowper and Burns—and in general these two only—had been continually named as the heralds of that resurrection of her poetry which makes glorious for England the crescent quarter of the nineteenth century. A third herald of that resurrection was undoubtedly William Blake; and although he was scarcely listened to at all, while his colleagues held in attention the whole kingdom, the fact may at length be recognised that by him, even more clearly than by them, was anticipated and announced both the event now already past and the event still in process of evolution.

If it be objected that one who was scarcely listened to at all could not exercise much influence, the reply is that we are concerned not with the influence, but with the accuracy and period of the presage. It is written that mankind did not heed Noah, or heeded only to mock, during the six-score years in which he foretold the Flood and built the Ark ready for it. If the Flood really came as he foretold, it attested the truth of his inspiration; but no one now would think that his prophecies were instrumental in accomplishing their own fulfilment, although this opinion must have been general among those who were being submerged. Or we may answer, applying a metaphor which has been with good reason much used, that the mountain-peaks which in any district first reflect the rays of the dawn exercise little or no influence on the dawn's development, even in relation to the country around them; they cast some glimmer of light into obscure valleys below (whose obscurity, on the other hand, their shadows make trebly deep when the sun is sinking); they prophesy very early of the coming noontide; we may judge as to their positions and altitudes by the periods of their reflection; but the dawn would grow and become noon, and the noon would sink and become night, just the same if they were not there. So the Spirit of the Ages, the *Zeitgeist*, is developed universally and independently by its own mysterious laws throughout mankind; and the eminent men from whom it first radiates the expression of what we call a new aspect (the continuous imperceptible increments of change having accumulated to an amount of change which we can clearly perceive, and which even our gross standards are fine enough to measure), the illustrious prototypes of an age, really cast but a faint reflex upon those beneath them; and while pre-eminently interesting in biography, are of small account in history except as prominent indices of growth and progress and decay, as early effects, not efficient causes. They help us to read clearly the advance of time; but this advance they do not cause any more than the gnomon of a sundial causes the procession of the hours which it indicates, or a tidal-rock the swelling of the seas whose oncoming is signalled in white foam around it and in shadowed waters over it.

The message of Cowper has been heard (it was not a very great announcement, and he uttered it neatly and distinctly and honestly), has been laid to heart by the many for whom it was sufficient, and is now in due season passing out of mind with the fulfilment of its purpose. Very little of his poetry can be expected to survive our century. Burns will live with the language; but it must be remembered that his poetry is not blossom and promise; it is consummate fruition; it points to the past more than to the future; it is the genial life, the heroism, the history, the song of his whole people for ages, gathered up and sublimated in and by one supreme man. This King of Scotland happened to come in the guise of a herald to England, but none the less was he a king, the last and greatest of a glorious line; and no other majesty than his own was behind the messenger. Shakespeare made perfect the English drama, and there has arisen no English drama since; Burns made perfect Scottish song, and there has arisen no Scottish song since. When the genius of a nation has attained (human) perfection in any one form and mode, it leaves to ambitious mediocrity all future rivalry with that monumental perfection, itself seeking to become perfect in some new form or mode.

Blake's first volume of poetry was printed (one cannot add *published)* in 1783, about the same time as the first volume of Cowper and a little before that of Burns; Crabbe's first popular poem, *The Village,* was printed in the same year. Seventeen years afterwards, Hayley was in high repute, and Blake went to live near him to engrave illustrations for some of his works. The *Lyrical Ballads* of Coleridge and Wordsworth did not appear until 1798; *The Lay of the Last Minstrel* until 1805. Byron was born in 1788, Shelley in 1792, Keats in 1796. The poems in this first volume had been written by Blake in the interval, 1768–1777, between the ages of eleven and twenty years.

Never, perhaps, was a book of verse printed more strange to the literature of its period; and one scarcely knows whether to account the novelty more or less wonderful because relative and not absolute, because the novelty of the long dead past come back to life rather than of a new future just born. The spirit of the great Elizabethan Age was incarnate once more, speaking through the lips of a pure and modest youth. "My Silks and Fine Array" might have been written by Shakespeare, by Beaumont and Fletcher, or by Sir Walter Raleigh. Its sweet irregular artless cadences are not more different from the sharp measured metallic ring of the rhymes of the scholars of Pope, than is its natural sentiment from the affected sentimentalities then in the mode. Of all the other eighteenth century writers, I think Chatterton alone (as in the Dirge in "Ella") has anything kindred to it; and Chatterton was archaic consciously and with intent. The "Mad Song" immediately reminds us of the character assumed by Edgar in *Lear* (a common character in Shakespeare's time, else Edgar would not have assumed it), and of the old Tom o' Bedlam songs. In the fine specimen of these, preserved by the elder Disraeli in his *Curiosities of Literature*, three main elements can easily be distinguished: the grotesque but horrible cry of misery wrung from the heart of the poor, half-witted, cruelly treated vagabond; the intentional fooling of the beggar and mountebank, baiting for the charity that is caught with a laugh in its mouth, maddening for his bread; the genuine lunacy of a wild and over-excited imagination, ungoverned so long that it is now quite ungovernable. The first gives us such lines as these:—

> In the lovely lofts of Bedlam,
> In stubble soft and dainty;
>> Brave bracelets strong,
>> Sweet whips ding-dong,
> And a wholesome hunger plenty.

The second such as these:—

> Of thirty bare years have I
> Twice twenty been enraged;
>> And of forty been
>> Three times fifteen
> In durance soundly caged.

The third such as these, which Edgar Allan Poe (a fine artist even in the choice of his mottoes) prefixed to his "Unparalleled Adventure of one Hans Pfaall"—

> With a heart of furious fancies
> Whereof I am commander;
>> With a burning spear,
>> And a horse of air,
> To the wilderness I wander.

Or these:—

> I know more than Apollo;
> For oft when he lies sleeping,
>> I behold the stars
>> At mutual wars,
> And the rounded welkin weeping.

As Tom o' Bedlams did not wander the country when Blake wrote, the elements of vagabondage and mountebankism are not in his piece; but as an expression of lunacy—the government of reason overthrown, and wild imagination making the anarchy more anarchic by its reign of terror—it is thoroughly of the old Elizabethan strain. Here is a stanza which Edgar might have sung in the storm by the hovel on the heath:—

> Like a fiend in a cloud,
>   With howling woe
> After night I do crowd,
>   And with night will go;
> I turn my back to the East
> Whence comforts have increased;
> For light doth seize my brain
> With frantic pain.

Mark the appalling power of the verb *crowd,* revealing, as by a lightning-flash, the ruins of sane personality, haunted and multitudinous, literally *beside itself.* Not one poet in twenty would have dared to use the word thus, and yet (although a careless reader might think it brought in merely for the sake of the rhyme) it was the very word to use. The address "To the Muses," sweet, calm, and masterly, as if the matured utterance of a conviction well pondered and of no recent date, yet written by a mere boy, embodies the essence of all that Coleridge, Wordsworth, Keats, and Shelley, many years afterwards, taught and sang in vindication of Pre-Drydenism.

The poems in blank verse "To the Evening Star," "To Spring," and "To Summer," are perhaps even more wonderful than those in rhyme, considering the age of the writer and the epoch of our literature in which they were produced. With the exception of the "Ode to Evening," I do not remember any blank verse of the century at all similar to them in tone. And the Ode of Collins, fine as it is, suffers greatly in the comparison with them; for it does not reach their noble breadth of conception and execution, and it is not quite free from then current affectations. These pieces are not perfect in art, but they are perfect in the spirit of their art; they have certain laxities and redundances of rhythm, and are here and there awkward in diction, but such youthful sweet errors rather grace than spoil "that large utterance of the early gods." They have the grandeur of lofty simplicity, not of laboured pomp, a grandeur like that which invests our imaginations of the patriarchs. By a well beneath a palm tree, stands one who wears but a linen turban and a simple flowing robe, and who but watches browsing sheep and camels drinking; yet no modern monarch, however gorgeously arrayed and brilliantly surrounded, can compare with him in majesty. . . .

Many years afterwards, in 1789, when Blake was thirty-two, the *Songs of Innocence* appeared; and we learn from them the strange fact that he who was mature in his childhood and youth became in his manhood a little child. A little child, pure in soul as the serenest light of the morning, happy and innocent as a lamb leaping in the meadows, singing all its joy in the sweetest voice with that exquisite infantine lisp which thrills the adult heart with yearning tenderness. The "Introduction," "The Lamb," "The Chimney Sweeper," the "Laughing Song," "A Cradle Song," "Holy Thursday," "Infant Joy," "The Divine Image;" what holy and tender and beautiful babe-lullabies, babe joy-songs, are these! The ideal Virgin Mother might have sung them to her infant; lambs and doves and flowers might comprehend them; they are alone in our language, which they glorify by revealing its unsuspected treasures of heavenly innocence and purity. I transcribe one of the shortest of them, "Infant Joy;" a sudden throb of maternal rapture which we should have thought inarticulate—expressible only by kisses and caresses and wordless cradle-crooning— marvellously caught up and rendered into song.

'I have no name,
I am but two days old,'
    What shall I call thee?
'I happy am,
Joy is my name.'
    Sweet joy befall thee.
Pretty joy!
Sweet joy but two days old,
    Sweet joy I call thee:
Thou dost smile,
I sing the while,
    Sweet joy befall thee.

Five years later come the *Songs of Experience,* and the singer is an older child, and even a youth, but not yet a man. The experience is that of a sensitive and thoughtful boy, troubled by the first perceptions of evil where he has believed all good, thinking the whole world cruel and false since some playmate-friend has turned unkind, seeing life all desolate and blank since some coveted object has disappointed in the possession; in short, through very lack of experience, generalising one untoward event into a theory of life that seems more bitterly hopeless than grey-haired cynical pessimism. Even the "Garden of Love," "The Human Abstract," "The Two Songs," "To Tirzah," and "Christian Forbearance" (one of the keenest arrows of Beelzebub shot straight back with wounding scorn at the evil-archer), are not in thought and experience beyond the capacity of meditative boyhood. "The Tiger" is a magnificent expression of boyish wonder and admiring terror; "The Crystal Cabinet" is a fairy dream of early youth; "The Golden Net" is a fine dream of adolescence. Perhaps in only three more of his briefer poems do we find Blake mature (it must be borne in mind that his second maturity unfolded itself in pictures rather than songs); "Broken Love," "Auguries of Innocence," and the Letter in verse, dated from Felpham, to his friend, Mr. Butts. These are mature as to their conception, as to the amount and quality of experience and thought involved in them, but occasionally very immature in execution. There is, indeed, one piece of twenty lines mature in every respect, although written so late as 1807: I mean the verses to Queen Charlotte with his illustrations of Blair's "Grave":—

> The door of death is made of gold,
> That mortal eyes cannot behold;
> But when the mortal eyes are closed,
> And cold and pale the limbs reposed,
> The soul awakes and wondering sees
> In her mild hand the golden keys.
> The grave is Heaven's golden gate,
> And rich and poor around it wait:
> O Shepherdess of England's Fold,
> Behold this gate of pearl and gold!
> To dedicate to England's Queen
> The visions that my soul hath seen,
> And by her kind permission bring
> What I have borne on solemn wing
> From the vast regions of the grave,
> Before her throne my wings I wave,
> Bowing before my sovereign's feet:
> The Grave produced these blossoms sweet
> In mild repose from earthly strife,
> The blossoms of eternal life!

And here are a few more lines almost as majestically mature as one of his inventions for the *Books of Job*:—

Jesus sat in Moses' chair;
They brought the trembling woman there:
Moses commands she be stoned to death;
What was the sound of Jesus' breath?
He laid his hands on Moses' law:
The ancient heavens in silent awe,
Writ with curses from pole to pole,
All away began to roll:
'To be good only, is to be
A God, or else a Pharisee.'

The man who wrote this might well proclaim: "I touch the heavens as an instrument to glorify the Lord."

"Broken Love" needs no comment here: Mr. W. M. Rossetti has done the best that could be done by the most subtle and patient sympathy to interpret it. I subjoin half-a-dozen lines from the "Auguries of Innocence":—

A Robin red-breast in a cage
Puts all Heaven in a rage;
A dove-house full of doves and pigeons
Shudders Hell through all its regions;
A skylark wounded on the wing
Doth make a cherub cease to sing.

It has been objected (strangely enough, in *Macmillan's Magazine*) to such couplets as these, that they express a truth with such exaggerated emphasis as wholly to distort it, as to make it virtually an untruth. No objection could be more unwise, for it is the result of reading the author's intention precisely *backwards*. His object was not to expand a small fact into a universal truth, but to concentrate the full essence of a universal truth into a small fact. He was intent on making great laws portable, not little events insupportable. "Are not two sparrows sold for a farthing? and one of them shall not fall to the ground without your Father. But the very hairs of your head are all numbered."— "But I say unto you, That every idle word that men shall speak, they shall give account thereof in the Day of Judgment." "For verily I say unto you, If ye have faith as a grain of mustard-seed, ye shall say unto this mountain, Remove hence to yonder place; and it shall remove; and nothing shall be impossible unto you." "But whoso shall offend one of these little ones which believe in Me, it were better for him that a millstone were hanged about his neck, and that he were drowned in the depth of the sea." These texts from the mouth of one of the sublimest of mystics realise the very same object in the very same manner. The sharply cut symbol leaves a distinct and enduring impression, where the abstract dogma would have perhaps made no impression at all. Briefly, in almost every couplet of this poem, Blake has attempted what all profound poets and thinkers have ever most earnestly attempted—to seize a rude but striking image of some sovereign truth, and to stamp it with roughest vigour on the commonest metal for universal circulation. To such attempts we owe all the best proverbs in the world; the abounding small currency of our intellectual commerce, more invaluably essential to our ordinary daily business than nuggets of gold, than rubies, and pearls, and diamonds.

As to the longer poems produced after the *Songs of Experience—Visions of the Daughters of Albion, Europe,]erusalem, Ahania, Urizen,* &c,—the Selections given by Mr. Gilchrist are not sufficient to enable one to form a settled opinion. This may be said, that a careful study of the whole of them, in the order of the years in which they were written, would probably reveal that they are much less wild and incoherent than even Mr. Gilchrist supposed. Every man living in seclusion and developing an intense interior life, gradually comes to give a quite peculiar significance to certain words and phrases and emblems. Metaphors which to the common bookwrights and journalists are mere handy counters, symbols almost as abstract and unrelated in thought to the things they represent as are the x and y and z used in solving an algebraic problem, are for *him* burdened with rich and various freights of spiritual experience; they are ships in which he has sailed over uncharted seas to unmapped shores, with which he has struggled through wild tempests and been tranced in Divine calms, in which he has returned with treasures from all the zones; and he loves them as the sailor loves his ship. His writings must thus appear, to any one reading them for the first time, very obscure, and often very ludicrous; the strange reader sees a battered old hull, where the writer sees a marvellous circumnavigation. But we ought not to be kept from studying these writings by any apparent obscurity and ludicrousness, if we have found in the easily comprehended vernacular writings of the same man (as in Blake's we certainly *have* found) sincerity and wisdom and beauty. Nor is it probable that even the most mysterious works of Blake would prove more difficult to genuine lovers of poetry than many works of the highest renown prove to nine-tenths of the reading public.

Sie haben dich, heiliger Hafis,
    Die mystische Zunge genannt;
Und haben, die Wortgelehrten,
    Den Werth des Worts nicht erkannt.

For many intelligent persons Carlyle at his best is almost or quite as unintelligible as if he were using an unknown language; and the same may be asserted of Shelley and Robert Browning. (I do not select lofty *old* names, because in their cases the decisions of authoritative judges accumulating throughout centuries overawe our common jurymen into verdicts wise without understanding; so that a dullard can speak securely of the sublimity of Milton, for example, although we are pretty certain that he never got through the first book of the *Paradise Lost,* and that he would find himself in a Slough of Despond when twenty lines deep in the opening passages of *Samson Agonistes.)* Indeed, I doubt whether it would be an exaggeration to assert that, for a very large majority of those who are accounted educated and intelligent people, poetry in itself is essentially an unknown tongue. They admire and remember a verse or a passage for its wit, its cleverness, its wisdom, its clear and brief statement of some fact, its sentiment, its applicability to some circumstance of their own life, its mention of some classic name, its allusion to some historical event; in short, for its associations and not for its poetry *per se.* Yet assuredly there are still men in England with an infallible sense for poetry, however disguised and however far removed from ordinary associations; men who know Shakespeare in despite of the commentators, and understand Browning in contempt of the critics, and laugh quietly at the current censures and raptures of the Reviews: and these men would scarcely consider it a waste of time to search into the meaning of the darkest oracles of William Blake.

I wish to add a few words on the relations subsisting between our author and succeeding English poets. In his early maturity, as a reincarnation of the mighty Elizabethan spirit, the first fruit of a constructive after a destructive period, his affinity to the great poets who flourished a few years before his death (he died in 1827) will be readily understood. Thus in the Minstrel's Song, before quoted, we at once discern that the rhythm is of the same strain as the largest utterance of Marlowe and Webster and Shakespeare precedent, and as the noblest modern exemplar, the blank verse of *Hyperion* subsequent.[2] It is not, however, in this early maturity, but in his second childhood and boyhood and youth, when he was withdrawn from common life into mysticism, when moonlight was his sunlight, and water was his wine, and the roses red as blood were become all white as snow, in the *Songs of Innocence,* the *Songs of Experience,* and the *Auguries of Innocence* (always *Innocence,* mark, not Virtue) that the seeds may be traced of much which is now half-consciously struggling towards organic perfection, and which in two or three generations may be crowned with foliage and blossoms and fruit as the Tree of Life for one epoch.

The essence of this poetry is mysticism, and the essence of this mysticism is simplicity. The two meanings in which this last word is commonly used—the one reverential, the other kindly contemptuous—are severally appropriate to the most wise and the least wise manifestations of this spirit of mysticism. It sees, and is continually rapturous with seeing, everywhere correspondence, kindred, identity, not only in the things and creatures of earth, but in all things and creatures and beings of hell and earth and heaven, up to the one father (or interiorly to the one soul) of all. It thus ignores or pays little heed to the countless complexities and distinctions of our modern civilisation and science, a knowledge of which is generally esteemed the most useful information and most valuable learning. For it "there is no great and no small;" in the large type of planets and nations, in the minute letters of dewdrops and worms, the same eternal laws are written; and merely as a matter of convenience to the reader is this or that print preferable to the other. And the whole universe being the volume of the Scriptures of the living word of God, this above all is to be heeded, that man should not dwell contented on the lovely language and illustrations, but should live beyond these in the sphere of the realities which they signify. It is passionately and profoundly religious, contemplating and treating every subject religiously, in all its excursions and discursions issuing from the soul to return to the soul, alone, from the alone, to the alone; and thus it is by no means strict in its theology, being Swedenborgian in one man and Pantheistic in another, while in the East it has readily assimilated Buddhism and Brahminism and Mohammedanism. Its supreme tendency is to remain or to become again childlike, its supreme aspiration is not virtue, but innocence or guilelessness: so that we may say with truth of those whom it possesses, that the longer they live the younger they grow, as if "passing out to God by the gate of birth, not death."

These few hints may serve as points of departure for some slender lines of relation between William Blake the Second and the principal subsequent poets. It must be borne in mind that the object here is not a survey of the full circle of the powers of any of these poets; they may be very great or very small in various other respects, while very small or very great in respect of this mystical simplicity. The heads of Da Vinci and Titian and Rembrandt, the bodies of Correggio and Rubens, would all count for nothing were we instituting a comparison between the old masters simply as painters of the *sky*.

Wordsworth ever aspired towards this simplicity, but the ponderous pedantry of his nature soon dragged him down again when he had managed to reach it. He was a good, conscientious, awkward pedagogue, who, charmed by the charms of childhood, endeavoured himself to play the child. Were it not rather too wicked, I could draw from Æsop another excellent illustration. He was not wrong when he proclaimed himself eminently a teacher; 'tis a pity that six days of the seven his teaching was of the Sunday-school sort.

Coleridge had much of this simplicity. In the *Ancient Mariner* it is supreme; in *Christabel* it does not lack, but already shows signs of getting maudlin; afterwards, *Lay Sermons* with Schelling and the Noetic Pentad, almost or quite extinguished it. He was conscious of the loss, as witness the lines in his great Ode:—

And haply by abstruse research to steal
From my own nature all the natural man.

Scott, a thoroughly objective genius, lived and wrote altogether out of the sphere of this simplicity. He had a simplicity of his own, the simplicity of truthfulness and power in his "magnificent and masculine grasp of men and things." Expansive not intensive, he developed no interior life, but diffused himself over the exterior life. His poetry is of action, not of thought; he is as a mighty and valiant soldier, whom we seek on the field of battle, not in the school of the prophets.

Byron had it not at all. He is great, exceedingly great; but great as the expression of intense life, and of such thought only as is the mere tool and weapon of life, never great as the expression of thought above and beneath life commanding and sustaining it. He had just ideality enough to shed a poetic glow upon powers and passions all essentially commonplace, but very uncommonly vigorous, overflowing with the energy of daemonic possession— an energy most mysterious, but in itself most impatient of mysticism.

Keats, who shall dare to judge? I doubt not that everything pure and beautiful would have had its season in him who, dying at twenty-four, wrote *Hyperion* a few years after *Endymion*. But this plastic genius would have proceeded in triumphant transmigrations through all fairest forms ere it could have found eternal tranquillity in the soul of all form. Had he been spared, all analogies, I think, point to this end.

Shelley possessed, or rather was possessed by, this simplicity to the uttermost. Although he and Keats were twin brothers, Greeks of the race of the gods, their works do not resemble but complement each other. The very childlike lisp which we remarked in Blake is often observable in the voice of Shelley, consummate singer as he was. The lisp is, however, not always that of a child; it is on several occasions that of a missionary seeking to translate old thoughts from his rich and exact native tongue into the dialect, poor and barbarous, of his hearers. He (while doing also very different work of his own) carries on the work begun by Blake, sinking its foundations into a deeper past, and uplifting its towers into a loftier future. Both Shelley and Keats are still so far beyond the range of our English criticism that they would not have been mentioned thus cursorily here had it been possible to omit them.[3]

Tennyson has no more of this simplicity than had Byron: his chief youthful fault was such a young ladyish affectation as could not exist together with it. But he is fully aware of its value, and woos it like a lover, in vain, as Byron wooed it in the latter parts of *Childe Harold* and in *Manfred*. Perhaps each of them should be credited with one great exception, in addition to a few short lyrics: Tennyson with the "Lotus Eaters," Byron with the "Dream." Scarcely any other artist in verse of the same rank has ever lived on such scanty revenues of thought (both pure, and applied or mixed) as Tennyson. While it cannot be pretended that he is a great sculptor, he is certainly an exquisite carver of luxuries in ivory; but we must be content to admire the caskets, for there are no jewels inside. His meditation at the best is that of a good leading-article; he is a pensioner on the thought of his age. He is continually petty with that littleness of the second degree which makes a man brag aloud in avoiding some well-known littleness of the first degree. His nerves are so weak that any largish event—a Crimean War or a Volunteer movement—sets him off in hysterics. Nothing gives one a keener insight into the want of robustness in the educated English intellect of the age than the fact that nine-tenths of our best-known literary men look upon him as a profound philosopher. When wax-flowers are oracular oaks, Dodona may be discovered in the Isle of Wight, but hardly until then. Mr. Matthew Arnold's definition of "distilled thought in distilled words" was surely suggested by the processes and productions of a fashionable perfumer. A great school of the poets is dying out: it will die decently, elegantly, in the full odour of respectability, with our Laureate.

Robert Browning, a really great thinker, a true and splendid genius, though his vigorous and restless talents often overpower and run away with his genius so that some of his creations are left but half redeemed from chaos, has this simplicity in abundant measure. In the best poems of his last two works, *Men and Women* and *Dramatis Personae,* its light burns so clear and steadfast through the hurrying clouds of his language (Tennyson's style is the polished reflector of a lamp) that one can only wonder that people in general have not yet recognised it. I cannot recommend a finer study of a man possessed by the spirit of which I am writing than the sketch of Lazarus in Browning's "Epistle of Karshish, an Arab Physician."

Elizabeth Barrett Browning, also, had much of it, yet never succeeded in giving it fair expression. The long study of her sick-bed (and her constant chafing against the common estimate of the talents and genius of her sex) overcharged her works with allusions and thoughts relating to books, and made her style rugged with pedantry. She was often intoxicated, too, with her own vehemence. *Aurora Leigh* sets out determined to walk the world with the great Shakespearian stride, whence desperate entanglement of feminine draperies and blinding swirls of dust. The sonnets entitled *From the Portuguese* reveal better her inmost simple nature.

Emerson stands closest of all in relation to Blake, his verse as well as his essays and lectures being little else than the expression of this mystical simplicity. Were he gifted with the singing voice we should not have to look to the future for its supreme bard. But whenever he has sung a few clear sweet notes, his voice breaks, and he has to recite and speak what he would fain chant. His studies, also, have somewhat injured his style with technicology, making him in his own despite look at Nature through the old church and school windows, often when he should be with her in the rustic air. In some of his shorter poems, however, and in the snatches of Orphic song prefixed to some of his essays (as "Compensation," "Art," "History," "Heroism"), any one with ears to hear may catch pregnant hints of what poetry possessed by this inspiration can accomplish, and therefore *will* accomplish; for no pure inspiration having once come down among men ever withdraws its influence until it has attained (humanly) perfect embodiment.

In eighty years the influence of this spirit has swelled from the *Songs of Innocence* to the poems of Emerson—a rapid increase of the tide in literature. Other signs of its increase meet us everywhere in the best books of verse published during the last few years. And perchance the increase has been even more rapid than the most of us have opportunity to learn, for we are informed by Mr. Rossetti that James John Garth Wilkinson has not only edited a collection of Blake's Poems, but has himself produced a volume of poems entitled "Improvisations of the Spirit," bearing a strong family likeness to those of Blake; and it may be that Wilkinson has the singing voice which Emerson has not. It would be a boon to the public, at any rate, to make these two volumes easily accessible. Emerson and Garth Wilkinson, the former undoubtedly the supreme thinker of America, the latter as undoubtedly second to none in England, are surely in themselves sufficient attestation to the truth and depth of the genius of their forerunner, William Blake.

He came to the desert of London town,
   Grey miles long;
He wandered up and he wandered down,

Singing a quiet song.
He came to the desert of London town,
    Mirk miles broad;
He wandered up and he wandered down,
    Ever alone with God.
There were thousands and thousands of human kind
    In this desert of brick and stone:
 But some were deaf and some were blind,
    And he was there alone.
At length the good hour came; he died,
    As he had lived, alone:
He was not missed from the desert wide,
    Perhaps he was found at the Throne.

Notes

1. *Life of William Blake, Pictor Ignotus, with Selections from His Poems and Other Writings.* By the late Alexander Gilchrist, author of the *Life of William Etty.* Illustrated from Blake's own works, in facsimile, by W. J. Linton, and in photolithography, with a few of Blake's original plates. In 2 vols. London: Macmillan & Co., 1863.

    I give the full title, in recommending the work to all good readers. The first volume contains the Life and a noble supplementary chapter by Mr. D. G. Rossetti; the second volume contains the Selections, admirably edited by Mr. D. G. Rossetti, with the assistance of Mr. W. M. Rossetti. There is magnificent prose as well as poetry in the selections, and the engravings in themselves are worth more than most books.

2. Keats avowed imitation of Milton in the structure of his rhythm. Similarity to the Council in Pandemonium there of course could not but be in the Council of the overthrown Titans; but the verse of Keats (if I have any ear and intelligence for verse) is as different from the verse of Milton as with the same language and the same metrical standard it possibly could be. It is in my judgment even more beautiful and more essentially powerful and sublime than Milton's.

3. Perhaps the astonishing difference in kind between these glorious poets and their contemporaries can best be put in clear light by thus considering them young Greeks of the race of the gods, born three thousand years after their time, in Christian England. Shelley has been called "The Eternal Child," and Keats "The Real Adonis;" and Novalis says well, "Children are ancients, and youth is antique " (Die *Kinder sind Antiken. Auch die Jugend*

ist antik, vol. iii. p. 190). The ideas and sentiments of the race among whom they were reared were naturally strange, and in many respects repugnant to them both. Keats, simply ignoring the Bumbleism and Christianity, except in so far as the Bumbleism obstructed his poetic career, unperturbed save by the first throes of creative art, developed himself in the regions from which he sprang—Pagan and Hellenic in his themes, his ideas, his perceptions, his objects. Shelley, on the other hand, started from the time and place of his birth to reach the old dominions of his ancestry. In this enterprise he had to conquer and destroy the terrible armies of fanaticism, asceticism, cant, hypocrisy, narrow-mindedness, lording it over England; and at the same time the spirituality of the new religion, the liberty and equality and fraternity of the new political systems, all things lovely and true and holy of the modern life, he would bear with him for the re-inspiration of the antique. He aspired not to a New Jerusalem in the heavens, but to a new Hellenic metropolis on earth: he looked for redemption and victory, not to Christ on Calvary, but to Prometheus on Caucasus.

These young Greeks could not live to old age. The gloom and chill of our English clime, physical and moral and intellectual, could not but be fatal to these children of the sun. England and France are so proudly in the van of civilisation that it is impossible for a great poet to live greatly to old age in either of them.

—James Thomson, from "The Poems of William Blake," 1864, *Biographical and Critical Studies,* 1896, pp. 240–269

HENRY G. HEWLETT "IMPERFECT GENIUS: WILLIAM BLAKE" (1876)

Henry G. Hewlett was an agnostic and a Gladstonian Liberal, concerned by the late Victorian religion of art and its appropriation of Blake as patron saint. His essay aims to debunk the idea that Blake enjoyed an out-of-the-ordinary genius or heaven-sent inspiration.

To do anything like justice to Blake it is requisite to deal separately with his pretensions as poet, prophet, and designer. His earliest appearance before the world was as a poet. Commencing with the question of originality, can it be justly claimed for him that his ideas and language are substantially underived, or that he has so assimilated the influences which he imbibed that their sources are undiscoverable? Remembering the language in which his first volume of *Poetical Sketches,* printed in 1783, but said to be written between 1768 and 1777, has been extolled as a literary phenomenon, not less unique than astonishing, we turn to the reprint in the Aldine edition of his works, and invite the unprejudiced reader to accompany us. If he be tolerably familiar with earlier English poetry, especially of the Elizabethan period, we shall be strangely mistaken if he does not pronounce the quality of the verse to be essentially imitative. That Blake was from boyhood a student of Elizabethan literature we know as a fact, upon the authority of Malkin,[1] whose information was derived from Blake himself. Traces of imitation Mr. Gilchrist does not deny, but would have us believe them superficial, and due to "involuntary emulation" of the great models which the youth set before him; while Mr. Swinburne throws a little critical dust in our eyes by suggesting comparisons which distract attention from the real nature of the resemblances. To show this adequately, we ought to put the whole volume in evidence, but the main proofs lie near the surface. The unfinished drama of *King Edward the Third* reads like a boy's crude effort to assume the manner and tone of Shakespeare. The types of character are drawn from his. The scene before Cressy is a modification of that before Agincourt *(Hen. V.,* Act IV.), the imitation being carried to the point of mimicking Fluellen's Welsh brogue. Some of the master's most characteristic and hackneyed phrases are reproduced almost unaltered, sprinkled with others from Milton and Ben Jonson. "Pass over as a summer cloud, unregarded," "deathy dust," "beaten brass," "rich as midsummer," "native seats," "feathered angels," "ribs of death," "silver Thames," are notable instances. Turning to the songs, we find still larger contributions levied from Shakespeare and Beaumont and Fletcher. "My silks and fine array," in point of form and tone, is modelled upon "Come away, come away, Death," Fletcher's *Constancy (Maid's Tragedy),* and *Dirge for the Faithful Lover (Knight of the Burning Pestle).* The lines—

> Bring me an axe and spade,
> Bring me a winding-sheet—

are simply copied from the Grave-digger's song in *Hamlet.* In the song of "Memory," "Tune your merry notes" is borrowed from *As You Like It;* "watery glass" from *Midsummer Night's Dream;* and "fish for fancies" was probably suggested by a phrase of Gratiano's in *The Merchant of Venice* (I.i.). Three other lines, "Places fit for woe," and

Walking along the darken'd valley,
With silent melancholy,

are adapted from a dirge in *The Nice Valour* of Beaumont and Fletcher—

Places which pale passion loves.
Then stretch our bones in a still gloomy valley;
Nothing's so dainty-sweet as lovely melancholy.

The "Mad Song," so rapturously praised for its originality by Mr. Gilchrist and Mr. Swinburne, is really a mosaic of reminiscences. The opening lines—

The wild winds weep,
And the night is a-cold—

were surely suggested by the scene in *Lear* (III. iv.), where Edgar, "disguised as a madman," enters, in a stormy night, with the words:
Through the sharp hawthorn blows the cold wind.

. . . . Poor Tom's a-cold.

The next lines—

Come hither, Sleep!
And my griefs enfold—

remind of the invocation to Sleep in Beaumont and Fletcher's *Woman-hater*. The two next lines—

But lo! the morning peeps
Over the Eastern steeps

—are obviously a remembrance of Milton's

Ere the blabbing Eastern scout,
The nice Morn on the Indian steep,
From her cabin'd loophole peep.

"The vault of paved heaven" is Shakespeare's, almost word for word. "Like a fiend in a cloud" is from Hecate's speech in *Macbeth* (III.v.)—

My little spirit, see,
Sits in a foggy cloud.

Either Beaumont and Fletcher or Shakespeare suggested another line, "I turn my back to the east;"[2] while its fellow, "From whence comforts have

increased," is from Desdemona's "comforts should increase" *(Othello* II. i.). In
some of the other poems, especially those addressed to the seasons, we have
reminiscences of Spenser and of the eighteenth-century poets who followed
him in their love of personification. The description of summer in the *Faery
Queene* ("Canto of Mutabilitie") as "dight in a thin silken cassock," no doubt
prompted the line, "Throw thy silk draperies off." That of autumn as "laden
with fruits" occurs in the same canto. Such property-epithets as "jolly," "lusty,"
"dewy," "buskined," and the like, are borrowed from the same master. The
description of morning—

> Roused like a huntsman to the chase, and with
> Thy buskined feet appear upon our hills—

is identical with Collins's picture of "Cheerfulness" in *The Passions,* who also
speaks of "Winter yelling" (Ode to Evening)—a phrase reproduced in Blake's
invocation to that season. Milton's *Comus* supplied the phrase, "chambers of the
east," which occurs both in "Morning" and "To the Muses." The opening verses
of "I love the jocund dance" are a diluted paraphrase of a passage in "L'Allegro."
To point out the evidences of Ossianic influence in other parts of the volume
would be superfluous, since none of Blake's commentators have ignored them.

We are far from intending to disparage the real merits of these verses.
Imitative to the verge of plagiarism as they are, they are often so skilfully
composed, and relieved by such graceful touches of fancy and sweet snatches
of melody, as to confer genuine pleasure in defiance of critical analysis. Here
Blake's artistic power makes itself felt, nor need we grudge him the praise that
belongs to it because his panegyrists perversely claim for him honours to
which he is entitled. It was most creditable to his taste that he rejected the
inferior models of contemporary poetry in favour of the great masters, but
from the pother that Mr. Gilchrist and Mr. Swinburne make about it, one
would suppose that he was the only one of his generation who manifested
such sympathy. In fact, his was an age of poetic revival, and he did but worship
at shrines newly set up by others. It was an age of active Shakespearian criticism
and study of Elizabethan literature, the age of Warburton, Tyrwhitt, Birch,
Farmer, Johnson, Garrick, Steevens, Warton, and Malone. The middle of
the century witnessed the publication of Dodsley's *Old Plays.* New editions of
Beaumont and Fletcher appeared in 1750 and 1778, of Ben Jonson in 1756.
Percy edited the poems of Surrey in 1763, and his *Reliques,* including many
of the choicest sixteenth and seventeenth-century lyrics, appeared in 1765.
Gray and Collins were disciples of Spenser and Milton; and avowed imitations
of the former were written by Thomson and Shenstone. In 1770, Chatterton,

whose influence on Blake is recognized by Mr. Gilchrist, put forth his elaborate mystifications; the product of an enthusiastic imagination kindled at antique fires. Was it very extraordinary that another youth of susceptible fancy and studious habit should display similar tendencies?

In Blake's next volume, the *Songs of Innocence,* printed in 1789, it would be needless to seek for proofs of originality, as it was avowedly addressed to children, for whom any but the tritest themes and simplest language would have been unsuitable. It bears evidence in its purity of style that his husbandry in the fields of classical English had not been profitless. There is little or no imitation of his old models, save that the "Laughing Song" is evidently prompted by Shakespeare's in *Troilus and Cressida,* or Beaumont and Fletcher's in *The Nice Valour.* On the other hand there is a flavour of the style of Dr. Isaac Watts, whose *Divine and Moral Songs for Children* were popular enough to have attracted Blake's notice, had he not been certain to meet with them in the Nonconformist circle in which he was bred. That this skilfully designed machinery for instilling Calvinistic ideas into infant minds suggested the plan of Blake's work seems probable, and perhaps no better method could have been devised of counteracting their influence than by competing in the choice of subjects and language, while substituting the ideas of a milder Theism and a larger humanity. On comparing the "Cradle Hymn" of the one series with the "Cradle Song" of the other, it is tolerably clear that this motive was present to his mind. Of the strange tenets put forth in his later works there is but the faintest trace in these verses, their prevailing sentiment being pitched in the amiable Theo-philanthropic key then in vogue among his republican associates. Pope's "Universal Prayer," modified to the capacities of children, might be a pattern for such poems as "The Divine Image" and "On Another's Sorrow," and probably Blake had this too in his mind when writing them.

In the *Songs of Experience* such proofs as there are of his originality must, we think, be sought, but we are unable to allow that the "find" is a large one. The design of the series is antithetical to that of the *Songs of Innocence,* most of the poems being addressed to youths upon subjects therein commended to the attention of children. The "Lamb" is thus contrasted with the "Tiger;" the "Little Boy Lost" and "Found," with the "Little Girl Lost" and "Found;" the "Divine Image," with the "Human Abstract," &c. To show by this comparison the "two contrary states of the human soul" was Blake's avowed object; and admitting from his point of view that he was justified in thus attempting to disillusionize the minds of his young disciples, the plan was ingenious. Of the new ideas hereby conveyed, which are substantially identical with those of the prophetic books, we shall speak presently; but it may suffice to say here that they are not of Blake's minting. The language, however, is his own, and in three or four poems reaches a high pitch either of condensed force or musical sweetness. Other poems, of which the meaning is enigmatical or the language weak, are redeemed by a melodious quatrain or graceful phrase. Taken together, however, these make up scarcely a ninth part of the whole, and, except for its unique flavour of heresy, there would be nothing to distinguish the little volume, in point of poetic originality, from many another collection of fugitive verse.

The majority of Blake's occasional poems, whether introduced into his prophecies or scattered among his note-books and letters, are so coloured by his peculiar notions of religion and morals that they cannot be considered apart. Herein, while there is no evidence of originality, its counterfeit, grotesqueness, does duty in its stead. No preliminary acquaintance with Blake's creed is requisite for the reader's appreciation from an artistic point of view of the following verses:—

> The fields from Islington to Marybone,
> To Primrose Hill and St. John's Wood,
>   Were builded over with pillars of gold,
> And there Jerusalem's pillars stood.
>
>   …
>
> The Jew's Harp house and the Green Man,
>   The pond where boys to bathe delight,
> The field of cows by Welling's farm,
>   Shine in Jerusalem's pleasant sight.

We doubt if many will be persuaded by Mr. Swinburne's ingenuity that any intention on the writer's part to indicate "the hidden spirit and significance of which the flesh or building is a type," and to vindicate the truth that "suburbs or lanes" have not less of a "soul than continents,"[3] can succeed in elevating ludicrous doggerel into serious poetry.

Notes

1. A *Fathers Memoirs of his Child.* Preface, p. 34.
2. "I turn thy head unto the east."—*Faithful Shepherdess.* "We must lay his head to the east."—*Cymbeline.*
3. *Critical Essay,* p. 197.

—Henry G. Hewlett, from "Imperfect
Genius: William Blake," *Contemporary
Review,* October 1876, pp. 763–767

Lucy Allen Paton "A Phase of William Blake's Romanticism" (1893)

Blake's place in the history of eighteenth-century cultural change was still exercising critics' attentions at the nineteenth century's end. With Robert Burns, Blake was considerably older than the pinup poets of British Romanticism (Coleridge and Wordsworth, and, later still, Shelley and Keats and Byron), yet his precocious defiance of classicist poetic convention suggests he is something of a Romantic vanguard. Certainly, Lucy Allen Paton argues, Blake was a Romantic by all important measures. Though she writes in 1893, the year that Edwin J. Ellis and William Butler Yeats offered their exposition of Blake's prophetic books, almost all of her quotations derive from Blake's *Songs of Innocence*, *Songs of Experience*, and *Poetical Sketches*, which were still the most read and the most accessible of Blake's works.

Mr. Walter Pater has described the romantic temper in its technical sense as one that possesses, in addition to the love of beauty, which is an integral part of every artistic nature, the element of curiosity. By virtue of this element, there exists a longing for fresh impressions, a sense of satiety of the old, and a seeking after a departure from precedent into untried regions and untrodden fields. This, which Mr. Pater calls the element of curiosity, may be said to exist in all romanticists, but in the higher types of the school it deserves the name of originality. In them the mere spirit of inquiry into the novel leads to creation. The classic temperament, on the contrary, clings to the models established by the artists of the past and sees in these alone the basis for all canons of true art. Its outcome is an adherence to form, unbalanced by an intuitive discernment of the prompting spirit. It is when the two are united in one man that the product of highest genius is given. Dante claims Virgil as his guide, and the five noble poets to whom he awards the meed of admiration are classic authors of greater or less repute; yet Dante can feel the charm of the "sweet new style," and can throw the light of romantic beauty around Francesca da Rimini and Ugolino. Shakespeare and Milton are by no means free from a debt to the past, but whatever their fancy touches—

> Doth suffer a sea-change
> Into something rich and strange

Since a blending, however, of the classic and romantic elements is as rare as genius, and in any age the preponderance of the one over the other is to be detected. It is as men's minds have been stirred with creative enthusiasm and a craving for true self-expression, or as conventionalism has satisfied them, and a subservience to the most minute of established details, that the romantic temper or its opposite has colored the age in which they have lived. The conditions of the present day with its gloomy death of romantic writers are closely akin to those prevailing in England during the latter part of the eighteenth and early in the nineteenth centuries. This was the age of classicism. The creative imagination must work strictly under the stern control of Reason. As in the pulpit the divines held out to their hearers no sweet high realms

Above the smoke and stir of this dim spot
Which men call earth,

but treated them instead to maxims of wise morality, so in the poetic world imagination must give way to the expression of sage truths and sententious utterances to which the prim couplet was essentially adapted.

In such a period as this, William Blake is a figure of peculiar individuality. He was a romanticist by nature, and no surrounding influences of classicism could completely control him. He rebelled against the very form of verse then in vogue, which was too confining a channel for his turbid imagination. He knew what it was

To see a world in a grain of sand,
And a heaven in a wild flower;
Hold infinity in the palm of your hand,
And eternity in an hour;

and to the rush and melody of his thoughts he forced the verse to conform. The workings of his inner nature were far from normal, and in proportion as they were complicated, it was necessary that the substance in which his thoughts were clothed should be pliant material in his imagination's hands. In no feature of Blake's style is this fact so strongly indicated as in his use of figures. They serve him in their proper province, as tools for the clear delineation of the pictures with which his fancy is teeming. He never forces them irrelevantly; with the tact of a writer in harmony with his theme, he omits them entirely where the simple narrative pictures the scene or object with sufficient vividness. Perhaps the poem of "Holy Thursday" furnishes as apt an illustration as any of his moderation. The description there is absolutely direct, yet the figures are so suggestive that their boldness does not in the least mar the simplicity of the whole—

The hum of multitudes was there, but multitudes of
    lambs,
Thousands of little boys and girls raising their innocent
    hands.
Now like a mighty wind they raise to heaven the
    voice of song,
Or like harmonious thunderings the seats of heaven
    among;
Beneath them sit the aged men, wise guardians of the
    poor,
Then cherish pity, lest you drive an angel from your
    door.

This use of a figure to suggest an entire scene is frequent in Blake's poems, and serves to connect him strikingly with the romantic movement. Where a classicist revels in a minute and detailed description, Blake with a word strikes the correct cord of association. He finds an adequate descriptive power in such expressions as,—

Tiger, Tiger, burning bright
In the forests of the night;
('The Tiger.')

and,—

Every tear from every eye
Becomes a babe in eternity;
The bleat, the bark, bellow and roar
Are waves that beat on heaven's shore;
('Auguries of Innocence.')

or again,—

When the silent sleep
Waves o'er heaven deep.
('A Little Girl Lost.')

In the poem of 'London,' too, there is a forcible expression of the same type:—

In every cry of every man,
In every infant's cry of fear,
In every voice, in every brain,
The mind-forged manacles I hear.

The last verse in its simplicity presents, as no detailed description could, the picture of a world "groaning and travailing together." In 'Broken Love,' also, whatever the poem may mean, there is no question that this characteristic pervades the figures of the lines:—

A dark winter deep and cold
Within my heart thou dost unfold;
Iron tears and groans of lead
Thou bindest round my aching head.

In Blake's personifications this suggestive power of which I am speaking, manifests itself very clearly. Personification was a pet figure with the classicists; they had found Fortuna, Pax, Concordia scattered through the pages of their Ovids and Horaces, and they flattered themselves that if only they gave an abstract quality a capital letter at the beginning of its name, they were classical. That the old mythology was a growth, that the existence of these gods was ever believed in, did not come within their mental ken, and as if the ancient models in cold blood had created a Pantheon, so these disciples sought to follow in the footsteps of their masters by simply turning out divinities by the line; the more capital letters the better poet. "Sweet Memory," sings Rogers,

From Thee gay Hope her airy coloring draws;
And Fancy's flights are subject to thy laws.
From Thee that bosom-spring of rapture flows,
Which only Virtue, tranquil Virtue, knows.

But Blake does not let Conscience speak, without allowing us to hear seraphic melodies and listen to angelic choirs singing in harmony with her tones.

When neither warbling voice
Nor trilling pipe is heard, nor pleasure sits
With trembling age, the voice of Conscience then,
Sweeter than music in a summer's eve
Shall warble round the snowy head, and keep
Sweet symphony to feathered angels, sitting
As guardians round your chair; then shall the pulse
Beat slow, and taste and touch and sight and sound
    and smell
That sing and dance round Reason's fine-wrought
    throne,

Shall flee away, and leave him all forlorn;
Yet not forlorn if Conscience is his friend.

(*King Edward III*)

Particularly noticeable, too, in contrast with the ponderous movement of classicism is the light, airy grace of his fancy in 'Memory, hither come,' and the peculiarly characteristic personification that occurs in the 'Cradle Song':—

Sleep, sleep; in thy sleep
Little sorrows sit and weep.

Not only abstractions, however, did Blake personify; but seeing as he did, with double vision, he could discern in all the objects of Nature a twofold essence:—

With my inward eye 't is an old man gray,
With my outward a thistle across my way.

The universe had for him a slender reality in comparison with the spiritual truths that, to his mind, it bodied forth; and just because it existed for him as an allegory, he was peculiarly apt in endowing abstractions and objects of Nature with a personal existence. Her every phase has a fantastic meaning of its own. She is a thesaurus from which he draws at pleasure:—

I walked abroad on a snowy day,
I asked the soft Snow with me to play;
She played and she melted in all her prime;
And the Winter called it a dreadful crime.

(*Couplets and Fragments*, I.)

In the 'Mad Song,' for example, not a single natural object nor an element is mentioned that is not endowed with a strange, wild life. If a man sees spirits, fiends, and angels lurking in the objects about him, a personification of Nature is absolutely essential to the expression of his imagination.

With a blue sky spread over with wings,
And a mild sun that mounts and sings;
With trees and fields full of fairy elves,
And little devils who fight for themselves,

. . .

With angels planted in hawthorn bowers,
And God himself in the passing hours.

Such a treatment of Nature as this stands in strong relief to that employed by the eighteenth century poets. They regarded her as a series of phenomena, so judiciously ordered as to be worthy of deep admiration and respect. Thomson, though undoubtedly a more intense lover of Nature than most of his contemporaries, handles her formally.

> These roving mists that constant now begin
> To smoke along the hilly country,

serves as an opportunity to discourse on theories of the sages in physical geography; nevertheless, he impresses us with his own careful observation of Nature, and shows plainly that he had watched the "father of the tempest" come forth "wrapped in black glooms," so that he is able to describe his actions with greater accuracy and feeling than the majority of his fellow-poets could have manifested. With Blake, however, the case is entirely different. With an imagination capable of seeing spiritual truths in the world about him, he does not surprise us when we find even in his figures that truest indication of a love of Nature, a susceptibility to her sympathy with human feeling. The 'Laughing Song,' for instance, fairly ripples with the sound of laughter:

> When the green woods laugh with the voice of joy,
> And the dimpling stream runs laughing by.
> When the air does laugh with our merry wit,
> And the green hill laughs with the noise of it.

But his imagination increased Blake's sympathy also, and gave him the power of understanding the aspirations of man for the ideal world. However complex and elusive his theory of Nature may be, this is plainly a moral truth that he finds her setting forth. To this theme he devotes, with a curious union of mystery and power, the 'Daughter of Thel,' and the shorter lyric, 'Ah! Sunflower,' which is so characteristic that it serves as its own apology for quotation.

> Ah! Sunflower! weary of time,
>   Who countest the steps of the sun;
> Seeking after that sweet golden prime
>   When the traveller's journey is done;
> Where the youth pined away with desire,
>   And the pale virgin shrouded in snow,
> Arise from their graves and aspire
>   Where my sunflower wishes to go.

In another and less subjective feature do Blake's figures indicate the extent to which he belonged to romanticism. Men were tired of cut and dried phrases in letters, bereft of meaning by incessant use; and when Macpherson's 'Ossian' appeared, they welcomed with keen delight its sonorous turns and rolling lines, vigorous with the sound of war and strife. Blake, with his sense of harmony and his need for the free expression of his boisterous imagination, readily imbibed the spirit of these poems, and in more than one place do we detect him using Ossianic figures. The thistle, that we have already found he saw as an old man, had appeared in the poems 'Carthon' and 'Lathmon' in the same guise; and just as in 'Gwin, King of Norway,' the hosts of men dash down the hillsides "like rushing mighty floods," or move along "like tempests black," so in 'Cath-Loda' and 'Temora' we have this same murmuring of waters and rolling of seas. There is, moreover, a general resemblance of thought which, perhaps, predominates over verbal similarity.

Thus, finally, by his literary taste as well as by his power in picturesque suggestion, in ideal delineation of a scene, and in spiritualizing Nature,—by his appreciation, also, of Nature's beauties,—Blake shows himself distinctly a romantic poet. The sense that his poems awaken, Rossetti's words describing that which Blake had attained best express: "Tenderness, the constant unison of wonder and familiarity, so mysteriously allied in nature; the sense of fulness and abundance, such as we feel in a field, not because we pry into it all, but because it is all there." He comes with the sunlight of poetic feeling through the heavy air of classicism, and while he eludes us with his imagery he fascinates us with an imagination of the most mystical type:—

For double the vision my eyes do see,
And double the vision always with me.

—Lucy Allen Paton, "A Phase of
William Blake's Romanticism," *Poet-Lore*,
October 1893, pp. 481–488

A.C. Benson "William Blake" (1896)

Arthur Christopher Benson (1862–1925), essayist and poet, is best known for his libretto to the 1902 coronation anthem, "Land of Hope and Glory". The anthology of essays in which the following critique of William Blake appears also deals with John Hales, John Earles, Henry More, Andrew Marvell, Vincent Bourne, Thomas Gray, John Keble, Elizabeth Barrett Browning, Henry Bradshaw, Christina Rossetti, and Edmund Gosse.

> Benson upholds an inflexible poetic standard throughout and judges
> Blake here, not on his own terms, but against Bensonian notions of
> poetic form (so that, for instance, half-rhymes are "incredibly careless").

—*vvv*— —*vvv*— —*vvv*—

Blake, in spite of the extravagant claims made for him by his admirers, must
be held to have been primarily an artist. If he had not been an artist his
poems could hardly have survived at all. Mr. D. G. Rossetti says of the *Songs
of Innocence* that they are almost flawless in essential respects. But few will be
found to endorse this verdict. The fact is, that those who are carried off their
feet by the magnificent originality of Blake's artistic creations, read in between
the lines of his delicate and fanciful, but faulty and careless verse, an inspiration
to which he laid no claim.

Blake's poetry is, from beginning to end, childish; it has the fresh simplicity,
but also the vapid deficiencies of its quality—the metre halts and is imperfect;
the rhymes are forced and inaccurate, and often impress one with the sense
that the exigencies of assonance are so far masters of the sense, that the word
that ends a stanza is obviously not the word really wanted or intended by the
author, but only approximately thrown out at it. This may be illustrated by a
line from the Nurse's song in the *Songs of Experience*, where he says

> Your spring and your day are wasted in play,
> And your winter and night in *disguise.*

where the sense requires some such word as "disgust" or "weariness." Again,
his use of single words is often so strained and unnatural as to rouse a
suspicion that really he did not know the precise meaning of some word
employed. We may cite such an instance as the following from "London"
(Songs of Experience)—

> I wander thro' each *chartered* street
> Near where the *chartered* Thames doth flow.

And also in the "Ideas of Good and Evil," the first two lines of "Thames and
Ohio"—

> Why should I care for the men of Thames
> And the cheating waters of *chartered* streams

Whatever the word 'chartered' means, it is obvious, from its iteration, that
Blake attached some importance to it; but what does it mean? In ordinary
speech the word of course means 'licensed,' in a metaphorical sense, 'enjoying

some special immunity,' as 'chartered buffoon.' Is it possible that Blake confused it with 'chart,' and meant 'mapped out' or 'defined'? Conjecture is really idle in the case of a man who maintained that many of his poems were merely dictated to him, and that he exercised no volition of his own with regard to them.

His rhymes too are incredibly careless—we have 'lambs' rhyming with 'hands,' 'face' with 'dress,' 'peace' with 'distress,' 'vault' with 'fraught,' 'Thames' with 'limbs,' and so forth, in endless measure.

It may be urged that it is hypercritical to note these defects in a poet like Blake; it may be said that he was a child of nature, and that it is in the untamed and untrained character of his poems that his charm lies. "I regard fashion in poetry," he wrote, "as little as I do in painting." But Blake was a foe to slovenliness in the other branch of his art; in his trenchant remarks upon engraving, in the "Public Address," he is for ever insisting on the value of form; he is for ever deploring the malignant heresy that engravers need not, nay ought not to be draughtsmen. He maintains that this degrading of the engraver into a mere mechanical copyist has killed the art; so had he devoted himself scientifically to poetry, he would have been the first to realise and preach that it is the duty of the artist to acquire a technical precision, so sure, so instinctive, that it ceases to hamper thought. . . .

The fact is that what Blake wanted was culture; in literature he is a good type of how ineffective genius may be, if it is too narrow in its republicanism. Blake was self-absorbed and obstinate. His sympathy with certain qualities and aspects of life—simplicity, innocence, natural purity, faith, devotion—was innate and deep; but he had no idea of making himself appreciate what he did not at once understand: he was his own standard. Consequently, within certain limits, he has left beautiful and refined work, though never with the added charm of elaborateness; the imagination is pleased with Blake's poetry as it may be attracted by an innocent face, a wild flower, a thrush's song; the heart may hanker after a purity that it has lost or possibly never enjoyed. But Blake can only charm idyllically: he can never satisfy intellectually: he has not the simplicity, let us say, of the Gospel, which enters into and subdues the complexity of human hopes and desires. Like the little maid that attended Guinevere, "who pleased her with a babbling heedlessness, that often lured her from herself," it is away from the true and myriad-sided self of man that he wins; his is not the poverty of spirit which comes of renunciation, but the cleanness of soul which results from inadequacy. Self-reverence he has, but not self-knowledge, nor the self-control, the need of which comes home to the human heart through its imperious passions. Wordsworth proposed the remedy of simplicity for healing the diseases of the soul, but Blake's simplicity is not medicinal; it is the calm of the untroubled spirit, not the deeper content which comes of having faced and cured the heaven-sent maladies of mortal nature. Thus it is that his *Songs of Innocence* have a charm denied to the *Songs of Experience,* because he was at home in the former region, and did not really understand the meaning of the latter. The critical faculty, the power of seeing the merits latent in work whose scope and aim is not sympathetic, the gift of delicate appreciation was, in Blake, almost wholly in abeyance. He praised and condemned wholesale, vehemently, violently, as a child might judge, deciding from the superficial aspect of the object. Occasionally, as for instance, when he said of Milton in the Spiritual world, "his house is Palladian, not Gothic," he uttered a deep and suggestive criticism. But such sayings are very rare. Probably his own work gained in originality. The man who could work from morning to night at his engraving, for a period of two years, in London, without ever stepping into the open air except to fetch his meat and drink, is to be congratulated no doubt upon his fund of steady enthusiasm, but he is not cast in the mould of other men, still less is he the prey of the temptations which, if they sometimes also degrade, are at least needed to develop in the artist the intimate sympathy with human passion which must be the basis of his work.

—A.C. Benson, "William Blake,"
Essays, 1896, pp. 150–162

HENRY JUSTIN SMITH "THE POETRY OF WILLIAM BLAKE" (1900)

Henry Justin Smith (1875-1936) was a historian, fiction writer, journalist, reporter and editor, working with the *Chicago Daily News* from 1899 until his death. "The Poetry of William Blake" won the *Century's* college graduates' essay prize for 1898, the year Smith graduated from the University of Chicago. Smith was widely read in Blake and well acquainted with the latest Blake criticism. His persistent envisioning of Blake as a child speaks to the Romantic celebration of childhood, as untouched by the sophisticating and corrupting influences of culture and society. Smith also stresses the complexity and ambition of Blake's poetry. His notion of childhood is at least as complicated as Blake's own.

—◇◇◇— —◇◇◇— —◇◇◇—

Blake's country, like the mythical ones of old, is shut away by a cloud, and a forest, and a fiery river. Luring the adventurous by its simple isolation, it has seemed always to hide behind impassable barriers, or even to float ahead and vanish, like a mirage. Those who have penetrated farthest into it have been least able to tell us coherently of what they saw; for, like the legendary land again, it seems to disturb the balance of its visitors. They come wandering back to us muttering of purple skies, and men walking upside down. Blake's country, too, is a rendezvous of quack explorers; of indolent empty-heads who show a relic or two of the enchanted land, and preach to our ignorance of things they never have seen or felt. In plain language, Blake, like Browning, Whitman, and a half-score other great personalities, has been too much in the hands of ill-poised theory-mongers on the one side, and of shallow sentimentalists on the other. When a startlingly isolated figure appears, there stands always ready a throng of proselyters eager to stamp their badge upon him; while there also stands ready a band of sickly admirers, who mask their want of penetration by their lavish tears and smiles. Blake never had, until recently, either the one or the other kind of "followers"; but now he has both, to his detriment. There may be virtue in a simple statement of Blake's more obvious qualities—a statement free, I trust, alike from preconceptions and blind loyalty, and certainly founded on the humility which intercourse with an exalted spirit always brings. The Blake I know is a child, grasping manhood at intervals. Childhood is mercury, manhood is strength. Blake, in the most of his art, is so mercurial, so instantaneous in following impulse, so airily positive, that childhood alone has types of mind corresponding with his. The note of youth is the most conspicuous quality in his lyrical poems—a youth divinely gifted, no doubt; seeing at a single glance what soberer heads reach only by steady shocks of reason; youth visited in dreams by truth unearthly. Certainly the results of Blake's mental processes are somewhat titanic. But the processes were essentially those of immaturity. Blake never grew up.

The man who declared, "All things exist in the human imagination," was merely a phrase-making continuation of the child who told a boasting traveler that *he* should call a city splendid "in which the houses were of gold, the pavements of silver, the gates ornamented with precious stones." It is the same hurried generalization, a like reliance upon the feathers of impulse as the rock of law. Individualism, clear of theory and forcible by reason of its innocent absoluteness, is hardly to be distinguished from childhood. Manhood brings with it not only caution, steadfastness, restraint, but a kind of knowing dependence on the rest of humanity. Blake's individualism, the most absolute, the most immutable, which the record of English poetry can show, kept him throughout life in that state of unthinking dependence upon his own impulse, that fleeting, quivering sensibility, which is the essence of the child temperament.

I

This brilliant immaturity of Blake accounts for many things in his career. It accounts especially for his perfect unlikeness to his age. People have said of him, in the stock phrases they use regarding any literary phenomenon, that he "reacted" against his age, and therefore was "evolved" from it. That was precisely what he did not do. He was too innocently and daintily set apart from his times to bear even a revolutionary relationship with that pedant period. Are we to suppose that in youth he read the works of John Wolcot, of Anne Seward,— the "Swan of Lichfield," who never grew out of the ugly duckling stage,—of Anne Barbauld, of divine Shenstone, and ineffable Akenside; and then, holding up his tiny hands, cursed the age and poised a lance against it? Not at all. Then, as always, his own tastes sufficed him, and his own impulses were inspiration enough. It is sufficiently remarkable not to find a gifted boy carried away by the atmosphere about him; but Blake's youth was the more remarkable still in that he totally ignored his opposites, and wrought from his own vein of metal. Having not a mood or a molecule in common with anybody else, he necessarily stood apart from his age. We must constantly remember, however, that he stands just as far apart from all other poets who ever wrote.

Of the essential Blake we make this assertion—not of the Blake who makes his appearance in the *Poetical Sketches* of 1783. Our twelve-year-old poet, though usually dwelling apart in an ideal realm, had moments of being as human and conventional a boy as any; hence, of trying to fashion himself after his heroes, to make himself big and pompous—in short, and in general, to labor for things beyond his reach. This lordly ambition of boyhood swerves Blake aside from his true element, and sets him to work upon tragedies, ballads, apostrophes, and the rest. He intends at one time to be Shakspere, and, kindly refraining from bettering the dramatist's account of Richard III and Henry VIII, lays hold of a royal personage Shakspere left untouched, and produces *King Edward III*. It is convincing to see how the boy, with all his command of a really beautiful and distinctive verse, misses the dramatic, misses sublimity, misses Shakspere. It is interesting too, to see how far, at this time, he could wander into Elizabethan conventionalities. The apostrophe to "Spring," followed dutifully by lines to the other seasons, is full of such lapses. In "The Evening Star" an occasional line or two—

Speak silence with thy glimmering eyes,
And wash the dusk with silver,

or,

the wolf rages wide,
And the lion glares through the dun forest—

give us a foretaste of his magic; but "Fair Eleanor" is fit for a lace-collared youngster to speak at a school entertainment. "Gwin, King of Norway," except for a few splendid lines, is forced and hollow; a certain "War Song" is parrot-talk; and "Samson," though it gives us the wonderful image,

He seemed a mountain, his brow among the clouds;
She seemed a silver stream, his feet embracing,

is a laborious struggle to express half-formed ideas.

But to do justice to the *Poetical Sketches* it is necessary to comment here upon a handful of songs which, cut clean apart from the fine frenzy generated out of other poets, come nearer to the essential Blake than the pure joyousness of any other boy of fourteen ever came to the utterance of his manhood. These songs, in mere precocity, lose nothing by comparison with the earliest work of Pope and Cowley. They are the more important for us because of their distinctively Blake-like quality. The analyst with note-book is at liberty to find any amount of "Elizabethan influence" in these verses, to lay a finger on this bit from Herrick, and that from Fletcher, and the other from Crashaw; but strip off every petal from these rose-leaf songs, and then say which one is accountable for the inmost fragrance. Nay, that fragrance is Blake. He gathers a dozen individualities into his own, and sends them forth laden with his essence.

How sweet I roamed from field to field,
    And tasted all the summer's pride,
Till I the Prince of Love beheld
    Who in the sunny beams did glide.
...
He loves to sit and hear me sing,
    Then, laughing, sports and plays with me;
Then stretches out my golden wing,
    And mocks my loss of liberty.

That, in purity, in height, in delicate breadth, is Blake and none other. And this is Blake spacious and austere:

Whether on Ida's shady brow,
  Or in the chambers in the East,
The chambers of the Sun, that now
  From ancient melody have ceased;

Whether in heaven ye wander fair,
  Or the green corners of the earth,
Or the blue regions of the air
  Where the melodious winds have birth;

. . .

How have you left the ancient love
  That bards of old enjoyed in you!
The languid strings do scarcely move,
  The sound is forced, the notes are few!

Yet even these always-quoted stanzas are as honey to snow compared with
the high, elusive notes that came later. They are too richly wrought, too
sweet by half. Still more absolutely Blake-like—more poignant, and sudden,
and full of his stinging ardor—are the lines of this "Mad Song," the metrical
liberty of which, for me, only connects the poem more closely with his
characteristic work:

The wild winds weep,
  And the night is a-cold:
Come hither, Sleep,
  And my griefs enfold!
But lo! the morning peeps
Over the eastern steeps,
And the rustling birds of dawn
The earth do scorn.

Like a fiend in a cloud,
  With howling woe
After night I do crowd
  And with night will go;
I turn my back to the east,
From whence comforts have increased,
For light doth seize my brain
With frantic pain.

So much for Blake at the age of experiment, and for the sole poems in which the faintest tendency to imitation is traceable. Fascinating as they are, significant as is this voice of melody in the stark deadness of the times, the *Poetical Sketches* are of highest interest by contrast with the Blake of a later growth. They count little more in the general scheme of his poetical career than his early fumblings with an engraver's tools counted with regard to his tremendous designs. They are products of ambition as well as of inspiration. When Blake grew ambitious, he lost his hold on the qualities most his own.

II

Arrived at its full power, Blake's mind dwelt mainly on two ideas: the reality of the spiritual world, and the divine nature of energy. From these radiated the complex and astounding mass of theories, or rather imaginative conceptions, which we may euphemistically term his system of philosophy. Blake was no thinker, in the ordinary sense, yet his philosophical development was a course of inductive reasoning—after his unique fashion. His data were his own states of mind, his own impressions, his own visions; the last most of all. Interesting explanations have been offered regarding this "abnormal insight" of Blake's; but the research is not of marked profit beyond the "Well done, good and faithful servant" of the class-room. Whether or not Blake "really saw" angels in a hay-field, or angels glittering in a tree, or fairies holding obsequies, or God's face at the window, he thought he saw them, he built a philosophy upon them, and he uttered the philosophy in verse. This is surely enough for discussion. There is no doubt that this temperamental extension of Blake's powers was the fundamental fact in his life, and that virtually the whole of his mystical theory results from it. There is no more common error in the world than generalization based upon one's individual abilities and tastes. Having some sort of insight into the supernatural, and an imaginative strenuousness which enabled him to see almost anything he wished to see, Blake, in the most innocent manner possible, laid down his laws that "all things exist in the human imagination"; that "imagination is the real and eternal world, of which this vegetative universe is but the faint shadow"; that "energy is the only life"; that "man has no body distinct from his soul"; and a host of more or less related dicta. These utterances are simply the records of Blake's spiritual experience; merely oracular statements of his individual perceptions and feelings. One may or may not accept them as divine revelation. One cannot avoid regarding them as expressions of a towering life, and as the testimony of a man who, by the grace of God, knew intuitively much that we shall never know by reasoning or by experience.

We are not trying to probe after the truth of mysticism, but to indicate what mental processes lay back of Blake's poetical work. Once realizing that he saw the earth and the heavens above as nothing in themselves, as mere hieroglyphs of a supernal reality, we may approach with sympathy the elate, floating, intangible poems, with a knowledge that their limitations are really their strength. It is doubtful if Blake will ever be taken on his own ground by a large number of readers. He touches life at so few points that his pen is usually dipped in mist or quicksilver, not blood. At times he is as the pure cloud that reaches its silken fringes to earth, but, subject to the waftings of its sky-element, hastily withdraws and floats intangibly over. At times he is that cloud darting lightnings, and sweeping past in dark, rolling vapor; always above, impenetrable. In both moods Blake is removed definitely from the clash of society, from tangible human things, from aught that the material and muscled can possibly grasp. Unless spiritual vision is to be granted to all mankind,—as, indeed, some prophets affirm,—or mysticism is to become as common as the spelling-book, a sympathetic understanding of Blake will never be broadspread. But it may keep some readers from snap judgments and hasty disgust if they remember the simple fact that he saw all things through the golden glass of symbolism, and necessarily missed some of the bold outlines.

There are some aspects of life which this method of vision exactly suits. Innocence in nature or humanity is chief of these aspects. Therefore, when Blake turned to the depiction of childhood, and the environment of childhood, he achieved poetry in which the expression is adequate, just, and wholly beautiful. Blake's most zealous interpreters have upbraided the general public for preferring the *Songs of Innocence* to anything else he wrote; but there is some right instinct in the preference, after all. These songs are not suggestive of heavy thought in the same degree that later poems are; perhaps they are less significant of "the true Blake." But certainly one finds here a mastery of the subjects which *are* treated, a lyrical correspondence between substance and form, and a simplicity which masks to esthetic perfection the spiritual suggestiveness for which the poems exist. In these respects few of Blake's poems reach the level of the *Songs of Innocence.*

We have already said that the less Blake's ambition to poetize, the finer poetry he wrought. Certain practical circumstances caused the *Songs of Innocence* to yield the poetry pure of the ambition. During the six years which passed between the *Sketches* and the *Songs,* Blake labored steadily at his trade of engraver and designer. In these years the artist side of his genius seems to have predominated. He became deeply engrossed in the technical part of his work.

He discovered, or, to be strictly accurate, there was revealed to him in vision, a new process of printing designs and verses together by a kind of reversed etching. So the poetical work of this period was, in his opinion, incidental to the founding of his reputation in art; and the verses, when published by the new method, seemed useful chiefly to fill in the vacant spots in the designs. To that very thing the Songs *of Innocence* doubtless owe much of their spontaneity and their elemental sweetness. Browning says, in a passage quoted by Gilchrist: "If there should arise a new painter, will it not be in some such way, by a poet now, or a musician (spirits who have conceived and perfected an ideal through some other channel), transferring it to this, and escaping our conventional roads by pure ignorance of them?" It is such a virgin power which appears in the *Songs of Innocence*. But for their lyrical quality they owe quite as much to the character of Blake at the time of writing. He did not yet wear the brow of a seer. His mystical philosophy was in the inchoate; his tremendous theories were then mere instincts and emotions, mingling insensibly with the pure joy of living. He himself had not felt the bitterness of deception, enmities, oppression. He had lived the free life of a child, and the rod of the taskmaster had not yet descended. He was innocence itself, and having cast aside all ambitions but the expression of his own impulses, he inevitably brought forth *Songs of Innocence*.

They are more than "child studies": they are childhood itself, for they are Blake. They are the mysterious raptures of a spirit which neither London smoke nor eighteenth-century sophistication could tarnish. And the medium of expression is refined to the vanishing-point. There is no more guile in the purest of these lays than speaks in the "O—o—oh" of a child's sudden wonder; no more, in fact, than speaks in the lighted countenance without the exclamation. But words are thick and blunt. Let the none too familiar "Lamb" suggest what it may:

> Little lamb, who made thee?
>   Dost thou know who made thee,
> Gave thee life, and bade thee feed
> By the stream and o'er the mead;
> Gave thee clothing of delight,
> Softest clothing, woolly, bright;
> Gave thee such a tender voice,
> Making all the vales rejoice?
>   Little lamb, who made thee,
>   Dost thou know who made thee?

> Little lamb, I'll tell thee;
> Little lamb, I'll tell thee:
> He is called by thy name,
> For He calls himself a Lamb;
> He is meek, and He is mild,
> He became a little child.
> I a child, and thou a lamb,
> We are called by His name.
> > Little lamb, God bless thee!
> > Little lamb, God bless thee!

Surely mysticism never assumed a daintier guise than this. With "The Lamb" may be mentioned "The Echoing Green," "The Blossom," "Spring," and "Infant Joy," as poems which have this rare note of innocent, sprightly wonder. From such an extreme of simplicity the *Songs* range downward all the way to "The Little Black Boy," which is over-subtle, and "The Divine Image," which is didactic. Perhaps the most perfect balance of thought and emotion is found in "A Cradle Song" and "Night," in both of which, as well, the melody exerts its utmost fascination. In the "Cradle Song" the most significant of a beautiful set of verses are the following:

> Sweet babe, in thy face
> Holy image I can trace;
> Sweet babe, once like thee
> Thy Maker lay, and wept for me:
> Wept for me, for thee, for all,
> When He was an infant small.
> Thou His image ever see,
> Heavenly face that smiles on thee!
> Smiles on thee, on me, on all,
> Who became an infant small;
> Infant smiles are His own smiles;
> Heaven and earth to peace beguiles.

It will need but a single stanza of "Night" to show what a spell the poem casts:

> The sun descending in the west,
> The evening star does shine;
> The birds are silent in their nest,
> And I must seek for mine.

The moon, like a flower
In heaven's high bower,
With silent delight,
Sits and smiles on the night.

It has been well said that "in Blake's poetry the finest expression of his genius is its power to open for the soul sudden vistas of immortality, to conduct it by means of a half-recognized emotion into fair fields whither it would lack the power to go of itself." This energy of suggestion is strongly marked in the *Songs of Innocence*. Blake has selected those figures and scenes which naturally symbolize the most; he has presented them with an artlessness which is the highest reach of art; he has insured a hearing by introducing an element of music which he never again recaptured; and he has infused, with that indescribable power granted only to the highest genius, the elusive, pervasive, and magical quality that we name "atmosphere." The effect of all this is to lead the reader to the verge of great discoveries, to give him a taste of the universal and ineffable, and then to leave him in the attitude of wonder and exaltation, which is, perhaps, all that human beings have a right to affect. Mystical poetry can achieve no higher victory than this.

III

In the memorable conflict which went on for some time between Blake's lyrical instincts and his didactic, "prophetic" tendencies, the former were bound to be eventually worsted. To retain the simple music of his soul is more than the average man can do, try as he may. And Blake, so far as we know, never made any such effort, but rather girded himself continually for his

> great task
> To open the eternal worlds! To open the miniature
>   eyes
> Of man inward; into the worlds of thought; into
>   eternity;
> Ever expanding in the bosom of God, the human
>   imagination.

Whitman, in his self-conscious and blustering assumption of responsibility as seer, hardly surpassed the determined endeavor of Blake to do the impossible. There is no need to say that Blake's labors as "prophet" were barren. But he certainly let his lyrical power go to waste while he was listening to thunderous voices from the mountain-top. For proof of this assertion, we have merely to bring forward the poems grouped as *Songs of Experience,* and place them where they belong, beside the lovely poems of childhood, of which they are the negation and the opposite.

How much of direct purpose there was in this attempt to present the same life with a blight upon it, we cannot know. The two books appeared together in Blake's time, with the description, "Two contrary states of the human soul"; but that is not conclusive. At any rate, Blake might have said to himself at the moment of writing,

> Turn wheresoe'er I may,
> By night or day,
> The things which I have seen I now can see no more.

Innocence is gone. Nature is no longer blithe and confiding; but earth raises up her head,

> Her light fled,
> Stony, dread,
> And her locks covered with grey despair;

while the burden of her song is:

> Break this heavy chain,
> That does freeze my bones around!
> Selfish, vain,
> Eternal bane,
> That free love with bondage bound.

The children of Holy Thursday now are pictured as
> reduced to misery,
> Fed with cold and usurous hand?

The chimney-sweep gives text for a sermon on hypocritical cruelty; the "little boy lost," for an outcry against persecution for freedom of belief; the babe of the new "cradle song" is warned against the "dreadful light" about to break; roses have invisible worms at the heart; gay little animals are slain in their pretty play; and in place of a lamb, we have the symbol of ferocity, a tiger,

> burning bright
> In the forests of the night.

Nature, then, may be considered ruined by "experience." But another ruination is apparent—that of Blake the lyrist. He does not fall into stiffness and hollowness; that were impossible. But, in place of simplicity, he gives us rude eloquence; in place of delicate suggestion, fierce stimulation; in place of melody, a rushing volume of emphasis. One may contend that this is precisely the value of the *Experience,* and that the great change in nature is accurately bodied forth by this harsh note. Unquestionably there is an austere might, a Hebraic spaciousness and a richness of coloring, not apparent in the *Innocence*. But Blake the singer is lost to us, nevertheless.

Some of the *Songs of Experience* are very powerful; others very trivial. Blake was always ineffectual the moment he deserted his ideal ground and attempted to cope with worldliness on its own terms. Our winsome poet is hard to recognize in this vein:

> Dear mother, dear mother, the Church is cold;
> But the Ale-house is healthy, and pleasant, and
> warm
> Besides, I can tell where I am used well;
> The poor parsons with wind like a blown bladder
> swell.

Thank fortune, there is not much of this, and we are just as likely to hit upon a beautiful fancy:

> Ah, Sunflower, weary of time,
> Who countest the steps of the sun;
> Seeking after that sweet golden clime
> Where the traveler's journey is done.

The weakest parts of the series are those which embody a remonstrance against oppression. In protest against specific ills, Blake shows the character of a sensitive man put beside himself by the brutal materialism of his opposites, and forgetting his own dignity in the heat of his anger. When attacking an abstraction, however, he rises to his idealistic vein, in which he is always superb. The most of "The Garden of Love," for example, seems to me extremely beautiful, not only in diction, but in versification:

> I laid me down upon a bank,
> Where Love lay sleeping;
> I heard among the rushes dank
> Weeping, weeping.
> Then I went to the heath and the wild,
> To the thistles and thorns of the waste;
> And they told me how they were beguiled,
> Driven out, and compelled to be chaste.

"The Angel" and "A Little Girl Lost" have much the same quality. But there is no comparison between these and the poems which embody a plea for a return to nature. This is really the central idea of the book, and, indeed, one of the principal ideas of Blake's philosophy in general. Almost all his "prophetical" books assert, in some manner, that all material things are holy, so they be under the dominion of the spiritual; that nature must be restored to its rightful place as the symbol of God's power and the medium of energy. In the *Experience* Blake embodies this thought in two wonderfully effective poems, "A Little Girl Lost" and "A Little Girl Found." The "little girl" evidently represents the human soul. She wanders for days in the desert, under the "frowning, frowning night," but falls placidly asleep at last, and is borne away to a cave of wild beasts. There, in her exquisite snow-whiteness, she is protected by leopards and tigers. So much for what nature will do for those who visit it in simplicity. But the parents also, seeking their child, "pale through pathless ways," come to the cave, are welcomed there, and

> To this day they dwell
> In a lonely dell,
> Nor fear the wolvish howl
> Nor the lion's growl.

This is the final teaching of the *Songs of Experience*—that nature, supposed sinful and accursed, and taking terrifying shapes, is permeated with divine goodness. Oppressed, it cannot live; but free, it yields blessing to those who approach it with pure hearts.

IV

Of all the English poets to whom the French Revolution had more than a far-away significance, Blake was the most profoundly stirred. Burns, indeed, with Cowper, Coleridge, and Wordsworth, viewed the great struggle with eyes aflame. But while to these men the Revolution was a lesson, to our humble engraver of Poland street it was a confirmation. By temperament, as we have seen, he was a revolutionist. When the monarchy fell, his ideas were just beginning to gain substance. Now, when he saw liberty raising its head in Paris, and men casting out magistrates, putting tyrants and degenerates to death, and glorifying passion and freedom to the uttermost, the effect upon his philosophy was to mold it into a white-hot, gigantic mass. With Blake exaltation always meant an ascent to dizzy heights of idealism. So this struggle became to him much more than a political movement, an affair of taxation and popular rights; it became symbolic of the struggle for free life in all phases. It touched his religion, his ethics, his esthetics. It brought his intellect and his emotional nature into energetic union. It transformed him from a suggestive singer into a furious declaimer and rhapsodist.

With extraordinary swiftness and ease, *Thel, The Marriage of Heaven and Hell, The French Revolution, The Vision of the Daughters of Albion,* and *America* streamed from Blake's brain and hand. There followed a descent into the comparative clarity of the *Songs of Experience;* and then, plunging his head among the clouds again, Blake produced, at intervals, *Urizen, The Song of Los, Ahania, Jerusalem,* and *Milton.* To the complacent and orderly mind, with a touch of imagination, these outpourings cause an indescribable shock. Tempest alone, with its whirling disorder, can produce the same sense of confusion and insecurity. And this "prophecy" is worse than tempest, for one cannot discern its center of force, or rely upon its beginnings and endings as such. There is, so far as one can tell after a considerable amount of study, nothing to be got from it but chaos. Genuine ethical suggestions, wonderful illuminations, and even beautiful glimpses of nature, appear in profusion. But they are always incomplete as they stand, and do not appear to be attached to anything else. In fact, the average reader, after a conscientious and determined attempt to discover what the rhapsody is about, will be apt to declare it all moonshine.

But returning day by day to these books, and gradually attaining a state of mind akin to that of the seer, the student will almost certainly declare that an immense meaning is wrapped up in them. One feels it rather than knows it. An intuitional faculty sufficiently broad and forceful cannot miss the perception that a vast mind is here speaking, and speaking truth drawn from Heaven knows what source. The wildness, the spluttering, the eery plunges, the shouting of names like Golgonooza, Kwantok, Kox, and Kotope, are not "faults"; they are parts of the phenomenon. They give not the effect of recklessness, but of being minor and outer manifestations of a tremendous force. No one has accomplished an unveiling absolutely satisfactory, and no one ever will. Mr. Swinburne's interpretation is elaborate, but fantastic and largely superimposed. In the monumental work of Messrs. Ellis and Yeats one cannot separate the philosophy of Blake from the philosophy of the commentators. One may accept these interpretations if he pleases, and fit them accurately to the subject-matter. But how be sure even then that the meaning is extracted? It is characteristic of Blake's loftiest work that there is always something beyond one's reach, something inexpressible. It is not "obscurity," it is simple vastness. He opens the avenues to knowledge of the divine, and our visions fail at the first turning. I think that in future time students will turn again and again to these prophecies, and penetrate farther and farther into their recesses; but I am positive that no explorer will ever reach the end and name the last nebulous idea dwelling there. These books are the soul of Blake, and souls stand aloof from the media by which mortals are intelligible to one another.

Assuredly this is not the place to attempt an interpretation of the "prophetical" books, or even to analyze the apparent subject-matter of each one. Some of them are not poetry, stretch the definition as you may. The rest require a lifetime of study, and a volume for elucidation. It may be said, merely to round out our study, that the titles bear no traceable relations to the text; that the books are not "prophecy" as we use the word; that they seem to be detailed copies of the visions of Blake as they swept across his mind; that they express in tortuous and terrific form, in somber, crowded images, Blake's philosophy of the fourfold nature of man, the divine nature of energy, and the reality of the spiritual. They are not to be approached in a spirit of easy skepticism, of impatience at their eccentricities, or of regret that they are not *Songs of Innocence*. To the gifted, the reverent, the thoughtful, the "eternal gates' terrific porter" will open these gloomy caverns, and the voice of a seer will issue forth.

V

My final word on Blake must be chiefly a bringing together of the scattered impressions already recorded. Blake, as I know him, was a child gifted with imaginative raptures lifting him to the plane of a seer. He had a child's self-sufficiency, a child's faith, a child's incompleteness. His inner life centered about two or three great ideas, all of which were more or less dependent upon his peculiar endowment of spiritual sight. Whatever else he taught was subsidiary to these two or three, or explanatory of them, or in conflict with them; for Blake held that "the man who never alters his opinions is like standing water, and breeds reptiles of the mind." These theories we find foreshadowed in *Songs of Innocence,* stated emphatically in *Songs of Experience,* repeated in stray poems like "The Golden Net," "The Land of Dreams," "Auguries of Innocence," and bursting into a dark torrent of amorphous imagery and suggestion in the "prophetical" books. The variety and pregnancy of his work proves not his immensity of thought, but his resources of personality. His philosophy was a mere starting-point for the great rush of his imagination. That philosophy was bold, brilliant, fascinating. It leaped beyond its times, and anticipated the individualistic conceptions of a half-century later. But the great ideas advanced by Blake were few; and, as far as the bare thought is concerned, one half of his work was a frank repetition of the other half.

King of the vague, Blake was powerless in the human, the dramatic, the concrete. There is flame in his poetry, but no blood. Of the material onset of society he knew nothing, and cared to know nothing. His interests were in an ideal and supernal world—the relations of God and man, spirit and flesh, good and evil. At his best, he either depicts those aspects of life ideally most suggestive, or lets humanity go altogether, and swims in an opaque element of his own. The same man whom we see "opening the eternal worlds" we behold mixing in trivial squabbles, and employing the cheap weapons of satire and bluster. He is neither consistent, nor self-mastered, nor true to any truth but his own. He is endowed with few of the solid, practical gifts which are the birthright of the commonplace. But his walk on earth was, nevertheless, a noble one, exhaling tenderness and strength, song and pure spirit, finding its nether joys in the most ethereal things in nature, and its higher joys in communion with the world of which this lower one seemed to him the imperfect reflection.

I do not suppose that Blake's influence either upon art or upon thought will ever be great. Not much in his verse is of a kind to be transferred from one personality to another; for one cannot "graft" spirit. Not much in his philosophy will outlast the swift changes and discardings and discoverings in the realm of ethics. Are not, indeed, one half of Blake's assertions already disproved or become obvious? Yet this philosophy has the surety of a sort of permanence in being directly the emanation of Blake's personality. As a man he will live; as one in whom energy attained great stature and absolute freedom; as one who saw the beauty of life, and draws us with him to the vision. He is, in a word, one of the great stimulators of modern times. He is shut away in his own world; shut away by a cloud, and a forest, and a river. But there are approaches to the mysterious land; and when one, using simplicity and steadiness and love, reaches the true Blake, he will find that the impact of that mind upon his own will be such an experience as to give life a different face.

—Henry Justin Smith, "The Poetry of
William Blake," *Century Magazine,*
June 1900, pp. 284–291

John Sampson "Bibliographical Preface to the *Songs of Innocence and of Experience*" and "Bibliographical Preface to Poems from the 'Prophetic Books'" (1905)

In 1905, John Sampson produced a new edition of the works of William Blake, according to what was then an innovative (and now an obvious) editorial principle: of recovering and presenting the author's own version of his writings, without attempts at emendation. Before Sampson, most editors had tried to "improve" Blake's works.

The bibliographical prefaces Sampson includes in his *Poetical Works of William Blake* do not attempt to interpret Blake's poems and books; rather, they offer textual histories, describing, where possible, the material qualities of the original texts, and the fate of those texts as they were redacted by various editors throughout the nineteenth century. Included below is the "Bibliographical Preface to the *Songs of Innocence and of Experience*," particularly interesting because of the several editions and variations Blake himself produced of the *Songs of Innocence* and *Songs of Experience*. Also the "Bibliographical Preface to Poems from the 'Prophetic Books,'" which presents a brief history of how editors invented the category of the "Prophetic Books," when Blake himself used no such term.

—————

Bibliographical Preface to the *Songs of Innocence and of Experience*
The *Songs of Innocence* (1799) was the first of Blake's works produced by the novel method which, in his prospectus of 1793, he styles 'illuminated printing.' The text and surrounding design were written in reverse, in a medium impervious to acid, upon small copper plates about 5" by 3", which were then etched in a bath of aqua fortis until the work stood in relief as on a stereotype. From these plates, which to economize copper were in many cases engraved upon both sides, impressions were printed, in the ordinary manner, in tints meant to harmonize with the colour scheme afterwards applied in water-colours by the artist. In the dexterous interweaving of text and design Blake anticipates the modern school of book illustration. Gilchrist's statement (*Life*, i. 68) that 'by the end of 1788 . . . the illustrated designs in colour . . . had been executed' conveys the impression that before engraving Blake had completed an entire series of coloured illustrations to the *Songs of Innocence*. This would seem to be pure assumption, and it is evident that no such sketches were known to Mr. W. M. Rossetti, or he would undoubtedly have included them in his exhaustive 'Annotated Catalogue of Blake's Pictures and Drawings' (Gilchrist, ii. 201–64). The only original designs known to the present writer are the following:—(1) In Quaritch's *General Catalogue* (1887, p. 935) there is an entry of three coloured sketches for the *Songs of Innocence* 'from the collection of a friend of Blake's.' These designs, which are described as being 'in Blake's usual rich style of colouring' and as 'differing considerably from the published engravings,' are the Piper frontispiece, the Introduction

('Piping down the valleys wild'), and a third drawing called 'An Ideal Hell,' which is probably attributed by a cataloguer's error to the *Songs of Innocence*. (2) There are besides in the Rossetti MS. Book the original designs for two of the *Songs of Experience*, 'The Angel' and 'The Sick Rose'—the latter different in many respects from the version subsequently engraved. We have no reason to believe that Blake first executed for all the songs coloured sketches which have since disappeared. Probably many of the originals were merely pencil drawings 'with nothing to seek'—to quote Blake's own phrase in his recipe for engraving on pewter—which would naturally be destroyed in the process of rubbing off on to the copper.

The engraved version of the *Songs*, issued by the author without change during a period of nearly forty years, must of course be regarded as the only authoritative text; even where, as in a few cases, the earlier manuscript readings seem preferable. Original autograph versions of three of the *Songs of Innocence* are found in the unpublished Blake manuscript known as *An Island in the Moon*. Manuscript versions of eighteen of the twenty-six *Songs of Experience* form some of the first entries in the Rossetti MS. Book. Several of the latter have the appearance of being fair copies, transcribed, at one time, from an earlier notebook or from loose scraps of paper, while others, such as 'The Tyger,' are evidently the first rough draft. All these variant readings are here given in the footnotes to the *Songs*.

The *Songs of Innocence* was at first issued as a separate work, complete copies of the little book in its original forest containing thirty-one plates. These include five—'The Little Girl Lost,' 'The Little Girl Found,' 'The Voice of the Ancient Bard,' and 'The School Boy'—which were afterwards generally transferred by Blake to the *Songs of Experience*, though the two last were still sometimes placed by him among the *Songs of Innocence*. With the exception of the frontispiece, title-page, and introduction, the plates in this earliest issue were printed upon both sides of octavo paper, the thirty-one plates occupying seventeen leaves. These loose leaves were then stitched by Mrs. Blake into paper covers, in most cases by the rough process known as 'stabbing,' a cord being laced through holes punctured an inch or two apart.

In 1793 Blake completed the engraving of the *Songs of Experience*. His prospectus, dated Oct. 10 of the same year, addressed 'To the Public,' and giving a list of ten works 'now published and on Sale at Mr. Blake's, no. 13 Hercules Buildings, Lambeth,' advertises the *Songs of Innocence and the Songs of Experience* as two separate books, each being priced at 5*s.* and described as containing twenty-five designs. Blake here, according to his practice in other cases, does not include either frontispiece or title-page, which would make the entire number of plates in the two series fifty-four. As this is the full number in a perfect copy of the *Songs of Innocence and of Experience*, including the general title-page which had not then been engraved, Blake in this prospectus must have reckoned 'A Divine Image' ('Cruelty has a Human Heart') among the number. Though this poem is inserted without question in all editions of Blake since Shepherd's, it would seem to have been deliberately rejected by the poet himself. The plate containing it is not found in any authentic copy of the *Songs* issued in the lifetime of the artist or his wife, and is known to us by only two examples. One of these is in the uncoloured copy of the *Songs* in the Reading Room of the British Museum, which, as the watermark shows, was printed not earlier than 1832, and the other is a proof impression in the possession of Mr. William Muir, which he has reproduced at the end of his facsimile of *The Marriage of Heaven and Hell*.

In 1794 Blake added a general title-page to both series, which thenceforward were issued by him as one work, the plates printed on one side of the leaf only and numbered by hand consecutively one to fifty-four. This is the form in which most copies of the *Songs* occur. It should be noted that there was never any true edition, in the ordinary sense of the term, of this or of any other of Blake's engraved works. Sets of impressions were struck off as required, the issue of the *Songs* extending from the completion of the *Songs of Innocence* in 1789 to the close of Blake's life. In 1863 ten of the original plates, yielding sixteen impressions (six being engraved on both sides of the copper), were still in existence, and were used by Mr. Gilchrist in the second volume of his *Life of Blake*. The outline designs there, as I learn from Mr. Frederick Macmillan, were printed from electrotypes which have every appearance of having been made from the actual plates engraved by Blake. The present whereabouts of these plates I have been unable to trace.

According to Gilchrist (*Life*, i. 125) a few copies were 'issued plain in black and white, or blue and white.' This agrees with the modest price (5*s.* each) at which Blake advertises the *Songs of Innocence and the Songs of Experience* in his Prospectus of 1793. The thirty shillings or two guineas which Gilchrist {i. 124) tells us the artist received for the first issue of the collected *Songs* probably refers to coloured impressions. The only uncoloured copy of the *Songs of Innocence and of Experience* known to the present writer is the very unworthy example, already referred to, in the Reading Room of the British Museum. This is a made-up copy, in which part of the plates at least were printed after the death of Blake and his wife, perhaps by Mr. F. Tatham, into whose possession they passed after Catherine Blake's death in October, 1831.

The earlier examples of the *Songs of Innocence* are distinguished by the simplicity and delicacy of their colouring, contrasting in this respect with some of the later more elaborately illuminated copies of the *Songs of Innocence and of Experience*. These last issues are printed upon larger paper and upon one side of the leaf only. The Monckton Milnes copy, produced after 1818, measures 13" x 10-5/8", and each plate has the additional embellishment of a wide wash border instead of the simple red line with which Blake ordinarily surrounded the designs. In a copy exhibited at the Grolier Club at New York in 1905, the plates are surrounded by delicate borders of trees, vines, and even drapery. These frames, which are not more than a quarter of an inch in width, were added with a fine brush.

Besides the sixteen plates reprinted by Gilchrist, which, as Mr. D. G. Rossetti points out, are 'as absolutely the *originals* as those appearing in the copies printed by Blake'—except of course in having been printed from electros instead of direct from the plates, and in lacking the superadded water-colour tinting—there are three modern facsimiles of the *Songs*. The first of these is given in *The Works of William Blake, reproduced in facsimile from the original editions* (100 *copies printed for private circulation*), 1876. This has evidently been prepared from the very poor uncoloured copy of the *Songs* acquired by the British Museum in January, 1864, and, while it affords a fairly good general idea of Blake's designs, is coarsely executed and exceedingly inaccurate as to the text. The second is the very beautiful reproduction made by Mr. William Muir in 1884 and 1885, the edition being limited to fifty copies. The outline drawings are here facsimilized by lithography, and the colouring added by hand from the finest examples accessible to the artist. The tinting of the *Songs of Innocence* is copied from the volume which Blake gave to Flaxman—though the plates, it may he noted, are arranged in a different order—that of the *Songs of Experience* from the famous Beckford Library copy, originally belonging to a Mr. Edwards, purchased by Mr. Quaritch at the Hamilton Palace sale. July 4, 1882, and now the property of Mr. W. A. White of Brooklyn. These exquisite facsimiles leave little to be desired in their general fidelity to the originals. Blake's cameo plates have, however, a sharpness and definiteness of outline impossible to achieve by printing from stone, and partly no doubt for this reason Mr. Muir fails in the difficult technical feat of reproducing the grace, beauty, and delicacy of Blake's lettering.

There is also a useful facsimile of the outlines of the *Songs*, edited by Mr. Edwin J. Ellis (Quaritch, 1903). The plates are here reproduced by a photographic process, which, as the editor points out, fails to represent the clearness of the originals where the copies have been made from tinted impressions. Neither of these facsimiles, however, though much more accurate than the reproduction of 1876, is a trustworthy guide for Blake's text.

In Blake's *Songs of Innocence* (including, as in the first issue, 'The Little Girl Lost', 'The Little Girl Found', and 'The School Boy') the body of the text is in minuscule roman, with the exception of 'The Voice of the Ancient Bard', which is in italic. In the *Songs of Experience*, on the contrary, Blake substituted for roman the more easily formed italic characters which he first adopted in the *Book of Thel* (1789) and used in all his subsequent works; only four songs, 'The Tyger', 'Ah! Sunflower', 'London', and 'A Poison Tree', with the introductory stanza to 'A Little Girl Lost', being written in the former style of lettering.

There is no engraved Table of Contents, and a collation of various copies of the *Songs* shows that the order in which the plates are arranged varies in almost every instance. The plates are without engraved foliation or pagination, and catchwords are only used where one of the longer songs is continued on to a second plate. The early issues of the *Songs of Innocence* are without manuscript pagination or border lines. Later issues of the two series, printed upon one side of the leaf only, are foliated at the top right-hand corner, in the same brown or red ink with which Blake added the border lines surrounding the plates.

Blake's earliest arrangement is found in the extremely rare first issue of the *Songs* printed upon both sides of the leaf. In Table I, I give the collations of five copies of the *Songs of Innocence* and in Table II of one copy of the *Songs of Innocence and of Experience*, plates printed upon the same leaf being bracketed together and those on the recto being placed first.

The first three plates of the *Songs of Innocence*, the frontispiece, title-page, and Introduction, are printed upon one side of the leaf only; the frontispiece was generally bound, as if printed on the verso, to face the title-page.

It will be seen from these tables that although the order of plates is not identical in any of these six copies, yet in four of these the same designs are invariably found either as recto or verso of the same leaf. A further instance of the same juxtaposition is the example in the Print Room of the British Museum. This is evidently a made-up copy, the deficiency of the original being supplied by two leaves of the earlier issue, in which, as in A, B, and C, 'The Ecchoing Green' (two plates) and the 'Nurse's Song' and 'Holy Thursday' are printed upon either side of the same leaf. In a sale at Sotheby's of the library of J. B. Ditchfield, M.D., April 24, 1893, among the books sold is recorded an incomplete copy of the *Songs of Innocence* in which these four plates are wanting. This volume was bound by C. Lewis in 1782, so that the two missing leaves, which we may reasonably conjecture have gone to supply the lacunae in the Print Room copy, must have disappeared at an early date. These coincidences of arrangement, however, are as likely to have arisen from the fact of a number of impressions having been printed at one time, as from any deliberate intention on the part of the author.

Bibliographical Preface to Poems from the "Prophetic Books"

In the present section I group together the lyrical poems from the works commonly known as the 'Prophetic Books.' This name, first employed by Gilchrist to describe Blake's Visionary Writings, is nowhere used by the poet himself, though he refers to them as 'inspired' or 'dictated,' and prefixes to two of the number the sub-title 'A Prophecy.'

The Prophetic Books fall under a category of their own. Either more or less than literature according to the point of view of the reader, it is impossible to subject them to any ordinary standard of criticism without ignoring the primary intention of the author. Broadly epic in character, they are in content a verbal and pictorial rendering of Blake's visions, a storehouse of his mythology, and a fervent exposition of his mystical gospel. In the earlier of these writings symbolism is wholly, or almost wholly, absent; in the later books nearly every phrase, name, and epithet must be interpreted symbolically.

The greater number of the Prophetic Books are written in a variety of forms of free verse. One book, *The Marriage of Heaven and Hell*, is almost entirely in prose; the others are composed in different measures, varying from the semi-rhythmic Ossianic verses of *Tiriel* to the short irregular metre of *Ahania* or the pseudo-hexameters of *Jerusalem*. The latter may possibly have been suggested to Blake's ear by the passages from Klopstock's *Messiah* which Hayley read and translated to him during his stay at Felpham. In Blake's 'Address to the Public' which serves as Introduction to the first chapter of *Jerusalem*, he furnishes, in imitation of Milton, the following account of the measure in which the poem is written:—

'We who dwell on Earth can do nothing of ourselves every thing is conducted by Spirits, no less than Digestion or Sleep.

'When this verse was first dictated to me, I consider'd a Monotonous Cadence, like that used by Milton & Shakspeare & all writers of English Blank Verse derived from the modern bondage of Rhyming, to be a necessary and indispensible part of Verse. But I soon found that, in the mouth of a true Orator, such monotony was not only awkward, but as much a bondage

as rhyme itself. I therefore have produced a variety in every line, both of
cadences & number of syllables. Every word and every letter is studied and
put into its fit place: the terrific numbers are reserved for the terrific parts,
the mild & gentle for the mild & gentle parts, and the prosaic for inferior
parts: all are necessary to each other. Poetry Fetter'd Fetters the Human Race!
Nations are Destroy'd or Flourish in proportion as Their Poetry, Painting, and
Music are Destroy'd or Flourish! The Primeval State of Man was Wisdom,
Art, and Science!'

The greater number of the Prophetic Books were produced by the method
of relief engraving which Blake first employed in the *Songs of Innocence*. The
labour of this must have been very great, and probably for this reason in two
works, *The Book of Los* and *Ahania*, both published in 1795, the artist appears
to have resorted to the simpler process of ordinary etching. The effect, however,
is less grand, and in Blake's next books, *Milton* and *Jerusalem*, he reverted to
his original method. In the works engraved in relief, pictorial design plays
an increasingly prominent part, ceasing to be mere illustration as in the
Songs of Innocence, and developing into a species of secondary symbolism,
complementary to and scarcely less important than the text itself.

A few of these engraved Prophetic Books are known to us by two or
three examples only, while one at least would appear to have been lost or
destroyed. This is the 'work called *Outhoon*,' included in a list of books by
Blake, offered for sale by his widow to a Mr. Ferguson (Gil. ii. 262). No copy
is known to exist.

Other of the Visionary Writings were never engraved. Two of these,
Tiriel and *The Four Zoas*, survive in MS.; but by far the greater number
were destroyed, on religious grounds, by Frederick Tatham, an 'Angel' of
the Irvingite church, into whose hands they passed after the death of Mrs.
Blake. A MS. attributed to Blake, forming part of the Lakelands Library
of Mr. W. H. Crawford, was sold at Sotheby's in March, 1891. This MS.,
which was purchased by Mr. Quaritch, was catalogued—'Blake (W.) Angels
and Devils, autograph manuscript, containing poems, inscriptions to the 7
sections, and 34 original drawings by this celebrated artist, neatly mounted
on cartridge paper, cf. 4to.' I am informed by Mr. Quaritch that the MS. was
proved to be not by Blake; it was put up again at Sotheby's, and resold for
a small sum.

Few of Blake's editors have endeavoured to grapple with the difficulties
of the Prophetic Books. In the absence, indeed, of any adequate apparatus
for the study of his text, notably through the want of legible and properly
indexed reprints, and of a concordance displaying in chronological

sequence the names, words, and phrases symbolically used, any attempt at interpretation must necessarily be of a somewhat tentative character. An initial step towards supplying the former want has been taken by Messrs. Russell and Maclagan, who print *Jerusalem* with a brief introduction, and an index which, however, is too incomplete to be of any real utility. In the exegetical field the only important names are those of Swinburne and Messrs. Ellis and Yeats. Swinburne's *Critical Essay* (1868) still remains the greatest and most readable introduction to the Prophetic Books. The latter editors, in their three-volume edition of Blake, devote much space to their theory of his symbolic system, and paraphrased commentaries of the different books. The value of their work, in many ways helpful and suggestive, is somewhat lessened by the omission of references to the passages upon which their conclusions are based, and by the introduction of private opinions not drawn from Blake's writings.

In the following list of the Prophetic Books the term is interpreted in its broader sense to include some of the earlier writings in which the mythological element is not very prominent. I append also, under the heading Dogmatic Writings, descriptions of two small early works, both entitled *There is no Natural Religion*, and two of the so called 'Sibylline Leaves.' The former consist of a series of propositions couched in purely abstract terms, the latter being small leaflets treating of art and classic poetry. Strictly speaking, as my introduction and footnotes to that poem show, 'The Keys of the Gates,' a sequel to *The Gates of Paradise*, should also be accounted one of the Prophetic Books.

> —John Sampson, *The Poetical Works
> of William Blake. A New and Verbatim
> Text from the Manuscript Engraved and
> Letterpress Originals, with variorum
> readings and bibliographical notes and
> prefaces*, Oxford: Clarendon Press, 1905

G.K. Chesterton (1910)

The following reflections on Blake's *Songs of Innocence and Experience* are typical of many early readings, which saw the apparent innocence of the poems' narrator as a reflection of Blake's own youthful exuberance.

To the same primary period of his life, boyish, romantic, and untouched, belongs the publication of his first and most famous books, "Songs of

Innocence and Experience." These poems are the most natural and juvenile things Blake ever wrote. Yet they are startlingly old and unnatural poems for so young and natural a man. They have the quality already described—a matured and massive supernaturalism. If there is anything in the book extraordinary to the reader it is clearly quite ordinary to the writer. It is characteristic of him that he could write quite perfect poetry, a lyric entirely classic. No Elizabethan or Augustan could have moved with a lighter precision than—

"O sunflower, weary of time,
That countest the steps of the sun."

But it is also characteristic of him that he could and would put into an otherwise good poem lines like—

"And modest Dame Lurch, who is always at church,
Would not have bandy children, nor fasting nor birch";

lines that have no sense at all and no connection with the poem whatever. There is a stronger and simpler case of contrast. There is the quiet and beautiful stanza in which Blake first described the emotions of the nurse, the spiritual mother of many children.

"When the voices of children are heard in the vale,
    And laughter is heard on the hill,
My heart is at rest within my breast
    And everything else is still."

And here is the equally quiet verse which William Blake afterwards wrote down, equally calmly—

"When the laughter of children is heard on the hill,
And whisperings are in the dale,
The days of my youth rise fresh in my mind,
My face turns green and pale."

That last monstrous line is typical. He would mention with as easy an emphasis that a woman's face turned green as that the fields were green when she looked at them.

—G.K. Chesterton, *William Blake*,
London: Duckworth & Co; New York:
E. P. Dutton & Co., 1910

D.J. Sloss and J.P.R. Wallis "America," "Europe," "The Book of Los," and "Milton" (1926)

The following extracts originally appeared as prefatory notes in an anthology of Blake's Prophetic Books, edited by Sloss and Wallis in 1926. The anthology was initially intended as a supplement to John Sampson's *The Poetical Works of William Blake* (1905), which offered the first truly scholarly edition of the lyrical poems, but it was delayed for two decades by the difficulty of the work and World War I. In the end, it was worth the wait: Sloss and Wallis produced a definitive edition, and their editing principles still set the standard (a 1978 edition of *The Four Zoas*, for instance, follows their precedent in putting one of the seventh Nights in an appendix). The Prophetic Books were still very little read in the 1920s—and approached with trepidation. The editors' careful entry-level synopses of each text were therefore invaluable in helping readers come to terms with the bare bones of the texts. These introductions also give detailed information about the material quantities of Blake's original texts, useful in the absence of facsimile editions.

⸻ ⸻ ⸻

AMERICA

INTRODUCTORY NOTE

Collation: 'frontispiece and title-page 1 plate each, 'Preludium' 2 plates, 'A prophecy' 14 plates; 18 plates relief engraving, about 9-1/4 x 6-5/8 inches' (Clar. Press, p. 334).

America is a fuller and less rhapsodic treatment of the theme of the *Song of Liberty*. Blake's purpose is to define the forces made manifest in the American Revolution, and to show the significance of that event in the spiritual history of man. He sees in the conflict between the English Government and the Colonies the commencement of the final struggle between the primal 'Contraries', Restraint and Passion or Desire, between 'the passive that obeys Reason' and 'the active springing from Energy' (M. H. H., p. 3). As elsewhere throughout the Lambeth books, these 'Contraries' are symbolized by Urizen and Orc, though in *America* the former does not appear till the close of the story, when his vice-regents have been compelled to give way before the forces of revolt. Up to this point the repressive 'religion' of Urizen operates through 'Albion's Angel', identified with the King of England (l. 29), 'the Guardian Prince of Albion'. It maybe mentioned in passing that here, as in the

Marriage, 'Angel' is used ironically to denote acceptance of the normal moral, civil, and religious codes.

Opposed to these are 'the souls of warlike men', Washington, Franklin, Paine, and others of the revolutionary leaders. They are roused by the quickening fires of Orc, who is for Blake the Liberator of mankind, but to the party of priest and king he is the 'Blasphemous Demon, Antichrist, hater of Dignities, Lover of wild rebellion and transgresser of God's Law' (ll. 56–57). In the conflict that ensues, the 'red flames' of Orc contend with the plagues and blighting winds of Urizen, and triumph over them. Then the spirit of revolt passes eastward over the Atlantic—here, as later, the symbol of the floods of error that 'poured in deluge over the earth-born man'—and reanimates the spiritually enfeebled, till

> They feel the nerves of youth renew, and desires of ancient times
> Over their pale limbs, as a vine when the tender grape appears.

But the time for the emancipation of Europe is not yet. By a supreme effort of the forces of repression, among whom Urizen descends in person, the incipient tendency to rebellion is crushed, and for twelve years 'Angels and weak men' tyrannize over the 'strong'. At the end of this period the unrest in France, Spain, and Italy presages for Blake the final overthrow of all forms of restraint.

From this brief summary it appears that in Blake's view political emancipation was but one, and not the greatest result of the American Revolution. Not the tyranny of the monarchical government alone, but that of all creeds and conventions was to end when men should rise and will their own freedom. Moreover, failure on the part of the colonists would have involved the loss of that undefined portion of truth represented symbolically by America.

> Then had America been lost, o'erwhelm'd by the Atlantic,
> And Earth had lost another portion of the infinite. (ll. 174–175)

Here too, as in the *Visions of the Daughters of Albion*, the perfect existence consists in the complete liberty of man to embody his impulses in act. Every attempt to interfere with this right is a violation of the eternal order, and a root of spiritual corruption. Lines 37–51 and 59–75 state Blake's view of this matter fully and unequivocally.

In an Appendix to the present text of *America* are printed what would seem to be portions of an earlier version of the Prophecy. The new matter consists of three pages, apparently displaced in the complete copies by plates

3, 4, and 12: a fourth, identical with plate 13, is not reprinted: for convenience of reference they are hereafter referred to as pp. 3*, 4*, 12*, 13* respectively. They occupy both sides of two sheets, bound up, along with other plates from the Prophetic Books and elsewhere, with a manuscript copy of Cunningham's *Life of Blake* now in the possession of Mr. B. B. Macgeorge of Glasgow. Printed by the familiar method of relief engraving and uncoloured, they may perhaps be proof sheets which Blake revised and altered, and finally re-engraved. Moreover, p. 12* has been worked over once or twice in pencil, and finally cancelled by a line drawn vertically through the middle of the text.

An examination of the symbolism of these pages seems to show that they are earlier than the corresponding pages in the complete work. One of the most constant features of the symbolism of the Lambeth books from *America* onwards is the association of the imagery of fire and flame with the spirit of ardent passion and desire, which is Orc, while the mythical embodiments of the contrary forces of moral and political tyranny, e.g. Urizen and Albion's Angel, are represented as cold demons of cloud and mist. We find, however, that in the pages under notice this distinction is not observed, but that in plate 3 in the complete work, and still more in the pencilled corrections on p. 12*, Blake sets himself so to alter his text as to bring it into line in this respect with the symbolism that characterizes the Lambeth books as a whole. Thus on p. 3*, l. 14, Albion's Angel, a spirit of error, is described as the 'fiery prince'; in the parallel passage on P. 3 Blake alters the phrase to 'wrathful prince'. The significance of the change from 'fierce' (p. 3*, l. 16) to 'red' meteors (p. 3, l. 16) is less certain, but there can be little doubt about the changes made on p. 12*. All the alterations are connected more or less directly with Albion's Angel. In l. 5 'flames' is altered to 'damp mists', 'shining limbs' (l. 6) to 'aged limbs', 'gleam' (l. 7) to 'cold', 'fires' (l. 9) rather awkwardly to 'chill and heavy flames' (l. 13) to 'clouds', 'ardors' (l. 15) to 'clangors', 'glowing' (l. 17) to 'mustering', and 'like a King' (l. 25) to 'like an aged King'. These changes seem clearly to prove that these pages belong to a period when Blake's symbolism was not as definitely established as it was when he made the perfected copies of *America*.

Further, on p. 3*, l. 4, the list of revolutionary leaders is given in this order: 'Washington, Hancock, Paine and Warren, Gates, Franklin and Green.' On p. 3 the names of Franklin and Hancock are transposed. This alteration could not have been made for metrical reasons; the run of the line remains unchanged. The only reason would seem to have been to give the more famous name a more prominent position; and this would be more likely to be done in the later than in the earlier version. Moreover, pp. 4*

and 12* describe the session of the King and his Council at such length as to impede the course, and obscure the main theme of the Prophecy, the spiritual significance of the revolt of the colonies; and the description comes nearer than anything else in Blake to passages in *The French Revolution* (1791). But in the corresponding pages 4 and 12 this prolixity is considerably reduced, the main thread of the argument is freed from distracting episodes, and the gist of the matter restated more symbolically. In fact, Blake in these pages seems to be treating the text of a Prophetic Book precisely as, at about the same time, he was treating poems like *To My Mirtle* in the Rossetti MS. (Clar. Press, pp. 166–167).

But the matter of what we may now call the rejected pp. 4* and 12* was afterwards utilized. The similarity of their text with that of *Europe*, ll. 60–126, would seem to suggest that Blake worked their substance into the body of the later Prophecy, inserting it between the first and the second sections of Enitharmon's song, perhaps the most remarkable parallel between the two works being the reference to the collapse of the roof of the Council Chamber upon the heads of those sitting within (p. 4*, ll. 20–24; *Europe*, ll. 63–67). Later still, Blake introduced passages reminiscent of these rejected pages into Nights VI and VII of *The Four Zoas*.

The existence of these two leaves is of interest by reason of the light they throw upon Blake's painstaking methods in producing his Prophetic Books, works which he rarely sold and which very few could have read. That he continually worked over his writings in their manuscript stage has been known ever since the publication of Sampson's edition of the Lyrical Poems; but now it is clear that he also undertook the much more arduous labour of re-engraving plates of text that for any reason did not satisfy him. These leaves also strengthen the theory that what are known as the extra pages in the copy of *Milton* belonging to the New York Public Library are rejected portions of an earlier and perhaps longer version of that poem which Blake, in part at least, re-engraved as he re-engraved plates 3, 4, and 12 of *America*.

The interest of *America* lies not in its range of ideas, as no new idea of value is developed, nor can it compare for vigour and quickness of mind with the *Marriage*. But perhaps better even than *The French Revolution* it shows how the outlines of events and personalities are modified and their aspects transformed as they were merged into the substance of Blake's dreams. As a foot-note to history its value is inconsiderable, but for the light it sheds on the workings of the mind of the mystic it is perhaps first among the non-lyrical works.

The following lines seem to have formed at one time part of *America*. Mr. A. G. B. Russell, who discovered them, gives them on p. 69 of his *Engravings of William Blake*.

> As when a dream of Thiralatha flies the midnight hour,
> In vain the dreamer grasps the joyous images, they fly,
> Seen in obscured traces in the Vale of Leutha; So
> The British Colonies beneath the woful Princes fade.

> And so the Princes fade from earth, scarce seen by souls of men,
> But tho' obscured, this is the form of the Angelic land.

The fragment cannot be related to *America* as it stands, nor is any symbolic or other value apparent in it.

EUROPE

INTRODUCTORY NOTE

Collation (B.M. copy): title 1 plate, Preludium 2 plates, text 11 plates, two full-page designs (pp. 6 and 7) = 16 plates, relief engravings, about 9-1/4 x 6-1/2 inches.[1]

The poem that we regard as a rejected Preludium to *Europe* is here printed in an appendix. That by which it was replaced has already been discussed in connexion with the cognate documents, the *America* Preludium and the *Song of Liberty*, in the Introductory Note to the latter work.

The 'Prophecy' itself has affinity with the other writings that bear the names of the continents, *America*, and the two parts of *The Song of Los*, *Africa*, and *Asia*. Its title 'Europe', used almost constantly in the later works to denote the state of subjection to the delusions of the normal metaphysic and ethic, has here in addition a particular reference to the social and political conditions that preceded the French Revolution. The work contains several very difficult passages. One of these is in the first fifty lines. It is possible that a vague suggestion of Milton's *Nativity Ode* in the rhythm and phraseology of the opening stanzas may point to the identity of the 'secret child' (l. 2), and Jesus. If this conjecture holds, the entire passage can be read as a part of Blake's earlier criticism of Christianity, for which the chief documents are other parts of *Europe* and ll. 20–27 of *Africa*. The same purpose would seem to underlie the lines (9–14) that tell how Urthona—an infrequent and obscure symbol in the early books—takes his rest, while Urizen, 'the primeval Priest', freed from his chains, appears in the north, the quarters to which the eternals banished him and his 'religion'. This apparently expresses Blake's opinion that, with the triumph of Christianity, the spiritual energy associated clearly enough in the later books, but not so clearly here, with Urthona becomes dormant, while its contrary, 'the passive that obeys reason', once more asserts itself. These lines are put into the mouth of Los, and it may prevent confusion to notice here that he and Urthona are nowhere related in the Lambeth books as they are in the later writings. Indeed, Blake's conception of Los in the early writings is difficult to determine. This may be due, in great measure, to the absence at this point of any idea of a divine purpose of regeneration, such as makes Los the central figure of the longer 'prophetic' books, from *The Four Zoas* to *Jerusalem*. In the present book it is not even possible to connect with any certainty the activities of Los and the emancipatory influence of Orc, though in the myth they are represented as father and son. An instance of what appears to be the distance between the early and later presentations of Los occurs in the lines following those already referred to. Los calls his children and bids them seize 'all the spirits of life' and bind 'their warbling joys' and 'all the nourishing sweets of earth' to the strings of their harps to give bliss to eternals—a presentation of the 'eternal prophet' and of the 'Eternals' that recalls the Epicurean idea of the nature of the gods (cp. ll. 19–23). Finally he commands Orc to rise in his chains, to be crowned, as in mockery, with vine leaves. So commences 'the Night of Enitharmon's joy', the triumph of the moral law. She summons her children by pairs, male and female, to aid her in her work of deluding man, bidding them

> Go, tell the human race that Woman's love is Sin;
> That an Eternal life awaits the worms of sixty winters,
> In an allegorical abode where existence hath never come. (ll. 37–39)

Her influence is represented as extending over the eighteen hundred years of the Christian dispensation, the duration of her 'sleep', the 'female dream', during which the life of man is an unreal existence beneath the 'Shadows of a woman', the delusion of sense-perception and repressive morality.

After briefly indicating this valuation of Christianity, the 'Prophecy' turns abruptly to the social and political conditions prevailing over Europe at the close of the eighteenth century. The action becomes centred in Britain, 'o'er-clouded by the terrors of struggling times' (l. 70), the first stirrings of the revolutionary spirit in the Old World. The symbols in this part of *Europe* are almost identical with those of America. On the side of repression is 'Albion's

Guardian', with his ministers, called in irony his 'Angels': against these, on the side of revolt, is Orc. The former derive their authority from Urizen, whose 'station', the 'Stone of night', is so described as to identify it with the human skull. The statement that it forms the 'southern porch' to the 'serpent temple' (l. 91)—as it were the citadel or sanctuary of the mundane error arising from reason and sense-perception—recalls the similar image in *The Human Abstract* (S. E., Clar. Press, p. 134), when the 'Tree of Moral Virtue', equivalent in its symbolic content to the 'serpent temple', is said to grow 'in the Human brain'. By reason of his exclusive dependence upon 'the natural organs of sense',

> man became an Angel,
> Heaven a mighty circle turning, God a tyrant crown'd. (ll. 92–93)

The Urizenic 'religion' triumphs in 'the night of Enitharmon':

> The youth of England, hid in gloom, curse the pain'd heavens, compell'd
> Into the deadly night to see the form of Albion's Angel.
> Their parents brought them forth, & aged ignorance preaches canting.
>
> Every house is a den, every man bound,
>
>   The shadows are fill'd
> With spectres, and the windows wove over with curses of iron
> Over the doors 'Thou shalt not' & over the chimneys 'Fear' is written.
> With bands of iron round their necks fasten'd into the walls
> The citizens;—in leaden gyves the inhabitants of suburbs,
> Walk heavy: soft and bent are the bones of villagers. (ll. 132–137)

But the tyranny that priest and lung exercise as Urizen's ministers is threatened by the increasing influence of the rebel Orc. There seems to be an allusion in ll. 120–130 to a popular rising in London, which, though successful at first, was ultimately repressed by the exercise of constitutional authority. It is perhaps worthy of passing notice, in connexion with what has been said above of the nature of Los in these early books, that two of his sons, Rintrah and Palambron, are represented as overwhelming this premature attempt to achieve freedom. Yet in spite of temporary repulse, the revolutionary spirit spreads in the quickening fires of Orc.

The concluding portion of the boot: is also the most difficult. Alarmed at the growing power of Orc, Albion's Angel

> Siez'd in horror and torment
>
> The Trump of the last doom: but he could not blow the iron tube.
>
> Thrice he assay'd presumptuous to awake the dead to judgment. (ll.
>   143–145)

Then

> A mighty Spirit leap'd from the land of Albion,
>
> Nam'd Newton: he siez'd the Trump & blow'd the enormous blast.
>
> Yellow as leaves of Autumn the myriads of Angelic hosts
>
> Fell thro' the wintry skies seeking their graves,
>
> Rattling their hollow bones in howling and lamentation. (ll. 146–150)

Nothing can be added to what has already been said of this passage in the General Introduction. What follows is equally obscure, and the utmost that can be attempted is to indicate the main points of the story. The sounding of the trumpet and the falling of the Angelic myriads evidently marks the beginning of the end of the old moral law. Yet this fact seems to be hidden from Enitharmon, who wakes from her sleep, not knowing that she had slept eighteen hundred years (ll. 151–153). She resumes her song as if it had suffered no interruption, and calls the remainder of her sons and daughters to her aid. Last of all she summons Orc, to smile upon her children and give her 'mountains joy of his red light' (ll. 190–192). This would seem to symbolize Blake's opinion that the ultimate purpose of the forces of empiricism and repressive morality symbolized by Enitharmon is to bring even passion and desire, their contraries, to minister to them. But again difficulty arises because Blake's statement of the matter makes it impossible to discover what response Enitharmon's children make to her call (ll. 193–195). Ultimately, however, the dawn appears; the morning of universal liberty begins to break. Enitharmon weeps, as Urizen does when, in the close of Asia, the Grave quickens beneath the fires of Orc. Apparently the final conflict between the opposed forces of Law and individual freedom is about to begin. Orc descends into France, the terrible agents of revolution begin their work, so that 'Enitharmon groans and cries in anguish and dismay'. The book closes with the descent of Los and his sons to 'the strife of blood'. Unfortunately his part in what is to follow, whether for or against Orc, is not discernible.

Note

1. In this copy quotations from the poets, from Shakespeare and Milton to Mrs. Ann Radcliffe, apposite to Blake's designs, have been written in a

hand very like that in the note signed 'F. Tatham' which is to be seen on the drawing in the Print-room, *Blake's Drawings*, vol. i (1874, 12.12.148), and in that signed 'Fred. Tatham' on the sheet on which are printed Blake's engravings of Venus, Hermes and the Laocoön group.

THE BOOK OF LOS

INTRODUCTORY NOTE

Collation: frontispiece and title-page, 1 plate each; 'Los', 3 plates; 5 plates, etched text.

Like *The Book of Ahania*, the present work is more an apparent than a real supplement to the myth of *The Book of Urizen*. Its first five stanzas, etched in a smaller hand than the body of the poem, seem to be in the nature of a Preludium, such as is found in the other books of this period. The theme is a criticism of conventional morality on the familiar lines, setting it over against what Blake exalted as the antinomianism of the 'times remote' before man fell.

The main myth opens at that point in the history of Urizen when the Eternals depute Los to watch over him, lest he should again attempt to establish his own power (B. U., chap. ii). Here Los has something of the attributes of Fuzon or of Orc: he is the spirit whose fiery energy is set against the deadening influence of the 'primeval Priest' and his 'Religion'. This dualism of energy and restraint is maintained throughout *The Book of Los*: the living 'flames of desire', eternal, intelligent, organized, are contrasted with the coldness, darkness and 'obstruction' of Urizen, and the fierce raging rivers of fire of the first are set against the petrific 'solid' of the other (chap. i, l. 54). A similar opposition is seen when in the wild deep into which Los falls there appear two elements: one, the baser, which is called the 'heavy', and sinks; the other, of apparently superior value, the 'thin', which tends towards the fires of the eternals (chap. iii).

At first the forces of restraint are represented as triumphing; for they shut in the 'clear expanding senses' of the Eternal Prophet, Los, obscuring his perceptions of eternity. But when 'impatience could no longer bear the hard bondage' (chap. ii, ll. 5–6), the 'Prophetic wrath, struggling for vent', burst its prison. From this point difficulties increase for the interpreter. In the first place, Los's breaking away from Urizen's restrictions is not, as might have been expected, the definite beginning of a higher condition of being. On the contrary, Los begins to fall into the 'horrid vacuity' of boundless error, and, stranger still, seems to become identified with 'the falling Mind', an aspect of the symbol not paralleled elsewhere, though it may be taken as affording some ground for the interpretation of part of this early myth in terms of psychology.

The 'falling Mind', after breaking from its prison, first manifests itself in wrath, which, subsiding, is succeeded by 'contemplative thought'. 'Contemplative thought' synchronizes with a modification in existence, of which the symbolic statement is that Los's downward fall becomes oblique. The next stage sees the undefined 'Human', apparently synonymous with Los, 'organized' into 'finite flexible organs', the beginnings of physical sensation. Thus the mind undergoes change until it is so far adapted to its new environment as to be able to traverse at will the 'abyss' or horrid vacuity of error. In this there may be implied the principle that objects of sense-perception have no inherent validity, being but illusions created by the physical organs supervening upon and distorting the pure visions of the immortal mind. But it is impossible to feel certainty as to whether Blake also intended that the changes in the falling Los are to be taken as indicating a regenerative purpose. Reading this episode in the light of the books of the post-Lambeth period, one can discern therein something that looks like an intention to attribute a value to the phenomena succeeding Los's fall; but there is not evidence in the Lambeth books themselves to establish this interpretation.

In the third chapter the processes of change continue. First the lungs appear, and from them is developed a 'fibrous form' wherein Los exists, as it were a 'polypus' in 'a vast world of waters'. All these expressions appear in the post-Lambeth books in association with the symbols of error, though it would be dangerous to say that the later meaning is intended here. What is perhaps the most decisive indication that this continual modification of the state of the fallen Los marks an improvement of spiritual conditions, is that at this point, by a definite act and for the first time since Urizen's succession, Los makes distinction between the two elements in the new world, between the 'heavy' which is of Urizen, and the 'thin' that has affinity with the quickening fires of eternals. Further, the 'thin' becomes the pure medium through which Light first manifests itself. At the same time, there appears in opposition to the Light, the Backbone of Urizen, an obscure expression, except in so far as it may be related to the commoner serpent symbol (see Index, *Serpent*).

The continuation of the conflict between the adverse powers Los and Urizen is full of doubtful points. Los concentrates his energies into 'a form of strength' and enters upon his characteristic labours at the furnaces and anvil. First he forms the light into an Orb, the sun (chap. iv, l. 35), a 'glowing illusion'. To this he binds the 'spine of Urizen', whose 'Brain' and 'Heart' ultimately become the sources of four rivers that obscure the 'Orb of fire' and so give rise to the 'Human Illusion'. There is evidently an intention in the contrasting of Los's 'glowing Illusion' and the 'Human Illusion' that is due to Urizen's influence. Neither represents a perfect vision, but that of Los is nearer to truth than Urizen's, which may perhaps be comparable with the body of error whose root is in the 'Human Brain' (cp. S. E., Clar. Press, p. 134, 'The Human Abstract').

Such is a brief summary of a book which it is difficult to epitomize and impossible to interpret. Its symbolism would seem to be, in its details, purely tentative, for Blake nowhere repeats its most characteristic features in any recognizable form.

MILTON

Milton is the first of the Prophetic Books belonging entirely to the later period of Blake's life. Yet though it was written under the inspiration of his maturer faith, when, out of great spiritual perturbation he had 'emerged into the light of the day', certain elements of his earlier symbolism occasionally appear in modified forms. There is, however, somewhat less of the confusion of styles that constitutes the peculiar difficulty of *The Four Zoas*, and in spite of considerable incoherences, chiefly in the first pages, the poem comes nearer to achieving unity than any other of Blake's longer writings. It contains many passages that read like transcripts from actual visionary experience, and shows how confidently Blake believed that he was the divinely appointed agent to expose and annihilate the fallacies of materialism in life and art. Further, the style is comparatively simple and direct; the incidents are varied and move rapidly, and there is something also of the re-awakened sense of wonder and delight in nature that marks his first letters from Felpham. For all these reasons, as well as on account of its more manageable bulk, *Milton* is more easily readable than *Jerusalem*.

Though the title-pages of both *Milton* and *Jerusalem* are dated 1804, an examination of the symbolism proves conclusively that the former is, as a whole, the earlier work. In the first place, the personages Orc and Urizen, the great protagonists of the Lambeth books, are of more importance in the development of the myths of *Milton* than of *Jerusalem*. Again in *Milton* and *The Four Zoas*, Nights VII and VIII, the chief 'feminine' symbols are Rahab and Tirzah. Vala is rarely mentioned, while the Daughters of Albion, who appear so constantly with her in *Jerusalem*, have no place at all.[1] So again Los is represented in *Milton* rather after the manner of the earlier works than of *Jerusalem*: his mythical functions are more developed and much more clearly defined in the last-named work. Finally, in the use of the curious topographical symbolism that is the mark of Blake's latest manner, *Milton*, except in p. 4, a later addition, and in p. 25 (also a late page, see p. 25, ll. 48–50 *note*), is clearly intermediate between *The Four Zoas* and *Jerusalem*.

It is not unlikely that an earlier and more extended form of *Milton* than the present is the poem referred to in Blake's letters of the years 1803–1805. He speaks of 'an immense number of verses on one grand theme, similar to Homer's *Iliad* or Milton's *Paradise Lost* the persons and machinery entirely new to the inhabitants of earth (some of the persons excepted)'. The phrase in parenthesis may refer to the presence of such names as Satan, Milton, Wesley, and Whitefield; or more probably the whole passage may merely state the fact that the myth of *Milton* is constructed on a different basis from that of the Lambeth books, and that in the main the personages are new. Again he says that this long poem is descriptive of the 'spiritual acts of [his] three years' slumber on the banks of ocean', and that he will soon publish it. *Milton* alone of Blake's works deals directly with his life at Felpham. Moreover, in the early part of these years he was engaged in engraving plates, after designs by Romney, Flaxman and himself, for Hayley's edition of Milton's poems (R., p. 120), and it may well be that this circumstance caused him to formulate the characteristic criticism of the theodicy of *Paradise Lost* that is the distinguishing feature of the present poem. But it is very unlikely that Blake would have spoken of the work as it now stands as containing an immense number of verses. There is, however, reason to think that a longer work was contemplated when the title-page was engraved in 1804. The title-page of the New York Public Library copy, reproduced as frontispiece to volume I of the present edition, reads: 'a Poem in 12 Books'. Indeed Blake seems to have been at pains to give special distinctness to the '1', though there are but two Books in all known copies of the poem. Doubtless the twelve was suggested by the number of the Books in *Paradise Lost*, just as the nine Nights of *The Four Zoas* (1797) are reminiscent of the Nine Nights of Young's *Night Thoughts*, for which Blake was making drawings in 1796 and 1797. But other evidence of a discarded purpose to compose a longer poem seems to be implicit in the supernumerary pages and in the Satan-Palamabron myth.

The extra pages, here printed as an appendix to *Milton*, are numbered 2, 3, 5, 8*, 17, and 32*. Of these, pages 2, 3 and 32* would seem on internal evidence to be later than the main body of the poem, and demand separate treatment. But the remainder show a comparatively early type of symbolism;

p. 2 is in part an almost verbatim repetition of the binding of Urizen (cp. B. U., chap. iv and F. Z. iv), and pp. 8* and 17 treat mainly of Orc and the Shadowy Female. In the body of the poem, however, the Shadowy Female has no place, and the other personage appears only in passages that cannot easily be reconciled with their contexts. The most striking of these is the 'old Prophecy in Eden', to the effect that

> Milton of the Land of Albion should up ascend
> Forwards from Ulro, from the Vale of Felpham, and set free
> Orc from the Chain of Jealousy. (M. 18. 59–61.)

These lines define the task which, according to the first intention, the reincarnate Milton was to perform; but in the work as it stands no such purpose is pursued. He comes, in fact, to annihilate his own 'self-hood', that is, to give example of the Divine law of brotherhood and self-sacrifice, and, in the person of Blake, to wipe out the evil effects of the erroneous doctrine of *Paradise Lost* by a new gospel and anew art based on vision and the life of the spirit. In the ending of the extant poem Orc is not mentioned. Again, the episode of Milton's wrestling with Urizen (M. 16. 36–17. 14), though referred to later (M. 41. 53–45 and 42. 4–5), is not specifically concluded Urizen disappears from the myth. It would seem as if these passages and others having a similar reference were either overlooked in revision or were allowed to remain because to remove them would have involved the removal of passages which for some special significance, rather than for their contribution to the story, Blake wished to retain.

The conclusion that suggests itself after an examination of the symbolism of the supernumerary pages is that *Milton* was originally based upon a myth closely resembling that of the later written parts of *The Four Zoas*, i.e. Nights VII and VIII, wherein Urizen or Satan, with Rahab and Tirzah, who combine into the Shadowy Female, appeared as the sources and symbols of all forms of mundane error. To Blake's mind, *Paradise Lost* had been singularly persuasive in advocacy of these errors; wherefore Milton descended from the region of Truth and united with Blake to release the enslaved spirit of man, Orc in the 'Chains of Jealousy'. The poem would have contained, probably in modified forms, much of the myths of Urizen and of the Los of the later-written parts of *The Four Zoas*, with a developed myth of Orc (cp. extra p. 17 *passim*). Such a story, treated after the manner of *The Four Zoas* or of the existing *Milton*, could have been wrought by Blake into 'a long poem'.

The occasion of the revision of *Milton* is obscure. In part it may be hidden in the dim symbolism of the Satan-Palamabron myth, in part it may be connected with the development of the doctrine of Self-annihilation, which supersedes the cruder theory of regeneration embodied in the combat between Milton and Urizen over the enchained Orc. A curious record of this change exists in the inscription beneath the design on p. 15. The drawing would seem to have been intended to illustrate Milton's struggle with Urizen (p. 17. 4–14), but, in revising the poem, Blake gave a new interpretation to the group. The figure of the aged man, forced to his knees and seeking to sustain himself by his tables of the law, is no longer Urizen but Milton's Spectre, as is shown by the words engraved beneath it, 'To Annihilate the Self-hood of Deceit and False Forgiveness'. The fact that this is the only clear instance in the engraved books where a design is interpreted by Blake is in itself significant. Another indication is the manner in which the poem is hurried to a close. Its last five lines are a most summary *précis* of *The Four Zoas*, ix. Probably they are all that Blake retained of an earlier account of the Last Judgment on the lines and scale of Night IX, like it wholly catastrophic and a sequel to the Urizen-Orc myth. But in the recension of *Milton* the doctrine of regeneration through the individual discipline of 'Self-annihilation' displaces most of the elaborate processes of a universal 'Harvest and Vintage of the Nations'. This may explain the exceedingly brief reference to this theme in the present text of *Milton*. At the same time it illustrates Blake's reluctance lightly to cast aside his outworn symbols.

It is practically certain that the Satan-Palamabron myth did not form part of the original poem.[2] In the first place it is complete in itself and has no organic connexion with the rest of the work. Secondly, it is this episode, here embodied in the 'Bard's prophetic song', that is said to have impelled Milton to descend a second time to earth; but this explanation is not sustained, and confusion arises later when Milton's act is attributed to a different cause, the conduct of the dwellers of Ololon, 'those who Milton drove down into Ulro' (19. 16–17). Finally, its doctrine, inculcating the iniquity of moral judgement, and its mythical representation of Satan, are not easily reconciled with the fragments of the Orc myth that remain, or with the identification of Urizen and Satan.[3]

Attention may be called at this point to extra page 3, which, unlike the three noticed above, belongs to the comparatively late period of Blake's return from Felpham: it mentions South Molton Street, where he went to live on 6th October 1803 (cp. l. 21). Yet the presence of the refrain (ll. 20, 26: cp. M. 3–25: 5. 17 and 49, &c.) would seem to show that it was intended to form a part of the Bard's song, although it is now impossible to place it satisfactorily. The matter is still further complicated by the presence of p. 4, which, on the evidence of symbolism and decoration, clearly belongs to the same period as *Jerusalem*.[4] It is evident that pp. 3 and 5 were originally consecutive and that Blake adapted the end of the added p. 4 to the opening lines of p. 5. But there is an awkward hiatus between pp. 3 and 4. In the Beckford copy extra p. 3 does in some sort bridge the gap, but in the Windus copy the sequence is again deranged by the intrusion of extra p. 5.

The last of the extra pages, 32*, is also later in its symbolism than the main body of the poem, and once more it is difficult to discover to what end Blake composed it. The page is of the first importance, however, as a document dealing with the theory of States and the symbolic significance of Milton.

To sum up: the discrepancies in symbolism show that in its present form *Milton* is the outcome of vital if unharmonized modifications. Primarily Blake meant to express, in extended form, the concepts he had been and was still striving to engraft upon the original stock of *The Four Zoas*, particularly in Nights VII and VIII. But as he worked, his position was changing. The older mythopoeic machinery was disintegrating; and the newly revealed importance of the principles of individual responsibility was extending its hold upon his mind and imagination. The mechanical complexities of the myths of Urizen, Luvah, Orc and the Shadowy Female fell away, and their places were taken by a succession of exemplary episodes emphasizing the fundamental obligations to unconditional and unremitted abstinence from judgement, and especially from moral censure, and to perpetual self-discipline and spiritual purgation. The details, or much even of the main history of this reconstitution must remain obscure and debatable. It may or may not have involved a contraction from twelve books to two. But unless the remarkably consistent development traceable in Blake's symbolic writings, from *Thel* to *The Ghost of Abel*, is to be gainsaid or ignored, it is impossible to deny that *Milton* bears the signs of being the product of a period of transition only less critical and significant than that which disorganized *The Four Zoas*.

The two main episodes in *Milton* are the Satan-Palamabron myth and the descent of Milton the Awakener. The first is more than usually difficult and calls for treatment in detail. In the first place, it speaks of the three classes into which mankind is divided. The first division is the Dead, the Elect, or the 'Spectrous' class, identified with Satan, who joins to his commoner Blakean attributes the spirit of 'officious brotherhood', uninspired benevolence that imagines itself competent to control the spiritual labours of the visionary. The second class, the Redeemed, 'live in doubts and fears, perpetually tormented by the Elect' (M. 25–26) until they are redeemed by Mercy from Satan's Law (M. 9. 23). Finally, the Reprobate are they who 'never cease to Believe' (M. 25–35). Rintrah, the typical Reprobate, a demon of wrath, may stand for the convinced and uncompromising mystic, but the evidence is too scanty and equivocal to admit of certain interpretation of either this or that preceding class.

The opening part of the myth defines Satan's prime offence. He seeks to usurp Palamabron's function, to guide the 'Harrow of the Almighty'. Los, arbiter of this sphere of existence, inadvertently permits him to do so, while Palamabron takes charge of the Mills of Satan. As in the earlier Urizen-Luvah myth, confusion follows the interchange of tasks, and the matter is referred to the Eternals for judgement. From this point difficulties increase rapidly.

> . . . Palamabron appeal'd to all Eden and reciev'd
> Judgment; and Lo! it fell on Rintrah and his rage,
> Which now flam'd high & furious in Satan against Palamabron,
> Till it became a proverb in Eden: 'Satan is among the Reprobate'
> (M. 7–9)

Satan accuses Palamabron of ingratitude and malice, and, shutting himself off from the Divine Vision, declares himself sole God, whose power is founded upon Moral Law in 'a world of deeper Ulro' or error. Providence intervenes on behalf of Palamabron, 'the wrath falling on Rintrah' (M. 7. 8–42): for

> If the guilty should be condemn'd, he must be an Eternal Death
> And one must die for another throughout all Eternity. (M. 9. 17)

The incident would seem to be an illustration, exaggerated for the sake of emphasis, of the iniquity of the exercise of moral judgement and of the cruelty of the law of punishment for sin. The true ethic demands that the innocent suffer for the guilty, in order that the law of brotherhood and mutual forgiveness may be fulfilled. The point of view is interesting and characteristic, even in its neglect of logic.

Rintrah's conduct, here and later, is perplexing. A curious point is his apparent unwillingness, the absence of spontaneity in his act of self-sacrifice. He

> rear'd up walls of rocks, and pour'd rivers & moats
> Of fire round the walls; columns of fire guard around
> Between Satan and Palamabron in the terrible darkness
> And Satan, not having the Science of wrath, but only of pity,
> Rent them asunder; and wrath was left to wrath & pity to pity.

He sunk down, a dreadful Death, unlike the slumbers of Beulah.
(M. 7. 43)

In passages like this, Pity has a sinister connotation. It involves an assumption of superiority and a passing of judgement; it is a spiritual trespass, infringing the sanctity of the individuality. The will must not be bended: each must keep his proper function.

Up to this point, Blake's purpose would seem to be to correct what he considered the errors of *Paradise Lost*, and, by means of the Bard's divinely inspired song, 'to justify the Ways of God to Men'. For in the first place, Satan did not fall through ambition, nor was the first sin that of rebellion against the Creator of Man and this world whom Blake always regarded, after the Gnostic fashion, as a disobedient 'Angel of the Divine Presence'. Satan fell because of 'officious brotherhood' or unenlightened benevolence. It has been suggested that the allusions to Satan's 'soft dissimulation of friendship',

Seeming a brother, being a tyrant, even thinking himself a brother
While he is murdering the just (M. 5. 23)

and the frequent denunciation of 'corporeal friends' glance at Hayley, whose 'genteel ignorance and polite disapprobation' of visionary enthusiasm appear to have disturbed Blake's peace of mind at Felpham. It is possible to support this identification by reference to passages in the letters, and particularly in those to Thomas Butts. But complete certainty on this point can only come with a much fuller knowledge of the relations existing between Blake and Hayley than is at present attainable. Indeed it would seem that the false friendship complained of in the Satan-Palamabron myth has reference to something of much longer standing than his acquaintance with Hayley. For in the *Advertizement* (Ross. MS., p. 52) Blake writes: 'The manner in which my Character has been blasted these forty years, both as an Artist and a Man, may be seen particularly in a Sunday Paper called the *Examiner*. Publish'd in Beaufort Buildings; . . . & the manner in which I have routed out the nest of villains will be seen in a Poem concerning my Three years' Herculean labours at Felpham, which I will soon Publish. Secret Calumny & open Professions of Friendship are common enough all the world over, but have never been so good an occasion of Poetic Imagery. When a Base Man means to be your Enemy, he always begins with being your Friend.' From this passage it is arguable that Blake intended to pillory not Hayley, but certain unknown persons who, like the critics in the *Examiner*, sought to pervert his spiritual labours, and that too, apparently, under the guise of friendship. But whatever the origin of the myth, Blake's meaning in this part of it would seem to be that Satan's error was not that he rebelled against the God of this world, but that he obstructed the Holy Ghost, the Poetic Genius, in others.

The remainder of the myth is chiefly concerned with the Miltonic fallacy of supposing Satan to have been punished by Providence for his fault. Blake deliberately sets himself to controvert this view by representing Divine Mercy as active from the first, and by means of several agents, to protect Satan from punishment. One instance of this, the suffering of Rintrah for the sin of Satan, has already been noticed. Another is the devotion of Enitharmon, who creates a 'Space' to shield the erring spirit; and the Eternals 'ratify the kind decision', giving 'a Time to the Space, even six thousand years' (M. 11. 16).[5] This divinely appointed purpose of regeneration in temporal existence is itself a manifestation of Mercy and Forgiveness.

The contrast between the Miltonic and Blakean points of view is still greater in the lines that follow (ll. 17–27). Not only is the notion of punishment entirely absent, but the 'solemn Assembly' of Eternals elects seven spirits, Lucifer, Molech, Elohim, Shaddai, Pahad, Jehovah and Jesus, to guard the newly created Space and to give themselves to 'Eternal Death' for Satan's sake. In spite of the obscure statement, found also in the corresponding passage in *The Four Zoas* viii, that all save Jesus fail, Blake's intention is clearly enough to emphasize the doctrine that the ideal ethic consists the dwellers in or by Ololon refuse to acquiesce in the act of the seven, who, combining with the form of Milton into a 'Starry Eight', are driven by Ololon into the Ulro. The subsequent relation of the 'Seven' to the descended Milton is quite obscure, unless they can be regarded as affording him spiritual guidance.

Ololon is almost immediately enlightened as to the error of its action, which involves an exercise of moral judgement. This appears from the repentant cry: 'Is Virtue a Punisher? O No!' Uniting with the Divine family in Jesus, they descend through the chaos or Ulro that lies about Los's world of time and space. But they are compelled to combine into a female form, lest they destroy that 'Vegetative world' they come to save. The significance of this change is difficult to discover; it may, however, represent the substitution of a mediate for an immediate presentation of truth, lest the latter should prove too great and terrible for man's comprehension. Some such idea, in a different connexion though still associated with the symbolic use of the 'Female', occurs in the description of Beulah (M. 30. 21 *seq.*) and in the important passage on the 'Female' and 'Human' forms on the extra p. 17. But whatever the explanation, Ololon is seen by Blake, as he walks before his cottage in Felpham, as 'a Virgin of twelve years'. She questions him concerning Milton, who straightway appears before her and commands her to aid him in his struggle against his Selfhood, the Spectre Satan. At this point the opposites are definitely revealed, ranged one against another. The Miltonic Shadow, Satan, the symbol of the entire body of mundane error, faces Milton the Awakener, who is associated with Los, now unequivocally the symbol of Divine inspiration. Following an elaborate symbolic description of the first of these comes a wholly obscure association of Ololon with Milton's 'Sixfold Emanation', which is identified with the source of Deism (M. 42. 4–16: 43. 30–36). In the succeeding lines confusion is worse confounded:

> The Virgin (Ololon) divided Six-fold & with a shriek
> Dolorous that ran thro' all Creation, a Double Six-fold Wonder,
> Away from Ololon she divided, & fled into the depths
> Of Milton's Shadow as a Dove upon the stormy Sea.
> Then as a Moony Ark Ololon descended to Felpham's Vale
> In clouds of blood, in streams of gore, with dreadful thunderings,
> Into the Fires of Intellect that rejoic'd in Felpham's Vale
> Around the Starry Eight: with one accord the Starry Eight became
> One Man, Jesus the Saviour, wonderful; round his limbs
> The Clouds of Ololon folded as a Garment dippèd in blood,
> Written within & without in woven letters; & the Writing
> Is the Divine Revelation in the Litteral expression,
> A Garment of War: I (Blake) heard it nam'd the Woof of
>   Six Thousand Years. (M. 44. 3–15.)

Then the trumpet sounded for the Last Judgement, and Blake came out from his trance; his soul

> return'd into its mortal state
> To Resurrection & Judgment in the Vegetable Body.

The poem closes with the preparations for 'the Great Harvest & Vintage of the Nations'.

The general significance of Ololon remains dark, and perhaps necessarily so, since so much of it appears to be a record of Blake's own mystical experience. All that can be attempted in the way of exposition is to notice the points of contact with the body of Blake's more familiar symbolism, and to suggest with all diffidence a possible line of interpretation. The initial conflict of Ololon with the Starry Eight repeats the main doctrine of this poem, the iniquity of any attempt at moral judgement such as is implied in the expulsion of the Light. Incidentally it illustrates the curious conception of the possibility of error even among Eternals, and this again is brought into relation to the notion that the principles of continual forgiveness and self-sacrifice are fundamental in the supreme state of existence. It is also noteworthy that, as in the earlier *Book of Urizen*, some at least among the Eternals act without foreknowledge: the dwellers in Ololon do not know that in banishing the Eight they are fulfilling part of the divine purpose of regeneration (M. 19. 31–57). All this is very confusing and not easily to be reconciled with the commoner statement of ideal unity in the supreme state of existence, expressed symbolically as the appearance of the 'Eternals' or of 'all Eternity' as 'One Man, Jesus', the 'Divine Humanity' or as a 'Divine Family'.

What is perhaps the surest clue to the interpretation of Ololon is to be found in the last lines of the passage quoted above, wherein the Clouds of Ololon that, like Luvah's 'robes of blood', enfold Jesus are compared to a 'Garment' whereon is woven 'the Divine Revelation in the Litteral expression'. This expression, taken in association with the further identification of Ololon with the 'Woof of Six Thousand Years', suggests that the symbol represents dramatically the revelation within temporal existence of the divine scheme of regeneration: its error is made the means to ultimate salvation for man. She is the 'Moony Ark' of the promise, the vehicle of the providential purpose. Evidently there is significance in the statement that she enfolds the Starry Eight whom before she had driven forth: it is a symbolic act of self-abasement to serve others. Yet so complete an identification of Eternals with the errors of mortality is singular.

In conclusion, one further matter of some interest may be noticed here. Though Blake's doctrinal antagonism to 'Nature' continues throughout *Milton* and the later writings, there are passages (M. 25. 26–M. 26. 12) where a definite modification of his attitude is faintly discernible. Though the 'created' universe is the world of Satan, Blake is conscious that aspects of it are beautiful. He remembers too that it is the world of Los and Enitharmon, of divinely given Time and Space, the place of human salvation. Hence the beauty of the universe may have its place in the scheme of human regeneration. The 'constellations in the deep and wondrous Night', the 'gorgeous clothed flies that dance and sport in summer', the trees that 'thunder thro' the darksom Sky'

> Uttering prophesies & speaking instructive words to the sons
> Of men; These are the sons of Los, These the Visions of Eternity.
> But we see only as it were the hem of their garments
> When with our vegetable eyes we behold these wondrous Vistas.

This passage and others on p. 31 not only are evidence of the renewed sense of the beauty in Nature which quickens the book of *Milton*, but suggest a basis for a mediate vision of truth that associates Blake with others of the Romantic poets. But when the vehemence of prophecy returns upon him, he finds no place for it:, and denounces the 'imitation of Nature's Images' as destructive of Imagination and an obstacle to truth.

Catchwords, answering in every instance to the initial word of the following page, are found on pp. 9, 10, 14, 16, 18, 20, 24, 25, 27, 30. and 31.

Notes

1. The fact that the Daughters of Albion are named in F. Z. ii. 268 shows that Blake still turned to that work even after he had written *Milton*. Cp. F. Z. ii. 263, the symbolism of which can be matched only in *Jerusalem*.

2. Though the Satan-Palamabron myth in F. Z. viii. 357 *seq.* is later than the body of that Night, being written on an added page, it is earlier than the Milton version. It is rudimentary; its later reference to Blake's Felpham experiences is only faintly adumbrated in an added line (l. 380), and it has not yet developed the elaborate system of complementary episodes that emphasize the obligation to continual sacrifice of self for others: see General Introduction, pp. 67–69.

3. Extra p. 8*, 1–2.

4. M. 4. 26 repeats, with slight alteration, J. 70. 32, and also bears a similar drawing of a Druid monument, a very late symbol.

5. Cp. M. 23. 72:
   Time is the mercy of Eternity: without Time's swiftness
   Which is the swiftest of all things, all were eternal torment.

—D.J. Sloss and J.P.R. Wallis, eds.,
The Prophetic Writings of William Blake,
Oxford: Clarendon Press, 1926,
reprinted in 1957 and 1964

Max Plowman "Two Examples" (1927)

Max Plowman (1883–1941) is best remembered as a World War I poet, the author of *A Lap Full of Seed*, an anti-war polemic, *The Right to Life*, and *A Subaltern on the Somme*. He was also a Romantic Socialist and a devotee of Shelley and Blake.

In this essay, "Two Examples," Plowman uses two major Blake poems, *The Book of Thel* (1789) and *Visions of the Daughters of Albion* (1793), to illustrate his claim that Blake rewards attentive reading and "is worth all the understanding we can give him."

Plowman reads *The Book of Thel* alongside the *Songs of Innocence* and the *Songs of Experience*. Thel, he argues, stands between the states of innocence and experience, perplexed over the relationship between what Plowman calls "generative life" and spiritual life.

Visions of the Daughters of Albion is often read as a sequel to *The Book of Thel*, both books concerned—at least at the narrative level—with female sexuality. Plowman is not interested in either poem as an essay on women's sexual experience (we are instructed, for instance, not to read Bromion and Theotormon as rapist and possessive husband, but as "states through which the soul in its mortal journey is compelled to pass"); they are highly allegorical, he argues, representing evocations of the soul.

Plowman reads the two texts in seamless sequence, writing: "In *The Book of Thel* Blake shows us the soul trembling on the threshold of experience. In *Visions of the Daughters of Albion*, Thel, who has become Oothoon, crosses the threshold." Blake's works, Plowman writes, should be read sequentially and in full, because he is "a progressive writer and his effects are cumulative."

———〜〜〜— —〜〜〜— —〜〜〜—

When Pilate, proudly, cynically, or with humble curiosity, put before Jesus the famous question, "What is truth?" he did the human race the greatest service that it lay in his power to perform. He apotheosized the reasoning faculty. At a crucial moment he put the crucial question. For if Jesus had been able to give a purely reasonable and wholly adequate answer to that question, not only Christianity, but every religion in the world would have been rendered superfluous. If, by effort of reason, man could in any wise encompass truth, then at that moment the perceptive or imaginative faculty of mankind would fall into abeyance; the riddle of the universe would be solved and, incidentally, man would lose his reason: it would die of starvation.

Of course, Pilate had for the moment forgotten himself. He was the representative of Roman law and, as the emissary of Law, facts and not the truth were his business. But Pilate's furtive soul crept out and made an infantile gesture, and by that gesture revealed for ever the impassable chasm that divides facts from truth. The world has been profiting by his moment of forgetfulness ever since; and though the Law still asks its witnesses to deliver "the truth, the whole truth, and nothing but the truth," no one is fool enough to suppose the Law to mean what it says, for everyone knows that it merely requires the facts even when they belie the truth. At Pilate's historic moment the embodiment of truth stood before the embodiment of reason and the challenge to truth was merely that of making itself explicable. This Truth failed to do, with consequences that turned the world upside down. Never again has it been possible for a reasonable being to suppose that truth can be encompassed by facts, though Science has had moments of delusion.

But every man, just in so far as he is not a poet (using that word in its widest and truest sense) is a descendant of Pilate, for truth of some kind the mind must have, and if it is not the truth of poetry then it will be the truth according to law. Jesus acted directly, but spoke indirectly by parables. When we do not apprehend the truth as poets apprehend, we feel we should prefer that Jesus had spoken directly and acted—as we even come to think he acted—parabolically. Why couldn't he have said what he meant and told men their duty in plain terms, instead of wrapping it all up in these parables of good Samaritans and grains of mustard seed? Then we could have tabled the seven deadly sins and fixed a code of behaviour that would have ensured to us the good things all men desire of this life and any other. And many, thinking thus, have translated the poetry of religion into their own legal prose. In so doing they have cursed the world with another substitute for truth.

Truth cannot be circumscribed. When Jesus described himself as the truth, we do not suppose that his physical body became the residuum of truth, but rather that in him truth found a focal point: he was the translucent prism of light, the means whereby light was made humanly appreciable. He was not a vessel which blotted out the sun by absorption. Pilate wanted the sun to come within his orbit. He did not see that his orbit shut out the sun.

His error lies persistently in wait for the reader of Blake, because of the unique degree to which Blake relied upon direct apprehension. Blake did not even try to understand the universe by the ordinary processes of reasonable deduction; yet, if the analogy may be pardoned, as the actions of Jesus were intelligible to the people who benefited by them while his words were a perpetual offence, so below the realm of Blake the visionary lies the plane of Blake the profoundly reasonable man; and seizing with our reasoning faculties upon his apparent reasonableness we are often tempted to believe the rest of his work is merely a puzzle to which he failed to supply the clue. When a man could express himself as Intelligibly as Blake in the "Proverbs of Hell," what but madness and delusion could have made him the elusive creature of symbolism?

There speaks sound common sense—and Pilate. Poetry is not the vehicle of sound common sense, but is a means of creating images, which like the prism, ray out innumerable aspects of truth. Blake did not choose from an alternative to write in verse: he wrote in verse because poetry was the only adequate means of conveying what he perceived. It was not optioned to him whether he should set out his philosophy in reasonable terms, or whether he should leave us to deduce his philosophy when our apprehensions failed to pursue his in the quest of vision; and the fact that must be grasped is that apart from the poetry which contains his ideas, what he wrote is, and will for ever remain, utterly unintelligible. It must remain unintelligible for this, the profoundest of all reasons, that poetry is an image of truth, and philosophy a rational statement of intellectual ideas. The greater contains the less, but not *vice versa*. Our perception of truth is not dependent upon fact, but upon intensity of imagination, and what Blake ultimately demands, and so far has demanded in vain, is power of vision equal to his own. The poet appeals to his peers.

It is necessary to say this because a little knowledge of Blake usually leads us to believe the fallacy that one very fine day we shall discover, or some other person who has been equally enchanted by Blake, will discover, the key to Blake—a key that will open all the hidden doors and let us into the two-and-thirty palaces like children following a guide at Hampton Court. We come to think of Blake as a sort of glorious conundrum which one day will be wholly and finally solved. And I verily believe that publishers and critics are at this moment keenly on the look-out for the book which promises some such grand solution.

They will look in vain. There is no such key. Blake is bigger and better than that. He lived in a realm we only enter at the happiest moments of insight. He habitually used a tongue we only speak at rare moments of keenest understanding. He flew where we walk or are wheeled in perambulators. He fed on manna while we soon cry out for solid quails. He moved about at ease in worlds unrecognized and gazed upon the sun's face almost without a veil.

This is perceived by those who understand him a little. By others it is denied: the irrational Blake is for them a man lost in his own terminology; but, like Vala destroying her heart's desire, they "only see his feet like pillars of fire travelling through darkness and nonentity."

It is perhaps time to justify such professions of faith, and this can best be done by instancing discoveries that have opened magic casements, not indeed in the belief that perception is a quality whose enjoyment can be communicated, but simply in the hope of showing that Blake is worth all the understanding we can give him. I must apologize for so doing, because there is no duller occupation than watching an angler, though few recreations are more enjoyable than landing one's own fish. Moreover, in Blake's great rivers there is room for any number of rods, and, be it noted, there are no reaches reserved for scholarship. He who declares he has fished a spot empty shows himself to be using the wrong bait.

Let us take the title page of *The Book of Thel*. It is a happy example of Blake's power of concentration. On the left of the page, beneath a tall sapling, arched so deeply that it embraces the whole design, stands a young girl with a shepherd's crook in her left hand. Her features bear an expression of reproach, for she turns to watch two tiny figures that have just escaped from the opening flowers. The male figure leaps to embrace the female, who raises her arms in a gesture of surprise and alarm. Above them, the arch formed by the tree is full of birds and other figures expressive of innocent delight: the letters of the title themselves put forth leaves.

This picture epitomizes the exquisite narrative poem that follows. The girl is Thel. She is full grown; but anything that pertains to the shepherd's calling is for Blake a symbol of innocence; so Thel must be the representative of adolescent youth. This is confirmed by the sapling under which she stands. Blake invariably uses the tree as a symbol of generation, and whatever stands beneath a tree is under the shadow of mortal life. Thel's tree, though young, is sadly bent, and is thus an apt emblem of the disillusionment and melancholy that come to youth at first sight of experience. And the sight of Experience is what Thel has as she stands watching the nuptials of the flowers.

Thel has been thought to be "a spirit not yet generated" and her experience, the descent into this world. But apart from our reading of the illustration, the opening lines of the poem quickly make it clear that Thel is already in this world. 'Tis from her "mortal day" she seeks to fade. "Our spring" is the time of childhood, and the watery bow, the cloud, the reflection in a glass, the shadow, and the dream, to all of which she likens herself, are all images of mortality. Those who heard "the voice of Him that walketh in the garden in the Evening time," though still in Eden, were generated mortals. *The Book of Thel* stands between the *Songs of Innocence* and the *Songs of Experience*, and that is Thel's position; between the two states. Innocence stands on the threshold of Experience.

What is the meaning of Thel's motto?

Does the Eagle know what is in the pit,
Or wilt thou go ask the Mole?
Can Wisdom be put in a silver rod?
Or Love in a golden bowl?

The eagle has the eye that can gaze upon the sun: the mole is reputed to be blind and lives underground. A cross-reference to a passage in *Visions of the Daughters of* Albion gives us,

> Does not the Eagle scorn the earth and despise the treasures beneath?
> But the Mole knoweth what is there and the worm shall tell it thee.

So the contrast is evidently between what is above the earth and what is beneath it, and we know that everywhere in Blake what is above the earth has spiritual significance and what is within, or beneath it, symbolizes the instinctive or generative powers. The sun, which in "The Little Black Boy" of the *Songs of Innocence* is the place where

> God does live
> And gives his light and gives his heat away,

is Blake's symbol of spiritual light; and is contrasted with the fires "that belch incessant from the summits of the earth." Hence we may suggest, with the partiality which is inherent in all prose renderings of poetry, the content of the first two lines to be something like this:

> Does spiritual life know of generation?
> Seek that in the blind instinctive life of the earth.

There now remain the symbols of the silver rod and the golden bowl. Silver is throughout Blake associated with the light of the moon, and gold with the light of the sun. Urizen, Prince of Light, has a golden crown. Luvah, Prince of Love, has a silver bow. Hence, gold is a metal of the mind, and silver a metal of the loins. From which we may infer this meaning:

> Can Wisdom (man's highest good) be found in the organ of procreation,
> Or Love (woman's life) be contained in the womb?

This motto has not the universal meaning of the motto to *Visions of the Daughters of Albion*: "The Eye sees more than the Heart knows." It is Thel's motto, not Blake's. There were treasures in the earth Thel had yet to discover, treasures which Oothoon (who is really Thel at a later stage) found despite her sufferings; but while Thel's motto does not deny the purpose or value of Experience, it suggests with great power Blake's fundamental belief in the unity and integrity of the soul apart from mortal life.

With sure instinct Blake shows the burden of Thel's grief to be the sense of her own mortality. Self-consciousness is an eating of the Tree of Knowledge—knowledge of separate individuality and hence isolation from surrounding life and consequent realization of death. So, from the Lily, the Cloud, the Worm and the Clod of Clay, Thel learns to understand that this isolation is but an appearance: all life is spiritual and therefore eternal: the meanest thing that lives owes its maintenance to divine prevision. As soon as Thel understands this, her fear of mortality is quelled. But now the matron Clay offers to show her the secrets of generative life in those caverns of the earth where the fires of instinct rage. She invites Thel to enter imaginatively, and not actually, and thus to retain her freedom to return to Innocence unharmed.

Immediately there is a change in the whole tenor of the poem. The words no longer ripple and flow like the tide of light at sunrise; dark clouds and a biting wind have suddenly sprung up. The keeper of the gates of vision lifts the bar that divides the spiritual from the instinctive world. Thel enters in and looks upon the realm that Blake afterwards identifies as Hell. She wanders on until she comes to "her own grave-plot" and her vision there is of her own descent into the pit of generation. From this, that the Eagle knows not of, a voice arraigns the five senses telling of the deceits of love in the flesh. This is more than Innocence can bear: only Experience could read this rune. Horrified, the virgin Thel flies back to her native state.

Why should Thel have such a vision? Why should she suffer such horror?

Blake lived in a sentimental age when Nature was regarded as a pleasant menial who ministered gracefully to the life of man. Rousseau was preaching the Return to Nature and Marie Antoinette was keeping her court of Dresden shepherdesses. Nowadays we know all about the war of instinctive life, but in his steady gaze upon the fertilization of flowers Blake was a hundred years before his time. Whatever he might have thought of sex-instruction via botany, it is clear that he would not have sentimentalized the lesson by omitting to show that pollenization is often a haphazard event begotten of fierce instinctive strife. Thel was not enabled to regard the marriage bed with graceful equanimity because she had received instruction from the matron Clay. For Blake knew that what implies mortal life implies death. He knew that except a corn of wheat fall into the ground and die, it abideth alone. He knew that youth cannot walk with single consciousness into the kingdom of imagination—that love implies supreme sacrifice and that without the recompensing consciousness only imagination can give, sexuality is a soul-destroying waste of life. Experience is for Blake the grave of self. So when, in lonely singleness, Thel contemplates "her own grave-plot," she neither murders her own innocence, nor dons the deceitful cloak of modesty: she does not even brazen it out with a mask that hides the quivering and lacerated soul: she flies in terror, and by her flight, proclaims her perfect integrity.

How shall the unloved give themselves to experience? Unless this realm be entered through the gates of love, what can it be but a place of lonely horror, since only by love can we find Imagination, the redeemer, in the grave?

Thel is finally no human girl, but the soul itself at the moment of its separation from the innocence of Eden. That moment is the moment of "the Fall," which Blake identified with the coming of self-consciousness.

The Book of Thel is perhaps the most beautiful narrative poem ever written. It has a peculiar iridescent colour of its own perfectly suited to its theme. Its atmosphere is the atmosphere of spring sunrise. It tells a tale as plainly as if it were written in prose, yet it moves as on wings of gossamer with a lightness and poise that betoken perfect control. Take the following passage and note with what perfect sympathy the movement hesitates, pauses and mounts, like an incoming wave, to break at last in sheer abandon on the shore of pity:

> Dost thou, O little Cloud? I fear that I am not like thee,
> For I walk through the vales of Har, and smell the sweetest flowers,
> But I feed not the little flowers: I hear the warbling birds,
> But I feed not the warbling birds, they fly and seek their food;
> But Thel delights in these no more, because I fade away,
> And all shall say, 'without a use this shining woman liv'd,
> Or did she only live to be at death the food of worms?'

The measure of Thel is like the long breath the freshening air takes at dawn: its human figures seem to have been just breathed into existence. For sheer lyric beauty Blake never did anything lovelier: the grace and tenderness are beyond comparison exquisite and magical. Did he, I wonder, write it to console his childless wife?

In The Book of Thel Blake shows us the soul trembling on the threshold of experience. In Visions of the Daughters of Albion, Thel, who has become Oothoon, crosses the threshold.

Too literal a reading of this book has dulled its significance. The theme has dramatized itself with such force that literal interpretations have been read into it which obscure Blake's subtle meaning. Here as everywhere, Blake's concern is wholly with the life of the soul. Oothoon is the soul in Experience and not a particular woman suffering a particularly harrowing experience. The visions are Blake's visions, and Oothoon's story is not a tale of coarse outrage and desertion, but an account of what the soul suffers in mortal incarnation. Bromion and Theotormon are not the traditional husband and lover of the old triangle theme, but evocations of the soul: states through which the soul in its mortal journey is compelled to pass. The whole drama takes place on the stage of the soul, and to drag it from thence to the open market-place, is to debase its value and distort its characters.

The title page to *Thel* showed us the first act of this drama. There we saw Thel gazing with wonder and reproach upon the nuptials of the flowers, herself no actor in the scene, but an absorbed onlooker whose eyes were opening. The title page to the *Visions* illustrates the third act of the same drama. Here she occupies the centre of the picture. Her love expressed has awakened the terrors of the deep, and now she flies naked over the tempestuous Sea of Time and Space to escape from a wrath that emerges in flames from the clouds behind her. As she flies she looks back upon the nude figure of a man who reclines high upon the clouds. He regards her not, but only looks with hungry terror upon the flames of the abyss below him. The woman is Oothoon. The bearded man is Bromion. The figure in the clouds is Theotormon.

> To find the Western path
> Right through the gates of wrath

Oothoon urges her way, and to mitigate the terror of her experience there is nothing but a rainbow—not the full completed bow, but the increasing arc climbing the sky—which symbolizes the promise that Imagination will yet redeem the soul from despair. The contrast between the two title pages gives us Blake's contrast between the Soul in Innocence and the Soul in Experience.

Oothoon we know, but who are Bromion and Theotormon?

The only way to read Blake is to read him from A to Z, for he is a progressive writer and his effects are cumulative. He worked like a spider throwing out the main lines of his web and then linking these together by a series of the most subtle connections. Once a vivid image occurred to him he seldom let it go. At its inception it is comparatively easy to recognize; but thenceforward he will apply it in a hundred contracted forms which are quite unrecognizable to those who have not seen the initial appearance. Take the flower, for example. The first flower mentioned in the *Songs of Innocence* is "The Blossom." Once we understand that the blossom is a symbol of love, then we shall find love symbolized throughout Blake as a garden in which the flowers are always symbols of human love. Blake was pre-eminently an expressionist in the sense that he was for ever pushing forward toward fuller and more precise expression of what he perceived. He did not pause to present the same image in half a dozen different lights as more static poets have loved to do. He was an adventurer, and those who read him must follow him, or he is quickly lost to sight. The track is strewn with clues to the road he took, but unless we accept them he is soon lost on mountain tops that have ravines and impassable chasms beneath them.

In the present instance, Bromion and Theotormon are likely to remain unintelligible figures to anyone who has not read the preceding *Marriage of Heaven and Hell*. But if we have given that work worthy attention we shall remember that Blake had much to say there about desire and restraint. In fact, if we turn to *plate 5* of *The Marriage of Heaven and Hell* we shall find in the opening sentences the characters of Bromion and Theotormon described in detail.

"Those who restrain desire do so because theirs is weak enough to be restrained; and the restrainer, or reason, usurps its place and governs; the unwilling. And, being restrain'd, it by degrees; becomes passive till it is only the shadow of desire."

Bromion is the Restrainer: Theotormon the Restrained, who by degrees becomes passive till he is only the Shadow of Desire.

Throughout the so-called Prophetic Books Blake's correspondences present intellectual difficulties which it would be foolish to deny; but whenever our sympathy and patience are sufficient to the task of recognizing these correspondences, the delicacy and precision of Blake's thought become evident. In the case of these three identities we see that by this method Blake has been able to identify and give a name to attributes of the soul which are perfectly recognizable, and hereafter immediately to be upcalled by their names in their exact significance, though they are essentially of such a character as almost to defy prose definition. They are attributes of consciousness, hitherto unnamed, that Blake saw as spiritual identities.

Oothoon is "the soul of sweet delight that can never be defiled." She is desire in its inherent purity. She is the soul in its incarnation. She is youth in perfect bud. She is the vindication of the senses. She is the means whereby the world is perpetually rejuvenated. Yet she is not the essential spirit. She is not Enitharmon. She is not the soul of poetry. Her love is the love of spontaneous self-expression, not of imaginative understanding. The soul of ideal aspiration is not the soul of all the world. Oothoon is the soul at a definite moment in its earthly history, wholly lovable, though her state is perhaps the most fleeting of all the states that make up the mortal life of man.

Bromion is the Restrainer. He is the embodiment of legal righteousness. He is man's passion for order in society. In the matter of sex, this passion for order has led him to prefer form to the life which creates form. Love outside the bonds of marriage is an offence to him, and where there is love he is ready to impose marriage, if need be against all human desire. He wants to fetter the soul in chains of logic:

And render that a lawless thing
On which the soul expands its wing.

But Bromion is not Urizen. Urizen is tyrannous in the spiritual realm: Bromion rules in the social world of state and law. He cannot pine, as Urizen does, for spiritual bliss, for he belongs to an inferior hierarchy. He is Roman, not Greek law. His habitation would be nearer Temple Bar than Lambeth Palace. Bromion is, above all else, fear of the consequences—a fear that in degree has its cave in every mind.

Theotormon is "the Shadow of Desire"—desire that, by reason of external restraint, has become as the shadow to the living body. The living body in this case is Los, the representative on earth of the Poetic Genius, Los the Time-Spirit, poet and seer, whose desire in its essence is desire for God. Theotormon is desire in experience suffering from self-consciousness. He is no longer of the giant race. But desire is always desire. Blake's plummet drops sheer from heaven down to hell: he does not break his line to measure the abyss. Desire does not become a perversion by coming into touch with the senses. It is solely by his contact with Bromion that Theotormon is nullified. Theotormon is desire in restraint, in contrast to Oothoon who is desire in freedom. Theotormon stands for man in the present state of society, torn between the yea of the senses and the nay of doubting intellect—a creature of infinite longing, spiritually emaciated by his fears, who permits his energy to be dissipated by assenting to laws other than those of his own being. He is the soul of religious compromise, compromise which cannot escape cognizance of the body, but is compelled to strive against it because, never having had the spiritual vigour fully to accept the body, it is never able truly to transcend it.

But as Restraint and Fear have no existence apart from Desire, so, in this poem, Bromion and Theotormon have no existence apart from Oothoon. That neither is to be regarded as an objective personality, but that both are animating principles which achieve identity, is clear if we observe carefully the time and manner of their appearance.

The argument spoken by Oothoon states that she loved Theotormon. But essentially Theotormon is only the shadow of herself, the materialized form of her aspirations. She is thus in love with her own ideal, and what better image could we have of a girl's first love? She hides "in Leutha's vale." Leutha, as we learn elsewhere, is "a daughter of Beulah," and Beulah being the realm of human love, Leutha stands for sex-attraction in the realm of experience.

She plucks Leutha's flower (the plucking of the flower being the old symbol of sexual experience) and rises up from the vale, but the terrible thunders of Bromion destroy her virgin innocence.

When we come to the poem itself, neither Theotormon nor Bromion is mentioned until after the principal event, the plucking of the flower. As the whole poem is a description of the state that event gives rise to, their omission is highly significant. All that happens subsequently is consequent upon Oothoon's action, and the chief consequences are Theotormon and Bromion themselves. Blake wanted to dramatize the events that transpire within the soul itself; so Oothoon is presented as, of her own volition, plucking the flower. It is inconceivable that if Blake had wanted to write a drama of three persons he should have omitted all mention of two of them until after the crucial action had taken place. Moreover, once the consequences of that act are fully apparent to Oothoon, Blake shows no further interest in Theotormon or Bromion as dramatic personalities. The stage is hers. They exist throughout only in relation to her. They are creatures of her environment and all the existence they have is subordinate to, and consequent upon, her action.

Visions of the Daughters of Albion is primarily Blake's passionate vindication of the inherent truth of the individual soul. Theotormon and Bromion generalize; but again and again Oothoon differentiates. All things are the same to Theotormon; for Oothoon everything has its own principle of being, its own law, its own individual identity. "One law for the Lion and Ox is oppression." Why? Because their instinctive activities being by nature opposite, obedience to a common law would destroy both types. Blake believed the purpose of creation to be the establishment of individual identities and whatever acted in opposition to that fundamental purpose was for him Satanic.

In a secondary degree the poem is a vindication of instinct. It is also an arraignment of man in his relations to woman. Inadequacy is written all over Theotormon. That inadequacy Blake particularly despised and years before had written in his notes on Lavater: "Let the men do their duty, and women will be such wonders. The female life lives from the light of the male. See a man's female dependents—you know the man."

Theotormon is the victim of his own weakness and a vacillation that destroys his character. Loved as the fulfilment of desire by a pure spirit, he is too weak to prevent the accomplishment of his own wishes from being annulled by an intellectual tyranny imposed upon him. Hence he remains "wretched Theotormon"—at once the prey of ungratified desire and fearful restraint. Therefore while the woman, passing through the terrors of experience, is able to achieve the imaginative height of

Arise, you little glancing wings, and sing your infant joy
Arise, and drink your bliss, for every thing that lives is holy!

he remains sitting

Upon the margin'd ocean conversing with shadows dire.

As was Thel, Oothoon is justified by her own integrity. Blake knew of no
other holiness. Conformity, alike to good or evil, is abhorrent alike to divine
and human love.

—Max Plowman, "Two Examples," in
An Introduction to the Study of Blake,
London: J. M. Dent, 1927

DOROTHY PLOWMAN "A NOTE ON WILLIAM BLAKE'S *BOOK OF URIZEN*" (1929)

The Book of Urizen (1794) is one of William Blake's so-called Prophetic
Books. It tells the story of the world's creation and of humanity's fall
from an eternal, spiritual state into transient material reality. Its narrative
is not meant to be read literally, but though undoubtedly allegorical, its
allegorical meaning is only tentatively guessed at in Dorothy Plowman's
early reading. She suggests, for instance, that "Urizen" derives from the
Greek verb meaning "to bound" or "limit" and from "Uranus," and later
refers to him as "the prime mover," allying him with a prohibitive God.
She seems less aware of how he might represent Reason, his name—as
later critics have pointed out—a homophone for "Your reason." But
Plowman has no intention of giving other than "faint indications" of what
Blake is saying; her aim in this essay is to encourage readers to linger in
the text. Like her husband, Max Plowman, another Blake enthusiast, she
advocates a personal acquaintance with Blake's works over any Blake
dictionary or key to Blakean symbology.

Plowman's essay is published as the explanatory note to a facsimile
edition of Blake's *Book of Urizen*, reproduced from an original copy
formerly in the possession of Baron Dimsdale. Her note is placed,
importantly, *after* Blake's plates, in the hope that those plates are allowed
to speak for themselves.

The Book of Urizen has long had the reputation of being one of the most
difficult of Blake's works to understand. We shall not, however, let this unduly

depress us if we remember that only within the last few years have his books begun to be republished as he himself first published them, engraved in his own handwriting and with his own colouring and decoration, each page a work of art, and each group of pages lively and expressive of meanings impossible to the printed page. Blake himself would probably find it hard to understand his own work if he saw it in that guise which is the only one most of us have ever known it in, namely, as pages of printed text.

Another reason for the legend of "difficulty" that has grown up round this book is the page order. There are six known copies of *Urizen*; two of them contain twenty-eight pages, the others less, in varying numbers, and the arrangement of the pages themselves varies from copy to copy. Which is the "right" number of pages, and what is their "proper" order?

Accustomed as we are to the printed word and the numbered page, our acceptance of the unvarying order of a book's contents is as implicit as our acceptance of order to the days of the week. Hence we suffer something like dismay at the prospect of books, apparently similar, with contents that vary from copy to copy.

Yet the dismay will quickly melt when we remember *The Book of Urizen* as Blake made it. That making was no mere act of repetition—bare sheets of paper fed into a machine, a roller inking a plate, paper and plate brought together, compressed and released—the whole process under the control of a mechanic whose chief concern is to turn out a constant quantity in a given time. Uniformity of production is, or should be, such a man's ideal. It was not so with Blake. Every copy of every book he made was as much a new act of creation as the bringing to birth of each successive child is to a mother. The process gone through each time is, generally speaking, the same: yet no two times are alike, and every child born is different from every other child. And a very small experience in the comparison of Blake's originals will show that he certainly intended them be different.

With such variety in the style of decoration and often of design in different copies of the same book it is not strange to find a varying order among the plates themselves. And in *The Book of Urizen* Blake allowed himself even more latitude in make-up than usual. For instance, it is clear that when he printed the title-page of the present copy he believed he would be printing a second, and possibly more, Books of Urizen. That bold inscription, "THE FIRST BOOK OF URIZEN," in large printed letters, has an endearing quality of its own, as it were letting us in to a secret of Blake's creative life. For on the second page there is evidence of modified intention. The word "First" has been painted over with a green flame, and throughout the book there are places where the figure "i" has escaped erasure. Besides this indication of change in the planning of the Urizen myth there are actual alterations and discrepancies in the text itself. For example, the last line of page 3 and the first two lines of page 5 are clearly (in the original) scored through, and in all but two copies of the work the intervening page 4 does not appear. This would seem to be an essential page, since chapter iii begins on it; yet it certainly has the appearance of being incorporated from another copy, and the scoring through of the last line on page 3 and the deletions, afterwards erased, on page 5 (because they were found to be, after all, unnecessary) show that Blake gave much care and thought to the structure of this book, even though, to a cursory glance, the arrangement might appear to be haphazard. Again, there is the problem of the duplicate chapter iv: surely, the purist might submit, an instance of carelessness. Yet we have only to turn to pages 8 and 10 of the present edition and let the eye rest so that the designs on those two pages sink through the "two little orbs" that help to "light the cavern'd man," and we shall know that Blake was right when he decided, in this copy at least, to cast to the winds "number" and "measure," and give us both chapter iv's in naked proximity, with the magnificent inventions of both pages intact—one excelling in grandeur of design and one in the terrific imagery of its verse. Such is the scale of the poem itself that the thirteen lines composing the first chapter iv are absorbed into the meaning of the whole without creating more than a surface ripple of disturbance. Indeed they might be said to announce the motif that is to be fully developed in the chapters immediately following.

And here we are face to face with the question which has probably been in the back of our minds since we first opened *The Book of Urizen*. What exactly is "the meaning of the whole"? Or, an even earlier and more urgent question: why did Blake apparently go out of his way to write in forms so remote from our ordinary comprehension?

The days are past, or rapidly passing, when the fact that Blake used a conscious disguise for the expression of his highest thought is offered as a proof of madness.

The common fate of all whose works or speech have led them beyond the bounds set by authority (or the average man) shows how necessary some protective form has always been to that living power of which they are the channel, and it becomes clearer with every reading of the great inventions of the Prophetic Books that they are what they are—forms of light clothed in semi-transparent veils of darkness—for this reason. They are in the tradition of the ancient mystery, the oracle and the rune: a tradition Christ honoured with the parable that left his hearers "questioning among themselves," and brought from him in explanation yet another dark saying: "He that hath ears to hear let him hear." Blake, seeker after truth eighteen centuries later, still had cause to follow the old mystical tradition.

All his life he had on him the mark of one set apart. In an age of orthodoxy he was born into a family with a "queer" religion (his father was a member of the Swedenborgian church, and the child's religious inheritance had wonder and a certain strange splendour of its own). As a boy of nine he refused to go to school any longer; as a young man he openly embraced a political creed that was throwing the government of his country into paroxysms, and when he had just established a reputation as a poet in a cultured circle, he threw away all his social chances by burning the very poems his friends had approved and even paid to have published.

This action, which probably cut him off from contemporary sympathy as much as anything he ever did, is, perhaps, the clue to our understanding of the Blake of the Prophetic Books. For by that time he knew, as prophets and poets have always known, that he had a message to deliver, and he did not want the value of that message to be lost or confused (at the hands of a few ignorant enthusiasts) with what he felt was merely derivative and experimental, however beautiful.

Being a poet, one that is who feels "not differently but more intensely" than other men, he could not be content to take only a vicarious interest in the greatest activities of the human soul, attaching to them some such label as religion, or love, or art, and then leaving them to be dealt with by unindividualised organisations such as the Church, or the Government, or Society. He knew that understanding of those powers of Light and Darkness, of Life and Death, of Love and Hate, from whose embrace we spring, is vital to human growth—that

> Thought is life
> And strength and breath,
> And the want
> Of thought is death.

Therefore, from the year 1788, when he published a series of propositions or aphorisms on religion, right on to the end of his life, this "mental fight" and these "stupendous visions" were his constant preoccupation. But being himself during most of this time socially, politically, and theologically suspect, it was necessary that he should create a vehicle for his thought which should carry it safely past the shoals of contemporary prejudice. He did this by drawing from all those sources and upon all those materials with which his most individual and eclectic education had provided him (some of them only very recently made known to us, notably through the work of Mr. S. Foster Damon), and the result was the Prophetic Books.

Reading these books to-day we find them "difficult" for two reasons. First, the magnitude of their themes, which is such as we are unused to and unprepared for. Secondly, because of their presentation in this symbolic dress.

A great deal of valuable work has been done and is still being done in the elucidation of Blake's symbols and the translation of his mystic "signatures" into the forms they represent.

Yet so much has been written about Blake and his Prophetic Books of recent years that probably the wisest thing now, if we really want to understand him for ourselves, would be to stop writing and reading *about* him altogether; to do nothing in fact but read him, as nearly as possible in the originals, and brood over his pictures.

That is the first and last word of advice I myself would offer to anyone opening this book. Read Blake, and as you read him, listen. What he has to say will unfold its meaning to the listening ear. Look into his pictures, and let them look into you. Remember how he saw, not "with" but "through" the eye. Keep the channel of vision clear and you will see all that you are capable of seeing; a capacity that grows, like any other, with use.

"The song is to the singer and comes back most to him. . . .
"And no man understands any greatness or goodness but his own, or the
    indication of his own."

These words of Walt Whitman are eternally true. Yet such is the magnetic power of greatness that the more we know it to be beyond us, the more it draws us after it. We are not content to leave it and busy ourselves only with what is within our reach. The peak that defeats us is the one we come back to again and again. The greatness or goodness we do not understand is the one we must inevitably make our own.

This, perhaps, is the secret of the strong fascination of these difficult Books, and the poet himself is our best guide in the reading of them. In that wonderful piece of writing from his MS. book describing his picture "The Last Judgment," Blake gives us his conception of Imagination or Vision (he uses the terms interchangeably) as "a representation of what eternally exists, Really and Unchangeably," and tells us how we may learn to know this for ourselves:

> If the Spectator could Enter into these Images in his Imagination,
> approaching them on the Fiery Chariot of his Contemplative
> Thought, if he could Enter into Noah's Rainbow or into his bosom,
> or could make a Friend and Companion of one of these Images of
> Wonder, which always intreats him to leave mortal things (as he
> must know), then he would arise from his Grave, then he would
> meet the Lord in the Air, and then he would be happy.

This is Blake's own invitation to us to enter into understanding, with him, of the greatest mysteries, and his clear direction how we may do so. To those who would have even more explicit guidance I commend the remainder of this same paragraph (page 364, *Poems and Prophecies of William Blake*, Everyman Edition), which also sheds much light on Blake's methods of creation.

But to return to *The Book of Urizen* itself.

> Eternals, I hear your call gladly.
> Dictate swift winged words, and fear not
> To unfold your dark visions of torment.

So Blake invokes his Inspiration in its opening lines. A Chariot of Fiery Thought is indeed the only vehicle in which to make the journey we contemplate—the following of those swift winged words and dark visions. For we are taken back straightway into the womb of Creation. Starting from original Unity ("Eternal Life" or the "Will of the Immortal"), before the evolution of the solar system, Blake traces the development of consciousness, now on the cosmic and now on the individual plane, but always through varying modes of duality, down to the birth of man as we know him, a moral being, living in organised communities on a historical earth.

"Without Contraries is no progression. Attraction and Repulsion, Reason and Energy, Love and Hate are necessary to Human Existence." This sentence from *The Marriage of Heaven and Hell* (composed at this same period, probably a little earlier), might be taken as the text of *The Book of Urizen*, for it gives in brief the whole theme of the later book. In fact, the whole of *The Marriage*, with its discussion of first principles, religion, the origin of evil, and the great prophetic vision in the *Song of Liberty* with which it ends, is so closely connected with the thought of *Urizen* that quite possibly the idea of such a book originated while *The Marriage* was being written. *Urizen* is almost certainly the first book of the "Bible of Hell" promised to the world in *The Marriage*. Its central figure (from one aspect, that of the God of the

Jews shown as the "Devourer"), as well as the chapter and verse form and the general scheme of the book, bear out this view.

We start with an inverted creation—"a shadow of horror"—and the whole of the first chapter is designed to show this new power as something sinister: "unknown" is the keyword to its nature (Blake uses this five times in five verses and twice in verse 1). Its origin is "dark," "unseen." In the original creative flux there is an intimation of another energy at work, a nucleating principle "self-closed, all-repelling," from which is laboriously evolved a separate entity, "abstracted," "brooding," "self-contemplating." This new "self" is full of pride in its Achievement, yet racked with fear of all that immense universe it is now enabled to regard (for the first time) as the "not-self." Something of the Lucifer myth is recognisable in this first phase, with Urizen mustering vast armies and hurling defiance at the hosts of Eternity. But Blake has developed and amplified the motives of his protagonist. He shows how this new form of life, the thought-form, though originally a creative "energy" in its work of distinguishing and separating, becomes a destructive force when it assumes that the whole cosmos exists merely as a field for its own activity.

The name "Urizen" is, I believe, intended to indicate this. Taking it (as we are entitled to in the absence of proof that Blake intended otherwise) as derived from the Greek word ourizein, meaning "to bound" or "limit," with the cognate form "Uranus," signifying the Lord of the Firmament, or that first self-imposed setter of bounds whose rule became a tyranny that his own sons were impelled to break and supplant, we have a symbolic name conveying exactly that state described in the opening lines of the Preludium:

Of the Primeval Priest's assum'd power
When Eternals spurn'd back his religion. . . .

In chapter ii Urizen becomes vocal and defends his position; and here we at once feel a strong instinctive sympathy with the prime mover in this clash of forces.

I have sought for a joy without pain,
For a solid without fluctuation. . . .

This—the *cri de coeur* of adolescence—finds an echo in every youthful heart. It is the voice of the eternal Peter Pan: "I want always to be a little boy and have fun": the passionate demand of youth for happiness and finality, made here by Urizen in the adolescence of the race. At this point the evolving self first looks out and recognises an alien world. Then comes the inevitable touch of change, translated by a quivering sensibility as cruelty or injustice; and from this the ego shrinks back into a defensive attitude, organising the family, the tribe, and the law. Hereafter all that is not reducible to the terms of Urizen's "wisdom" is condemned and labelled "sin," while all that is must conform strictly to

> One command, one joy, one desire,
> One curse, one weight, one measure,
> One King, one God, one Law.

The words toll like a doom, alienating sympathy and foretelling disaster. We recognise in them the sin of pride, which brings about its own "fall." For Urizen himself has not learnt to accept the law of change, or suffering, through which one form of life perpetually dies into and becomes another. To him, with his merely analytic power of thought, death is simply an objective fact, a calamity. He cannot understand and will not allow pain its place as a portion "of eternity too great for the eye of man." But pain *has* this part to play in the eternal plan; as Keats knew when he denounced the labelling of this world as "a vale of tears" and demanded that it should be called instead "the vale of soul-making." For pain has this one gift for man, if he will take it: the gift of growth. Joy is an angel with dancing feet and the face of morning: pain, one with the very shape and clutch of darkness. Yet pain, not merely borne with bitterness or resignation, but met and grasped and wrestled with till it is finally known as Jacob knew his angel, is a power that opens the way to still greater joy—to a stair-way into heaven, with angels ascending and descending the steps.

So that Urizen's ideal of a joy without pain is of a joy without growth or increase. The same is true of his intellectual ideal, the attempt to subdue nature, or to explain the universe by a rationalistic system. Scientific and theological controversy about first principles was probably as active in Blake's day as it is now. Nevertheless Science has now come to the position held long ago by those great rationalists and mystics, the Greeks, and enshrined by them in their aphorism "πάντα ῥεῖ," "All flows."

We no longer talk of "dead matter," or divide it into "organic and "inorganic," or attempt to visualise the atom. We have begun—tardily perhaps, but still begun—to realise the joy of "dying" with the "Eternals" into eternally new life; and our preoccupation with compact theories of origin is noticeably, and wholesomely, less.

Yet the scientific or purely mental point of view has an invincible bias towards a mechanistic theory, to which there is always strong, if silent, opposition on the part of the individual consciousness. Thus Urizen has become, through his great objectifying effort, the spokesman of general intelligence. He represents the known, the proveable, the "right." He is the intellectual autocrat, the priest, the king.

There is, however, the whole spontaneous, intuitive life to be reckoned with, *out* of which he took form; and this is still to be found in every manifestation of *individual* purpose. The eternal verity of the "sparrow that falleth to the ground" is not impugned by the dogma of the "greatest possible good of the greatest possible number." And what Urizen calls the "seven deadly sins of the soul" are no more than exclusive assertions of individuality. The Eternals, or elemental forces of life, have been forced into a narrow channel by Urizen's passion for objectifying. He has "condensed" all things—fire, winds, waters, earth—and it is this very restraint which actually calls sin (the bursting of restraining bonds) into being. The irony is complete. From this moment Urizen is the chief contributor to the cosmic duality he had set out to displace and disprove.

The four plates that follow the title-page of *The Book of Urizen* show the four steps taken by the embryo soul on its way to this state. First there is the Babe in Eternity being invited by Nature to enter Time.[1] ("Lord teach these souls to fly" is the beautiful and touching inscription given to one copy of this illustration.) The figure on the next plate is usually mistaken for Los. But Los has not yet appeared, since Urizen has not yet reached that state of tension where his opposite is inevitably called forth. Besides, the picture very clearly represents the youthful Lucifer Urizen surrounded by "black winds of perturbation," and "combustion, blast, vapour, and cloud," in the creative attitude "self-balanc'd, stretched o'er the void," when he "fought with the fire consum'd Inwards" (chapter ii, v. 5).

The next stage of creative strife is represented in the fourth plate.

I alone, even I! the winds merciless
Bound, but condensing in torrents
They fall and fall: strong I repell'd
The vast waves. . . .

We see Urizen in the throes of reducing the fluctuating, unquenchable burnings" of Eternity to a "solid" intellectual-material formula. In the previous plate we saw him as a youth with radiant limbs and "Head sublime": here his beauty is dimmed and thought has become agony. In the fifth plate we have Jehovah-Urizen, the aged figure, with snowy locks "hoary, age-broke, and bent," with his enormous book representing the unfluctuating and irrefragible law.

The sixth plate shows us the stage inevitably following upon this—the fall, necessary, as Blake explains in the Vision of the Last Judgment, whenever error has become enthroned and must be cast out. Directly after this there is a tremendous representation of the element that stands in direct opposition to the Urizen element, now called into action for the first time. This is Los, the individual spark, the breath of immortal energy, the artist in man, forever in conflict with the metaphysical rationalising power that would hedge in humanity with a herd-morality on the one hand and intellectual dogma on the other.

Chapter iii describes the clash and rebound of the two forces. All the original "energies" now assume huge forms, and appear violent and evil, so that barriers and ramparts (structures of logic and morality) are inevitably raised by Urizen, and even Los—the poetic genius of the race, and therefore the true formative principle as contrasted with the false limiting one—is shown as weeping, howling, and "cursing his lot." "A fathomless void for his feet" we read in verse 9, and knowing (from a *Proverb of Hell*) that the "hands and feet are proportion" we realise, through this compact symbol, how Los suffers by Urizen's usurpation of all the intellectual powers. But handicapped as he is, Los is impelled by his own spiritual ardour to grapple with the formless death that Urizen has become; and in chapter iv there follow the seven ages of Creation, when Los forges a body for Urizen and plays (though unconsciously) the part of the "Comforter or Desire, that Reason may have ideas to build on" (*vide The Marriage of Heaven and Hell*).

Los's great task—the binding of Urizen—represents the penetration and illumination of scientific formulae by the creative fires of poetry and prophesy: as Shelley so well understood and pointed out in an early letter; work that is done anew by every artist who enters imaginatively ("on the Fiery Chariot of Contemplative Thought") into the world about him, by his sympathetic perception animating and synthesising that which the egoist can only see as objective matter, and can only handle for purposes of analysis.

Yet when this work is done, again there comes a period to the output of spiritual energy; the hammer falls from Los's hand; his fires sink, and he is silent. Again we realise that a powerful duality underlies human existence; that truth is, not an achievement or a possession, but rather a vibration between "contraries," and that all life is built upon a divine equipoise of forces.

When the poet lacks inspiration and the seer loses sight of the Divine Vision, it is their humanity only which will save them from being "cut off from life and light, frozen into horrible forms of deformity." This was already happening to Los when he looked on Urizen, and seeing him with the penetrative insight of sympathy, he wept. So Pity was born. And in the world of matter, Eve was created. By taking on himself the task of "providing Reason with ideas to build on" and forging the chain of Time in the process, Los had already cut himself off from Eternity ("his eternal life like a dream was obliterated"); but it is only with this last duality, the birth of the female form, that the Eternals finally cut themselves off from him. For they represent original creative unity, and this division of spiritual energy is abhorrent to their nature. (We see some of them looking out across the "Abyss of Los" in plate 15, their "expanding eyes," which Blake likens to the telescope with its power of discovering new worlds, beholding the new world and visions of Los—to them nothing but "shadows" and "appearances"—"with wonder, awe, fear, and astonishment.") But human life derives from this very division. The creation of Enitharmon may be nothing but an appearance in Eternity, but in Time, and to man, she is the other half of his soul (as Plato also tells in the *Phaedrus*) and the new life that blossoms from the marriage of Los and his Pity is life as we know it on this earth.

In chapter vi Blake again gives us (as he did in chapter iv) one of his marvellous panoramas of evolution, flashing before us, in fewest words and rapid succession, little pictures of the origin and history of species, each one a marvel of economy and insight. The chapter ends with the birth of the man-child, and in plate 20 we see this child, Orc, "delving earth in his resistless way." His limbs are haloed with "clouds of glory," part of the original creative fire, and he plunges like a comet, downward and eastward, beginning anew the circle of incarnation.

The story of Orc is only touched upon in this book, in the first four verses of chapter vii, though his influence is the main-spring of all that follows. Orc is, essentially, the spirit of youth. He represents the energy and innocence of all new life; his element is revolt, and his consummation the eternal irony of growth into all that he has rebelled against. We meet him first in the Song of Liberty as, alternately, the "new-born fire," the "new-born terror," and the "new-born wonder"; while *Europe* and *America*—the books that preceded *Urizen*—show that a myth of Orc was already a familiar part of Blake's cosmogony.

In plate 21 of The Book of Urizen the duality of Los and Enitharmon has become a trinity. The human family—beautiful but pathetic figures, with sad, anxious faces—stands grouped under a lowering sky, hemmed in by rocks and vegetation (symbols of error and materialism), Los already girt with the chain of jealousy. He sees in his son merely an heir to supplant him. This danger he evades by subjecting the child to a repressive and exclusively mental form of education, cut off from all communion with natural life—typified by the chaining of Orc to the rock "beneath Urizen's deathful shadow": an interesting commentary on educational systems a hundred (and less) years ago.

The remaining chapters of the book describe the effect of Orc upon his cosmic opposite, Urizen. Once more a new duality is in being.

> The dead heard the voice of the child
> And began to awake from sleep.

Urizen begins to measure and explore the universe of nature from a new angle; he is even moved to a sentimental pity when confronted with "facts" of life and death which he sees cannot be reconciled under any arbitrary and external law of unity. But his conclusions are still false—as it is obvious they must be from his choice of a lamp to guide him on his journeyings (plate 23). His disgust at his own limited efforts at creation, his despair at any solution to this eternal problem of duality and his own inability to accept the Law of Contraries lead him to a final act that cannot be called creative because it is in essence involuntary. He leaves behind him a trail wherever he goes, like a spider spinning a web. But this web, his net, is the product of all the negations of his soul; it is "dark" and "cold" with "meshes knotted and twisted like to the Human Brain." It is Urizen's last, great, and most successful attempt to ensnare mankind with that ancient snare of unity, "One King, one God, one Law": and its name is "The Net of Religion." Blake makes a fitting close to Urizen's book by showing him in the last plate, an awful snow-covered figure, crouched in the north, his arms still supported on the stone tables of the law, bound in the icy meshes of his own giant net.

But though we read in Blake's beautiful writing above this picture "The End of the Book of Urizen," this is not, we realise, the end of Urizen. Indeed in the last stanzas of the poem a new balance of power is already preparing; and in *The Four Zoas*, the great epic which Blake began to write soon after this, we have the further history of Orc and Urizen, carried on through alternating phases of conflict and growth, to its wonderful conclusion in a twofold sublimation.

But *The Four Zoas* was not what I had in mind when I said this is not the end of Urizen. I was thinking of this book of Blake's, now at last made accessible to the public, for whom it was intended. Those who will be opening it and reading in it for the first time may indeed feel sometimes as if, having set out to cross a mountain stream, they are in danger of being carried away by a torrent. And losing courage they may decide to come back and find a bridge, and cross it by motor, in safety and comfort. It is quite possible to do so. I have tried it. There are books that will explain to you the meaning of every word Blake wrote; but when you have read them all through you will not know as much about *The Book of Urizen* as if you had spent half an hour poring over one of Blake's own pages.

A working knowledge of the most important symbols is certainly a help, but this can be gathered as you go, and will come as it is wanted. Only do not set out armed beforehand with a chart and a dictionary and then, as it were, defy Blake's meaning to elude you. Because that is the snare of Urizen, and from that, life always escapes. The first time I read *The Book of Urizen* there was only one image in it that meant anything to me at all; and I think that was only because those were the days of the "great Somme offensive," and my son was two months old.

The globe of life blood trembled . . .

At least I understood what that meant; and knowing that, I believed I should, some day, understand the rest as well. Eleven years later I took into my hands the lovely copy of *The Book of Urizen* belonging to Baron Dimsdale, and with the gentle shock of delight that always comes at the touch of living beauty, came the memory of my first reading of it. I still did not understand all the rest; I do not even now. But I knew then that my belief had not been vain. Understanding had come, and is still coming, in its own way, and its own time. So it will come to all who want it.

Such faint indications of it as I have tried to write down here are no more than one individual's stepping-stones across the mountain torrent; of no great use to anyone but the maker, but set here as tokens of godspeed to those about to attempt their own crossing.

And to them, as a parting talisman, I would offer these words of Walt Whitman, one who, like Blake, looked through shadow and appearance and saw heaven in the "vision of what eternally exists, Really and Unchangeably":

> "Were you thinking that those were the words—those upright lines,
>   those curves, angles, dots?
> No, these are not the words—the substantial words are in the ground
>   and sea,
> They are in the air—they are in you."

Note

1. That the woman represents Nature and not, as I had at first thought, one of the Eternals, was suggested to me by Mr. J. Wicksteed, who pointed out

that she seizes the babe with her left hand. He adds: "It is Blake's suggestion that the origin of 'division' is the lure of Nature. It is reminiscent of *Thel*; of the mandrake in the *Gates of Paradise*, and of the lines in *Auguries of Innocence*:

> Every Tear from Every Eye
> Becomes a Babe in Eternity;
> This is caught by Females bright
> And return'd to its own delight."

—Dorothy Plowman, "A Note on William Blake's *Book of Urizen*," in *The Book of Urizen by William Blake: Reproduced in Facsimile from an original copy of the work printed and illuminated by the author in 1794, formerly in the possession of the late Baron Dimsdale*, London and Toronto: J.M. Dent & Sons; New York: E.P. Dutton & Co., 1929

Chronology

~w~ ~w~ ~w~

1757   Born November 28 in London.

1771   Apprenticed to James Basire, an engraver.

1782   Married to Catherine Boucher.

1783   *Poetical Sketches* published, containing poems written from 1769 to 1778.

1787   Death of Robert Blake, the poet's beloved younger brother.

1789   Engraving of *Songs of Innocence* and *The Book of Thel.*

1790   Writes *The Marriage of Heaven and Hell.*

1791   Printing of *The French Revolution* by left-wing publisher Joseph Johnson, but the poem is abandoned after the proof sheets stage.

1793   Engraving of *America* and *Visions of the Daughters of Albion.*

1794   Engraving of *Songs of Experience, Europe,* and *The Book of Urizen.*

1795   Engraving of *The Book of Los, The Song of Los,* and *The Book of Ahania.*

1797   Begins to write *Vala,* or *The Four Zoas.*

1800   Moves with his wife to Felpham, Sussex, to live and work with William Hayley.

1803   Quarrels with Hayley and returns to London.

1804   Is tried for sedition and acquitted after being accused by a soldier, John Scholfield. Blake's epics, *Milton* and *Jerusalem,* are, according to him, completed in this year but are believed to have been actually finished later.

1809   Exhibits his paintings but fails to attract buyers. *A Descriptive Catalogue,* written for the exhibition contains his criticism of Chaucer.

1818	Becomes a mentor to younger painters: John Linnell, Samuel Palmer, Edward Calvert, and George Richmond.
1820	Woodcuts to Virgil's *Pastorals* produced.
1825	Completes engravings of the biblical book of Job.
1826	Finishes his Dante illustrations.
1827	Dies on August 12.

Index